Evolutionary Synthesis of Pattern Recognition Systems

T0205433

Monographs in Computer Science

Abadi and Cardelli, **A Theory of Objects**

Benosman and Kang [editors], **Panoramic Vision: Sensors, Theory and Applications**

Broy and Stølen, **Specification and Development of Interactive Systems: FOCUS on Streams, Interfaces, and Refinement**

Brzozowski and Seger, **Asynchronous Circuits**

Cantone, Omodeo, and Policriti, **Set Theory for Computing: From Decision Procedures to Declarative Programming with Sets**

Castillo, Gutiérrez, and Hadi, Expert **Systems and Probabilistic Network Models**

Downey and Fellows, **Parameterized Complexity**

Feijen and van Gasteren, **On a Method of Multiprogramming**

Herbert and Spärck Jones [editors], **Computer Systems: Theory, Technology, and Applications**

Leiss, **Language Equations**

McIver and Morgan [editors], **Programming Methodology**

McIver and Morgan, **Abstraction, Refinement and Proof for Probabilistic Systems**

Misra, **A Discipline of Multiprogramming: Program Theory for Distributed Applications**

Nielson [editor], **ML with Concurrency**

Paton [editor], **Active Rules in Database Systems**

Selig, **Geometric Fundamentals of Robotics, Second Edition**

Tonella and Potrich, **Reverse Engineering of Object Oriented Code**

Bir Bhanu
Yingqiang Lin
Krzysztof Krawiec

Evolutionary Synthesis of Pattern Recognition Systems

 Springer

Bir Bhanu
Center for Research in
Intelligent Systems
University of California
at Riverside
Bourns Hall RM B232
Riverside, CA 92521

Yingqiang Lin
Center for Research in
Intelligent Systems
University of California
at Riverside
Bourns Hall RM B232
Riverside CA 92521

Krzysztof Krawiec
Center for Research in
Intelligent Systems
University of California
at Riverside
Bourns Hall RM B232
Riverside CA 92521

Series Editors
David Gries
Dept. of Computer Science
Cornell University
Upson Hall
Ithaca NY 14853-7501

Fred B. Schneider
Dept. Computer Science
Cornell University
Upson Hall
Ithaca NY 14853-7501

Library of Congress Cataloging-in-Publication Data
Bhanu, Bir.
  Evolutionary Synthesis of Pattern Recognition Systems /Bir Bhanu, Yingqiang Lin, and Krzysztof
  Krawiec.
     p. cm. –(Monographs in Computer Science)
     Includes bibliographical references and index.

ISBN 978-1-4419-1943-4   Printed on acid-free paper.
e-ISBN 978-0-387-24452-5
© 2010 Springer Science+Business Media, Inc.

Printed in the United States of America.   (BS/DH)

9 8 7 6 5 4 3 2 1

springeronline.com

Contents

List of Figures

Chapter 2

Chapter 3

Chapter 4

Chapter 5

Chapter 6

Chapter 7

List of Tables

Chapter 4

Chapter 5

Chapter 7

Preface

Designing object detection and recognition systems that work in the real world is a challenging task due to various factors including the high complexity of the systems, the dynamically changing environment of the real world and factors such as occlusion, clutter, articulation, and various noise contributions that make the extraction of reliable features quite difficult. Furthermore, features useful to the detection and recognition of one kind of object or in the processing of one kind of imagery may not be effective in the detection and recognition of another kind of object or in the processing of another kind of imagery. Thus, the detection and recognition system often needs thorough overhaul when applied to other types of images different from the one for which the system was designed. This is very uneconomical and requires highly trained experts. The purpose of incorporating learning into the system design is to avoid the time consuming process of feature generation and selection and to lower the cost of building object detection and recognition systems.

Evolutionary computation is becoming increasingly important for computer vision and pattern recognition fields. It provides a systematic way of synthesis and analysis of object detection and recognition systems. With learning incorporated, the resulting recognition systems will be able to automatically generate new features on the fly and cleverly select a good subset of features according to the type of objects and images to which they are applied. The system will be flexible and can be applied to a variety of objects and images.

This book investigates evolutionary computational techniques such as genetic programming (GP), linear genetic programming (LGP), coevolutionary genetic programming (CGP) and genetic algorithms (GA) to automate the synthesis and analysis of object detection and recognition systems. The ultimate goal of the learning approaches presented in this book is to lower the cost of designing object detection and recognition systems and build more robust and flexible systems with human-competitive performance.

The book presents four important ideas.

First, this book shows the efficacy of GP and CGP in synthesizing effective composite operators and composite features from domain-independent primitive image processing operations and primitive features (both elementary and complex) for object detection and recognition. It explores the role of domain knowledge in evolutionary computational techniques for object recognition. Based on GP and CGP's ability to synthesize effective features from simple features not specifically designed for a particular kind of imagery, the cost of building object detection and recognition systems is lowered and the flexibility of the systems is increased. More importantly, a large amount of unconventional features are explored by GP and CGP and these unconventional features yield exceptionally good detection and recognition performance in some cases, overcoming the human experts' limitation of considering only a small number of conventional features.

Second, smart crossover, smart mutation and a new fitness function based on the minimum description length (MDL) principle are designed to improve the efficiency of genetic programming. Smart crossover and smart mutation are designed to identify and keep the effective components of composite operators from being disrupted and a MDL-based fitness function is proposed to address the well-known code bloat problem of GP without imposing severe restriction on the GP search. Compared to normal GP, smart GP algorithm with smart crossover, smart mutation and a MDL-based fitness function finds effective composite operators more quickly and the composite operators learned by smart GP algorithm have smaller size, greatly reducing both the computational expense during testing and the possibility of overfitting during training.

Third, a new MDL-based fitness function is proposed to improve the genetic algorithm's performance on feature selection for object detection and recognition. The MDL-based fitness function incorporates the number of features selected into the fitness evaluation process and prevents GA from selecting a large number of features to overfit the training data. The goal is to select a small set of features with good discrimination performance on both training and unseen testing data to reduce the possibility of overfitting the training data during training and the computational burden during testing.

Fourth, adaptive coevolutionary linear genetic programming (LGP) in conjunction with general image processing, computer vision and pattern recognition operators is proposed to synthesize recognition systems. The basic two-class approach is extended for scalability to multiple classes and various architectures and strategies are considered.

The book consists of eight chapters dealing with various evolutionary approaches for automatic synthesis and analysis of object detection and recognition systems. Many real world imagery examples are given in all the chapters and a comparison of the results with standard techniques is provided.

The book will be of interest to scientists, engineers and students working in computer vision, pattern recognition, object recognition, machine learning, evolutionary learning, image processing, knowledge discovery, data mining, cybernetics, robotics, automation and psychology.

Authors would like to thank Ken Grier, Dale Nelson, Lou Tamburino, and Bob Herklotz for their guidance and support. Many discussions held with Ed Zelnio, Tim Ross, Vince Velten, Gregory Power, Devert Wicker, Grinnell Jones, and Sohail Nadimi were very helpful.

The work covered in this book was performed at the University of California at Riverside. It was partly supported by funding from Air Force Research Laboratory during the last four years. Krzysztof Krawiec was at the University of California at Riverside on a temporary leave from Poznan University of Technology, Poznan, Poland. He would like to acknowledge the support from the Scientific Research Committee, Poland (KBN). Authors would like to thank Julie Vu and Lynne Cochran for their secretarial support.

Riverside, California
November 2004

Bir Bhanu
Yingqiang Lin
Krzysztof Krawiec

Chapter 1

INTRODUCTION

In recent years, with the advent of newer, much improved and inexpensive imaging technologies and the rapid expanding of the Internet, more and more images are becoming available. Recent developments in image collection platforms produce far more imagery than the declining ranks of image analysts are capable of handling due to human work load limitations. Relying on human image experts to perform image analysis, processing and classification becomes more and more unrealistic. Building object detection and recognition systems to take advantage of the speed of computer is a viable and important solution to the increasing need of processing a large quantity of images efficiently.

1.1   Object Detection and Recognition Problem

The object detection and recognition problem is one of the most important research areas in pattern recognition and computer vision [7], [18]. It has wide range of applications in surveillance, reconnaissance, object and target recognition, autonomous navigation, remote sensing, manufacturing automation, etc. The major task of object detection is to locate and extract regions that may contain objects in an image. It is an important intermediate step to object recognition. The extracted regions are called regions-of-interest (ROIs) or object chips. ROI extraction is very important to object recognition, since the size of an image is usually large, leading to the heavy computational burden of processing the whole image. By extracting ROIs, the computational cost of object recognition is greatly reduced, thus improving the recognition efficiency. This advantage is particularly useful to real-time applications, where the recognition speed is of prime importance. Also, by extracting ROIs, the recognition system can focus on the extracted regions that may contain potential objects and this can be very helpful in improving the recognition accuracy. Generally, the extracted ROIs are identical to their corresponding regions in the original image, but sometimes, they may be images that result from applying some image processing operations to the corresponding regions in the original image. No matter what ROIs are, they are passed to an object recognition module for further processing. Usually, in order to increase the probability of object detection, some false alarm ROIs, which do not contain an object, but some natural or man-made clutter, are allowed to pass object detection phase.

The task of object recognition is first to reject the false alarm ROIs and then recognize the kinds of objects in the ROIs containing them. It is actually a signal-to-symbol problem of labeling perceived signals with one or more symbols. A solution to this problem takes images or the features extracted from images as input and outputs one or more symbols which are the labels of the objects in the images. Sometimes, the symbols may further represent the pose of the objects or the relations between different objects. These symbols are intended to capture some useful aspects of the input and in turn, permit some high level reasoning on the perceived signals.

It is well known that automatic object detection and recognition is really not an easy task. The quality of detection and recognition is heavily dependent on the kind and quality of features extracted from the image, and it also highly relies on the representation of an object based on the extracted features. The features used to represent an object are the key to object detection and recognition. If useful features with good quality are unavailable to build an efficient representation of an object, good detection and recognition results cannot be achieved no matter what detection and recognition algorithms are used. However, in most real images, there is always some noise, making the extraction of features difficult. More importantly, since there are many kinds of features that can be extracted, so what are the appropriate features for the current detection and recognition task or how to synthesize composite features particularly useful to the detection and recognition from the primitive features extracted from an image? There is no easy answer to these questions and the solutions are largely dependent on the intuitive instinct, knowledge, previous experience and even the bias of human image experts. Object detection and recognition in many real-world applications is still a challenging problem and needs further research.

1.2   Motivations for Evolutionary Computation

In the past, object detection and recognition systems are manually developed and maintained by human experts. The traditional approach requires a human expert to select or synthesize a set of features to be used in detection and recognition. However, handcrafting a set of features requires human ingenuity and insight into the objects to be detected and recognized since it is very difficult to identify a set of features that characterize a complex set of objects. Typically, many features are explored before object detection and recognition systems can be built. There are a lot of features available and these features may be correlated. To select a set of features which, when acting cooperatively, can give good performance is very time consuming and expensive. Sometimes, simple features (also called primitive features) directly extracted from images may not be effective in detecting and recognizing objects. At this point, synthesizing composite features useful for the current detection and recognition task from those simple ones becomes imperative.

Traditionally, it is the human experts who synthesize features to be used. However, based on their knowledge, previous experience and limited by their bias and speed, human experts only consider a small number of conventional features and many unconventional features are totally ignored. Sometimes it is those unconventional features that yield very good detection and recognition performance. Furthermore, after the features are selected or designed by human experts and incorporated into a system, they are fixed. The features used by the system are pre-determined and the system cannot generate new features useful to the current detection and recognition task on the fly based on the already available features, leading to inflexibility of the system. Features useful to the detection and recognition of one kind of object or in the processing of one kind of imagery may not be effective in the detection and recognition of another kind of object or in the processing of another kind of imagery. Thus, the detection and recognition system often needs thorough overhaul when applied to other types of images that are different from the one when the system was devised. This is very uneconomical.

Synthesizing effective new features from primitive features is equivalent to finding good points in the feature combination space where each point represents a combination of primitive features. Similarly, selecting an effective subset of features is equivalent to finding good points in the feature subset space where each point represents a subset of features. The feature combination space and feature subset space are huge and complicated and it is very difficult to find good points in such vast spaces unless one has an efficient search algorithm.

Hill climbing, gradient descent and simulated annealing (also called stochastic hill climbing) are widely used search algorithms. Hill climbing and gradient descent are efficient in exploring a unimodal space, but they are not suitable for finding global optimal points in a multi-modal space due to their high probability of being trapped in local optima. Thus, if the search space is a complicated and multi-modal space, they are unlikely to yield good search results. Simulated annealing has the ability to jump out of local optimal points, but it is heavily dependent on the starting point. If the starting point is not appropriately placed, it takes a long time, or even could be impossible, for simulated annealing to reach good points. Furthermore, in order to apply a simulated annealing algorithm, the neighborhood of a point must be defined and the neighboring points should be somewhat similar. This requires some knowledge about the search space and it also requires some smoothness of the search space.

It is very difficult, if not impossible, to define the neighborhood of a point in the huge and complicated feature combination and feature subset spaces, since similar feature combinations and similar feature subsets may have very different object detection and recognition performance. Due to the lack of knowledge about these search spaces, a variety of genetic programming techniques and genetic algorithms [6], [36], [57], [58], [66] are employed in this book. In order to apply GP and GA, all that needs to be known are how to define individuals, how to define crossover and mutation operations on the individuals and how to evaluate individuals. GP and GA are very much capable of exploring huge complicated multi-modal spaces with unknown structures. Maintaining a large population of individuals as multiple searching points, GP and GA explore the search spaces along different directions concurrently. With multiple searching points and the crossover and mutation operations' ability to immediately move a searching point from one portion of the search space to another faraway portion, GP and GA are less likely to be trapped at local optimal points. All these characteristics greatly enhance the probability of finding global optimal points, although they cannot guarantee the finding of global optima. It is to be noted that GP and GA are not random search algorithms, they are guided by the fitness of the individuals in the population. As search proceeds, the population is gradually adapted to the portion of the search space containing good points.

1.3   Evolutionary Approaches for Synthesis and Analysis

In this book, the techniques necessary for automatic design of object detection and recognition systems are investigated. Here, the object detection and recognition system itself is the theme and the efficacy of evolutionary learning algorithms such as genetic programming and genetic algorithm in the feature generation and selection is studied. The advantage of incorporating learning is to avoid the time consuming process of feature selection and generation and to automatically explore many unconventional features. The system resulting from the learning is able to automatically generate features on the fly and cleverly select a good subset of features according to the type of object and image to which it is applied. The system should be somewhat flexible and can be applied to a variety of objects and images. The goal is to lower the cost of designing object detection and recognition systems and build more robust and flexible systems with human-competitive performance.

This book investigates evolutionary computational techniques such as genetic programming (GP), coevolutionary genetic programming (CGP), linear genetic programming (LCP) and genetic algorithm (GA) to automate the synthesis and analysis of object detection and recognition systems.

First, this book shows the efficacy of GP and CGP in synthesizing effective composite operators and composite features from domain-independent primitive image processing operations and primitive features for object detection and recognition. It explores the role of domain knowledge in evolutionary computation. Based on GP and CGP's ability to synthesize effective features from simple features not specifically designed for a particular kind of imagery, the cost of building object detection and recognition systems is lowered and the flexibility of the systems is increased. More importantly, it shows that a large amount of unconventional features are explored by GP and CGP and these unconventional features yield exceptionally good detection and recognition performance in some cases, overcoming the human experts' limitation of considering only a small number of conventional features.

Second, smart crossover, smart mutation and a new fitness function based on minimum description length (MDL) principle are designed to improve the efficiency of genetic programming. Smart crossover and smart mutation are designed to identify and keep the effective components of composite operators from being disrupted and a MDL-based fitness function is proposed to address the well-known code bloat problem of GP without imposing severe restriction on the GP search. Compared to normal GP, a smart GP algorithm with smart crossover, smart mutation and a MDL-based fitness function finds effective composite operators more quickly and the composite operators learned by a smart GP algorithm have smaller size, greatly reducing both the computational expense during testing and the possibility of overfitting during training.

Third, a new MDL-based fitness function is proposed to improve the genetic algorithm's performance on feature selection for object detection and recognition. The MDL-based fitness function incorporates the number of features selected into the fitness evaluation process and prevents GA from selecting a large number of features to overfit the training data. The goal is to select a small set of features with good discrimination performance on both training and unseen testing data to reduce both the possibility of overfitting the training data during training and the computational burden during testing.

Fourth, linear genetic programming (LGP) and coevolutionary genetic programming (CGP) techniques are used to synthesize a feature extraction procedure (FEP) to generate features for object recognition. FEP consists of a sequence of instructions, which are primitive image processing operators that are executed sequentially one after another. Each instruction in a FEP is composed of an opcode determining the operator to be used and arguments referring to registers from which to fetch the input data and to which to store the result of the instruction. LGP is a variety of GP with simplified, linear representation of individuals and it is a hybrid of GA and GP and combines their advantages. LGP is similar to GP in the sense that each individual actually contains a sequence of interrelated operators. On the other hand, a FEP has a fixed number of instructions and an instruction is encoded into a fixed-length binary string at the genome level, which is essentially equivalent to GA representation. LGP encoding is, therefore, more positional and more resistant to destructive crossovers. When CGP is applied, the problem of feature construction can be decomposed at different levels. We explore decomposition at the instruction, feature, class and decision levels. Our experiments show the superiority of decomposition at the instruction level. With different segments of a FEP evolved by sub-populations of CGP, a better FEP can be synthesized by concatenating the segments from sub-populations. The benefits we expect from the decomposition of feature construction by CGP include faster convergence of the learning process, better scalability of the learning with respect to the problem size and better understanding of the obtained solutions.

1.4   Outline of the Book

The outline of the book is as follows:

Chapter 1 is the introduction. It describes object detection and recognition problems, provides motivation and advantages of incorporating evolutionary computation in the design of object detection and recognition systems.

Chapter 2 discusses synthesizing composite features for object detection. Genetic programming (GP) is applied to the learning of composite features based on primitive features and primitive image processing operations. The primitive features and primitive image processing operations are domain-independent, not specific to any kind of imagery so that the proposed feature synthesis approach can be applied to a wide variety of images.

Chapter 3 concentrates on improving the efficiency of genetic programming. A fitness function based on the minimum description length (MDL) principle is proposed to address the well-known code bloat problem of GP while at the same time avoiding severe restriction on the GP search. The MDL fitness function incorporates the size of a composite operator into the fitness evaluation process to prevent it from growing too large, reducing possibility of overfitting during training and the computational expenses during testing. The smart crossover and smart mutation are proposed to identify the effective components of a composite operator and keep them from being disrupted by subsequent crossover and mutation operations to further improve the efficiency of GP.

In Chapter 4, genetic algorithms (GA) are used for feature selection for distinguishing objects from natural clutter. Usually, GA is driven by a fitness function based on the performance of selected features. To achieve excellent performance during training, GA may select a large number of features. However, a large number features with excellent performance on training data may not perform well on unseen testing data due to the overfitting. Also, selecting more features means heavier computational burden during testing. In order to overcome this problem, an MDL-based fitness function is designed to drive GA. With MDL-based function incorporating the number of features selected into the fitness evaluation process, a small set of features is selected to achieve satisfactory performance during both training and testing.

Chapter 5 presents a method of learning composite feature vectors for object recognition. Coevolutionary genetic programming (CGP) is used to synthesize composite feature vectors based on the primitive features (simple or relatively complex) directly extracted from images. The experimental results using real SAR images show that CGP can evolve composite features that are more effective than the primitive features upon which they are built.

Chapter 6 presents a coevolutionary approach for synthesizing recognition systems using linear genetic programming (LGP). It provides a rationale for the design of the method and outlines main differences in comparison to standard genetic programming. The basic characteristic of LGP approach is the linear (sequential) encoding of elementary operations and passing of intermediate arguments through temporary variables (registers). Two variants of of the approach are presented. The first approach called, evolutionary feature programming (EFP), engages standard single-population evolutionary computation. The second approach called, coevolutionary feature programming (CFP), decomposes feature synthesis problem using cooperative coevolution. Various decomposition strategies for breaking up the feature synthesis process are discussed.

Chapter 7 presents experimental results of applying the methodology described in chapter 7 to real-world computer vision/pattern recognition problems. It includes experiments using single-population evolutionary feature programming (EFP), and selected variants of coevolutionary feature programming (CFP) cooperating at different decomposition levels. To provide experimental evidence for the generality of the proposed approach, it is verified on two different real-world tasks. First of them is the recognition of common household objects in controlled lighting conditions, using the widely known COIL-20 benchmark database. The second application is much more difficult and concerns the recognition of different types of vehicles in synthetic aperture radar (SAR) images.

Finally, Chapter 8 provides the conclusions and future research directions.

Chapter 2

FEATURE SYNTHESIS FOR OBJECT DETECTION

2.1   Introduction

Designing automatic object detection and recognition systems is one of the important research areas in computer vision and pattern recognition [7], [35]. The major task of object detection is to locate and extract regions of an image that may contain potential objects so that the other parts of the image can be ignored. It is an intermediate step to object recognition. The regions extracted during detection are called regions-of-interest (ROIs). ROI extraction is very important in object recognition, since the size of an image is usually large, leading to the heavy computational burden of processing the whole image. By extracting ROIs, the recognition system can focus on the extracted regions that may contain potential objects and this can be very helpful in improving the recognition rate. Also by extracting ROIs, the computational cost of object recognition is greatly reduced, thus improving the recognition speed. This advantage is particularly important for real-time applications, where the recognition accuracy and speed are of prime importance.

However, the quality of object detection is dependent on the type and quality of features extracted from an image. There are many features that can be extracted. The question is what are the appropriate features or how to synthesize features, particularly useful for detection, from the primitive features extracted from images. The answer to these questions is largely dependent on the intuitive instinct, knowledge, previous experience and even the bias of algorithm designers and experts in object recognition.

In this chapter, we use genetic programming (GP) to synthesize composite features which are the output of composite operators, to perform object detection. A composite operator consists of primitive operators and it can be viewed as a way of combining primitive operations on images. The basic approach is to apply a composite operator on the original image or primitive feature images generated from the original one; then the output image of the composite operator, called composite feature image, is segmented to obtain a binary image or mask; finally, the binary mask is used to extract the region containing the object from the original image. The individuals in our GP based learning are composite operators represented by binary trees whose internal nodes represent the pre-specified primitive operators and the leaf nodes represent the original image or the primitive feature images. The primitive feature images are pre-defined, and they are not the output of the pre-specified primitive operators.

This chapter is organized as follows: chapter 2.2 provides motivation, related research and contribution of this chapter; chapter 2.3 provides the details of genetic programming for feature synthesis; chapter 2.4 presents experimental results using synthetic aperture radar (SAR), infrared (IR) and color images. Various comparisons are given in this section to demonstrate the effectiveness of the approach, including examples of two-class and multi-class imagery; finally, chapter 2.5 provides the conclusions of this chapter.

2.2   Motivation and Related Research

2.2.1   Motivation

In most imaging applications, human experts design an approach to detect potential objects in images. The approach can often be divided into some primitive operations on the original image or a set of related feature images obtained from the original one. It is the expert who, relying on his/her experience, figures out a smart way to combine these primitive operations to achieve good detection results. The task of synthesizing a good approach is equivalent to finding a good point in the space of *composite operators* formed by the combination of primitive operators.

Unfortunately, the ways of combining primitive operators are infinite. The human expert can only try a very limited number of conventional combinations. However, a GP may try many unconventional ways of combining primitive operations that may never be imagined by a human expert. Although these unconventional combinations are very difficult, if not impossible, to be explained by domain experts, in some cases, it is these unconventional combinations that yield exceptionally good results. The unlikeliness, and even incomprehensibility of some effective solutions learned by GP demonstrates the value of GP in the generation of new features for object detection. The inherent parallelism of GP and the high speed of current computers allow the portion of the search space explored by GP to be much larger than that by human experts. The search performed by GP is not a random search. It is guided by the fitness of composite operators in the population. As the search proceeds, GP gradually shifts the population to the portion of the space containing good composite operators.

2.2.2   Related research

Genetic programming, an extension of genetic algorithm, was first proposed by Koza [55], [56], [57], [58] and has been used in image processing, object detection and object recognition. Harris and Buxton [39] applied GP to the production of high performance edge detectors for 1-D signals and image profiles. The method is also extended to the development of practical edge detectors for use in image processing and machine vision. Poli [92] used GP to develop effective image filters to enhance and detect features of interest and to build pixel-classification-based segmentation algorithms. Bhanu and Lin [14], [17], [21], [69] used GP to learn composite operators for object detection. Their experimental results showed that GP is a viable way of synthesizing composite operators from primitive operations for object detection. Stanhope and Daida [114] used GP to generate rules for target/clutter classification and rules for the identification of objects. To perform these tasks, previously defined feature sets are generated on various images and GP is used to select relevant features and methods for analyzing these features. Howard et al. [44] applied GP to automatic detection of ships in low-resolution SAR imagery by evolving detectors. Roberts and Howard [103] used GP to develop automatic object detectors in infrared images. Tackett [115] applied GP to the development of a processing tree for the classification of features extracted from images.

Belpaeme [5] investigated the possibility of evolving feature detectors under selective pressure. His experimental results showed that it is possible for GP to construct visual functionality based on primitive image processing functions inspired by visual behavior observed in mammals. The inputs for the feature detectors are images. Koppen and Nickolay [54] presented a special 2-D texture filtering framework, based on the so-called 2-D-Lookup with its configuration evolved by GP that allowed representing and searching a very large number of texture filters. Their experimental results demonstrated that although the framework may never find the globally optimal texture filters, it evolves the initialized solutions toward better ones. Johnson et al. [50] described a way of automatically evolving visual routines for simple tasks by using genetic programming. The visual routine models used in their work were initially proposed by Ullman [121] to describe a set of primitive routines that can be applied to find spatial relations between objects in an input image. Ullman proposed, that given a specific task, the visual routine processor compiled and organized an appropriate set of visual routines and applied it to a base representation. But as Johnson et al. [50] pointed out, Ullman did not explain how routines were developed, stored, chosen and applied. In their work, Johnson et al. [50] applied typed genetic programming to the problem of creating visual routines for the simple task of locating the left and right hands in a silhouette image of a person. In their GP, crossover was performed by exchanging between two parents the subtrees of the same root return type. To avoid the code bloat problem of GP, they simply canceled a particular crossover if it would produce an offspring deeper than the maximum allowable depth. Rizki et al. [102] use hybrid evolutionary computation (genetic programming and neural networks) for target recognition using 1-D radar signals.

Unlike the prior work of Stanhope and Daida [114], Howard et al. [44] and Roberts and Howard [103], the input and output of each node of a tree in the system described in this chapter are images, not real numbers. When the data from node to node is an image, the node can contain any primitive operation on images. Such image operations do not make sense when the data is a real number. In our system, the data to be processed are images, and image operations can be applied to primitive feature images and any other intermediate images to achieve object detection results. In [114], [44], [103], image operations can only be applied to the original image to generate primitive feature images. Also, the primitive features defined in this chapter are more general and easier to compute than those used in [114], [44]. Unlike our previous work [17], in this chapter the hard limit of composite operator size is removed and a soft size limit is used to let GP search more freely while at the same time preventing the code-bloat problem. The training in this chapter is not performed on a whole image, but on the selected regions of an image and this is very helpful in reducing the training time. Of course, training regions must be carefully selected and represent the characteristics of training images [11]. Also, two types of mutation are added to further increase the diversity of the population. Finally, more primitive feature images are employed. The primitive operators and primitive features designed in this chapter are very basic and domain-independent, not specific to a kind of imagery. Thus, this system and methodology can be applied to a wide variety of images. For example, results are shown here using synthetic aperture radar (SAR), infrared (IR) and color video images.

2.3   Genetic Programming for Feature Synthesis

In our GP based approach, individuals are composite operators represented by binary trees. The search space of GP is huge and it is the space of all possible composite operators. Note that there could be equivalent composite operators in terms of their output images. In the computer system, a pixel of an image can assume only finite values, the number of possible images is finite, but this number is huge and astronomical. Also, if we set a maximum composite operator size, the number of composite operators is also finite, but again this number is also huge and astronomical. To illustrate this, consider only a special kind of binary tree, where each tree has exactly one leaf node and 30 internal nodes and each internal node has only one child. For 17 primitive operators and only one primitive feature image, the total number of such trees is 17^{30}. It is extremely difficult to find good composite operators from this vast space unless one has a smart search strategy.

2.3.1   Design considerations

There are five major design considerations, which involve: determining the set of terminals; the set of primitive operators; the fitness measure; the parameters for controlling the evolutionary run; and the criterion for terminating a run.

• **The set of terminals:** The set of terminals used in this chapter are sixteen primitive feature images generated from the original image: the first one is the original image; the others are mean, deviation, maximum, minimum and median images obtained by applying templates of sizes 3×3, 5×5 and 7×7, as shown in Table 2.1. These images are the input to composite operators. GP determines which operations are applied on them and how to combine the results. To get the mean image, we translate a template across the original image and use the average pixel value of the pixels covered by the template to replace the pixel value of the pixel covered by the central cell of the template. To get the deviation image, we just compute the pixel value difference between the pixel in the original image and its corresponding pixel in the mean image. To get maximum, minimum and median images, we translate the template across the original image and use the maximum, minimum and median pixel values of the pixels covered by the template to replace the pixel value of the pixel covered by the central cell of the template, respectively.

Table 2.1. Sixteen primitive feature images used as the set of terminals.

No.	Primitive feature image	Description	No.	Primitive feature image	Description
0	PFIM0	Original image	8	PFIM8	5×5 maximum image
1	PFIM1	3×3 mean image	9	PFIM9	7×7 maximum image
2	PFIM2	5×5 mean image	10	PFIM10	3×3 minimum image
3	PFIM3	7×7 mean image	11	PFIM11	5×5 minimum image
4	PFIM4	3×3 deviation image	12	PFIM12	7×7 minimum image
5	PFIM5	5×5 deviation image	13	PFIM13	3×3 median image
6	PFIM6	7×7 deviation image	14	PFIM14	5×5 median image
7	PFIM7	3×3 maximum image	15	PFIM15	7×7 median image

- **The set of primitive operators:** A primitive operator takes one or two input images, performs a primitive operation on them and stores the result in a resultant image. Currently, 17 primitive operators are used by GP to form composite operators, as shown in Table 2.2, where A and B are input images of the same size and c is a constant (ranging from −20 to 20) stored in the primitive operator. For operators such as ADD, SUB, MUL, etc., that take two images as input, the operations are performed on the pixel-by-pixel basis. In the operators MAX, MIN, MED, MEAN and STDV, a 3×3, 5×5 or 7×7 neighborhood is used with equal probability. Operator 16 (MEAN) can be considered as a kind of convolution for low pass filtering and operator 17 (STDV) is a kind of convolution for high pass filtering. Operators 13 (MAX), 14 (MIN) and 15 (MED) can also be considered as convolution operators. We do not include edge operators for several reasons. *First*, these operators are not primitive and we want to investigate if GP can synthesize effective composite operators or features from simple and domain-independent operations. This is important since without relying on domain knowledge, we can examine the power of a learning algorithm when applied to a variety of images. *Second*, edge detection operators can be dissected into the above primitive operators and it is possible for GP to synthesize edge operators or composite operators approximating them if they are very useful to the current object detection task. *Finally*, the primitive operator library is decoupled from the GP learning system. Edge detection operators can be added in the primitive operator library if they are absolutely needed by the current object detection task.

Some operations used to generate feature images are the same as some primitive operators (see Table 2.1 and Table 2.2), but there are some differences. Primitive feature images are generated from original images, so the operations generating primitive feature images are applied to an original image. A primitive operator is applied to a primitive feature image or to an intermediate image output that is generated by the child node of the node containing this primitive operator. In short, the input image of a primitive operator varies.

Table 2.2. Seventeen primitive operators.

No.	Operator	Description
1	ADD (A, B)	Add images A and B.
2	SUB (A, B)	Subtract image B from A.
3	MUL (A, B)	Multiply images A and B.
4	DIV (A, B)	Divide image A by image B (If the pixel in B has value 0, the corresponding pixel in the resultant image takes the maximum pixel value in A).
5	MAX2 (A, B)	The pixel in the resultant image takes the larger pixel value of images A and B.
6	MIN2 (A, B)	The pixel in the resultant image takes the smaller pixel value of images A and B.
7	ADDC (A)	Increase each pixel value by c.
8	SUBC (A)	Decrease each pixel value by c.
9	MULC (A)	Multiply each pixel value by c.
10	DIVC (A)	Divide each pixel value by c.
11	SQRT (A)	For each pixel with value v, if $v \geq 0$, change its value to $\sqrt{v}$. Otherwise, to $-\sqrt{-v}$.
12	LOG (A)	For each pixel with value v, if $v \geq 0$, change its value to ln(v). Otherwise, to –ln(-v).
13	MAX (A)	Replace the pixel value by the maximum pixel value in a 3×3, 5×5 or 7×7 neighborhood.
14	MIN (A)	Replace the pixel value by the minimum pixel value in a 3×3, 5×5 or 7×7 neighborhood.
15	MED (A)	Replace the pixel value by the median pixel value in a 3×3, 5×5 or 7×7 neighborhood.
16	MEAN (A)	Replace the pixel value by the average pixel value of a 3×3, 5×5 or 7×7 neighborhood.
17	STDV (A)	Replace the pixel value by the standard deviation of pixels in a 3×3, 5×5 or 7×7 neighborhood.

- **The fitness measure:** It measures the extent to which the ground-truth and the extracted ROI overlap. The fitness value of a composite operator is computed in the following way. Suppose G and G' are foregrounds in the ground-truth image and the resultant image of the composite operator respectively. Let $n(X)$ denote the number of pixels within region X, then $Fitness = n(G \cap G') / n(G \cup G')$. The fitness value is between 0 and 1. If G and G' are completely separated, the value is 0; if G and G' are completely overlapped, the value is 1.

- **Parameters and termination:** The key parameters are: the population size M; the number of generations N; the crossover rate; the mutation rate; and the fitness threshold. The GP stops whenever it finishes the pre-specified number of generations or whenever the best composite operator in the population has fitness value greater than the fitness threshold.

2.3.2   Selection, crossover and mutation

GP searches through the space of composite operators to generate new composite operators, which may be better than the previous ones. By searching through the composite operator space, GP gradually adapts the population of composite operators from generation to generation and improves the overall fitness of the whole population. More importantly, GP may find an exceptionally good composite operator during the search. The search is done by performing selection, crossover and mutation operations [2], [71], [118]. The initial population is randomly generated and the fitness of each individual is evaluated.

- **Selection:** The selection operation involves selecting composite operators from the current population. In this chapter, we use tournament selection, where a number of individuals (in this case five) are randomly selected from the current population and the one with the highest fitness value is copied into the new population.

- **Crossover:** To perform crossover, two composite operators are selected on the basis of their fitness values. The higher the fitness value, the more likely the composite operator is selected for crossover. These two composite operators are called parents. One internal node in each of these two parents is randomly selected, and the two subtrees rooted at these two nodes are exchanged between the parents to generate two new composite operators, called offspring. The offspring are composed of subtrees from their parents. If two composite operators are somewhat effective in detection, then some of their parts probably have some merit. The reason that an offspring may be better than the parents is that recombining randomly chosen parts of somewhat effective composite operators may yield a new composite operator that is even more effective in detection.

It is easy to see that the size of one offspring (i.e., the number of nodes in the binary tree representing the offspring), may be greater than both parents. So if we do not control the size of composite operators when implementing crossover in this simple way, the sizes of composite operators will become larger and larger as GP proceeds. This is the well-known code bloat problem of GP. It is a very serious problem, since when the size becomes too large, it will take a long time to execute a composite operator, thus, greatly reducing the search speed of GP. Further, large-size composite operators may overfit the training data by approximating various noisy components of an image. Although the results on the training image may be very good, the performance on unseen testing images may be bad. Also, large composite operators take up a lot of computer memory. Due to the finite computer resources and the desire to achieve a good running speed (efficiency) of GP, we must limit the size of composite operator by specifying its maximum size. In our previous work [17], if the size of one offspring exceeds the *maximum size* allowed, the crossover operation is performed again until the sizes of both offspring are within the limit. Although this simple method guarantees that the size of composite operators does not exceed the size limit, it is a brutal method since it sets a *hard size limit*. The hard size limit may restrict the search performed by GP, since after randomly selecting a crossover point in one composite operator, GP cannot select some nodes of the other composite operator as a crossover point in order to guarantee that both offspring do not exceed the size limit. However, restricting the search may greatly reduce the efficiency of GP, making it less likely to find good composite operators.

One may suggest that after two composite operators are selected, GP may perform crossover twice and may each time keep the offspring of smaller size. This method can enforce the size limit and will prevent the sizes of offspring composite operators from growing large. However, GP will now only search the space of these smaller composite operators. With a small number of nodes, a composite operator may not capture the characteristics of objects to be detected. How to avoid restricting the GP search while at the same time prevent code-bloat is the key to the success of GP and it is still a subject of intensive research. The key is to find a balance between these two conflicting factors.

In this chapter, we set a composite operator size limit to prevent code-bloating, but unlike our previous work, the size limit is a *soft size limit*, so it restricts the GP search less severely than the hard size limit. With a soft size limit, GP can select any node in both composite operators as crossover points. If the size of an offspring exceeds the size limit, GP still keeps it and evaluates it later. If the fitness of this large composite operator is the best or very close to the fitness of the best composite operator in the population, it is kept by GP; otherwise, GP randomly selects one of its sub-trees of size smaller than the size limit to replace it in the population. In this chapter, GP discards any composite operator beyond the size limit unless it is the best one in the population. By keeping the effective composite operators exceeding the size limit, GP enhances the possibility of finding good composite operators, since good composite operators usually contain effective components (sub-trees) and these effective components are kept by the soft size limit and they may transfer to other composite operators during crossover. Also, by keeping some large composite operators, the size difference between composite operators in the population is widened and this is helpful in reducing the possibility of fitness bloat (in which an increasing number of redundant composite operators in the population evaluate to the same fitness value), although it cannot get rid of it. With a hard size limit, many composite operators in the population have size equal or very close to the hard size limit in the later generations of GP. This increases the possibility of fitness bloat. However, large composite operators kept by the soft size limit take a long time to execute and many of them have redundant branches. By getting rid of the redundant branches, we can reduce the size and running time of composite operators without degrading their performance. But, in order to identify the redundant branches, the fitness of each internal node has to be evaluated and this is a time-consuming process. Moreover, some redundant branches are effective components. They are redundant just because they are in an inhospitable context and their effect is cancelled by other nodes. Eliminating them does no good to the GP search since these effective components may go into other friendly composite operators via crossover operation. Also, composite operators with redundant branches are more resistant to destructive crossover and mutation. Without redundant branches, each part of a composite operator is important to its performance and breaking any component may have a major impact on the performance of the composite operator.

- **Mutation:** In order to avoid premature convergence, mutation is introduced to randomly change the structure of some individuals to maintain the diversity of the population. Composite operators are randomly selected for mutation. In this system, there are three types of mutation invoked with equal probability:

1. Randomly select a node of the binary tree representing the composite operator and replace the subtree rooted at this node, including the node selected, by a new randomly generated binary tree
2. Randomly select a node of the binary tree representing the composite operator and replace the primitive operator stored in the node with another primitive operator of the same arity as the replaced one. The replacing primitive operator is selected at random from all the primitive operators with the same arity as the replaced one.
3. Randomly select two subtrees within the composite operator and swap these two subtrees. Of course, neither of the two sub-trees can be the sub-tree of the other.

2.3.3   Steady-state and generational genetic programming

Both steady-state and generational genetic programming are used in this chapter. In *steady-state GP*, two parent composite operators are selected on the basis of their fitness for crossover. The children of this crossover replace a pair of composite operators with the smallest fitness values. The two children are executed immediately and their fitness values are recorded. Then another two parent composite operators are selected for crossover. This process is repeated until the crossover rate is satisfied. Finally, mutation is applied to the resulting population and the mutated composite operators are executed and evaluated. The above cycle is repeated from generation to generation. In *generational GP*, two composite operators are selected on the basis of their fitness values for crossover and generate two offspring. The two offspring are not put into the current population and do not participate in the following crossover operations on the current population. The above process is repeated until the crossover rate is satisfied. Then, mutation is applied to the composite operators in the current population and the offspring from crossover. After mutation is done, selection is applied to the current population to select some composite operators. The number of composite operators selected must meet the condition that after combining with the composite operators from crossover, we get a new population of the same size as the old one. Finally, combine the composite operators from crossover with those selected from the old population to get a new population and the next generation begins. In addition, we adopt an *elitism* replacement method that keeps the best composite operator from generation to generation. Figure 2.1 and Figure 2.2 show the pseudo code for steady-state and generational genetic programming algorithms, respectively.

Steady-state Genetic Programming Algorithm:

1. *randomly generate population P of size M and evaluate each composite operator in P.*
2. *for gen = 1 to N do loop 1 // N is the number of generation.*
3.   *keep the best composite operator in P.*
      repeat
4.   *select 2 composite operators from P based on their fitness values for crossover through tournament selection.*
5.   *select 2 composite operators with the lowest fitness values in P for replacement.*
6.   *perform crossover operation and let the 2 offspring replace the 2 composite operators selected for replacement.*
7.   *execute the 2 offspring and evaluate their fitness values.*
      until crossover rate is met.
8.   *perform mutation on each composite operator with probability of mutation rate and evaluate mutated composite operators.*
      // After crossover and mutation, a new population P' is generated.
9.   *let the best composite operator from population P replace the worst composite operator in P' and let P = P'.*
10. *if the fitness value of the best composite operator in P is above fitness threshold value, then stop.*
11. *for each composite operator in P, do loop 2*
12.   *if its size exceeds the size limit and it is not the best composite operator in P, then replace it with one of its subtrees whose size is within the size limit.*
       endfor // loop 2
       endfor // loop 1

Figure 2.1. Steady-state genetic programming algorithm.

Generational Genetic Programming Algorithm:

1. *randomly generate population P of size M and evaluate each composite operator in P.*
2. *for gen = 1 to N do loop 1 // N is the number of generation*
3.   *keep the best composite operator in P.*
4.   *perform crossoveron the composite operators in P until crossover rate is satisfied and keep all the offspring from crossover separately.*
5.   *perform mutation on the composite operators in P and the offspring from crossover with the probability of mutation rate.*
6.   *perform selection on P to select some composite operators. The number of selected composite operators must be M minus the number of composite operators from crossover.*
7.   *combine the composite operators from crossover with those selected from P to get a new population P' of the same size as P.*
8.   *evaluate offspring from crossover and the mutated composite operators.*
9.   *let the best composite operator from P replace the worst composite operator in P' and let P = P'.*
10.   *if the fitness of the best composite operator in P is above fitness threshold, then stop.*
11.   *for each composite operator in P, do loop 2.*
12.   *if its size exceeds the size limit and it is not the best composite operator in P, then replace it with one of its subtrees whose size is within the size limit.*
    endfor // loop 2
   endfor // loop 1

Figure 2.2. Generational genetic programming algorithm.

2.4   Experiments

Various experiments are performed to test the efficacy of genetic programming in extracting regions of interest from real synthetic aperture radar (SAR) images, infrared (IR) images and RGB color images. We provide detailed results using examples from remote sensing, target recognition, and survallence/monitoring application areas. We give several comparisons to demonstrate the effectiveness of the approach. These include comparisons with the image-based genetic programming and the traditional ROI extraction algorithm. We also provide the performance of the GP with hard limit on the composite operator size. The results from the hard size limit GP are compared with those from the MDL-based GP in chapter 3. We provide examples of both two-class classification and multi-class classification.

The size of SAR images is 128×128, except the tank SAR images whose size is 80×80, and the size of IR and RGB color images is 160×120. GP in chapter 2.4.1 Examples 1-5, 2.4.2, 2.4.5 and 2.4.6 is not applied to a whole training image, but only to a region or regions carefully selected from a training image, to generate the composite operators. The generated composite operator (with the highest fitness) is then applied to the whole training image and to some other testing images to evaluate it. The advantage of performing training on a small selected region is that it can greatly reduce the training time, making it practical for the GP system to be used as a subsystem of other learning systems, which improve the efficiency of GP by adapting the parameters of GP system based on its performance. Our experiments show that if the training regions are carefully selected from the training images, the best composite operator generated by GP is effective. In the following experiments in sections 2.4.1, 2.4.2, 2.4.3, and 2.4.6, the parameters are: population size (100), the number of generations (70), the fitness threshold value (1.0), the crossover rate (0.6), the mutation rate (0.05), the soft size limit of composite operators (30), and the segmentation threshold (0). In each experiment, GP is invoked ten times with the same parameters and the same training region(s). The coordinate of the upper left corner of an image is (0, 0). The ground-truth is used only during the training, it is not needed during testing. We use it in testing only for evaluating the performance of the composite operator on testing images. The size, orientation or shape of the objects in testing images is different from those in the training images.

2.4.1   SAR Images

Five experiments are performed with real SAR images. The experimental results from one run and the average performance of ten runs are given in Table 2.3. We select the run in which GP finds the best composite operator among the composite operators found in all ten runs. The first two rows show the average values of the above fitness values over all ten runs. The third and fourth rows show the fitness value of the best composite operator and the population fitness value (average fitness value of all the composite operators in the population) on *training region (s)* in the initial and final generations in the selected run. The fitness values of the best composite operators on the entire training image (numbers with a * superscript) and other testing images in their entirety are also given. The regions extracted during the training and testing by the best composite operator from the selected run are shown in the following examples.

Example 1 — Road extraction: Three images contain road, the first one contains horizontal paved road and field (Figure 2.3(a)); the second one contains unpaved road and field (Figure 2.10 (a)); the third one contains vertical paved road and grass (Figure 2.10(d)). Training is done on the training regions of training image shown in Figure 2.3(a). After the training, the learned composite operator is evaluated on the whole training image and testing images. There are two training regions, locating from (5, 19) to (50, 119) and from (82, 48) to (126, 124), respectively. Figure 2.3(b) shows the ground-truth provided by the user and the training regions. The white region corresponds to the road and only the training regions of the ground-truth are used in the evaluation during the training. Figure 2.4 shows the sixteen primitive feature images of the training image.

Table 2.3. The performance on various examples of SAR images

	Training Performance									
	Road		Lake		River		Field		Tank	
	f_{op}	f_p	f_{op}	f_p	f_{op}	f_p	f_{op}	f_p	f_{op}	f_p
Ave. $f_{initial}$	0.55	0.27	0.59	0.32	0.48	0.18	0.54	0.37	0.61	0.17
Ave. f_{final}	0.83	0.60	0.95	0.92	0.85	0.77	0.76	0.59	0.86	0.68
$f_{initial}$	0.68	0.28	0.56	0.32	0.65	0.18	0.53	0.39	0.51	0.16
f_{final}	0.95 0.93*	0.67	0.97 0.93*	0.93	0.90 0.71*	0.85	0.78 0.89*	0.64	0.88 0.88*	0.80
	Testing Performance									
	Road		Lake		River		Field		Tank	
f_{test}	0.90, 0.93		0.98		0.83		0.80		0.84	

f_{op}: fitness of the best composite operator on selected region(s),
f_p : fitness of population on selected region(s),
*: indicate fitness on the *entire* training images,
$f_{initial}$: fitness of the initial generation on selected region(s),
f_{final}: fitness of the final population on selected region(s),
f_{test}: fitness of the best composite operator on the *entire* testing images.

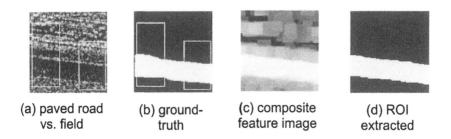

(a) paved road   (b) ground-   (c) composite   (d) ROI
   vs. field   truth   feature image   extracted

Figure 2.3. Training SAR image containing road.

The generational GP is used to synthesize a composite operator to extract the road and the results of the best of the ten runs (sixth run) are reported. The fitness value of the best composite operator in the initial population is 0.68 and the population fitness value is 0.28. The fitness value of the best composite operator in the final population is 0.95 and the population fitness value is 0.67. Figure 2.3(c) shows the output image of the best composite operator on the whole training image and Figure 2.3(d) shows the binary image after segmentation. The output image has both positive pixels in brighter shade and negative pixels in darker shade. Positive pixels belong to the region to be extracted. The fitness value of the extracted ROI is 0.93. The best composite operator has 17 nodes and its depth is 16. It has only one leaf node containing 5×5 median image. The median image is less noisy, since median filtering is effective in eliminating speckle noises. The best composite operator is shown in Figure 2.5, where PFIM14 is 5×5 median image. Figure 2.6 shows how the average fitness of the best composite operator and average fitness of population over all 10 runs change as GP explores the composite operator space. Unlike [17] where the population fitness approaches the fitness of the best composite operator as GP proceeds, in Figure 2.6, population fitness is much lower than that of best composite operator even at the end of GP search. It is reasonable, since we don't restrict the selection of crossover points. The population fitness is not important since only the best composite operator is used in testing. If GP finds one effective composite operator, the GP learning is successful. The large difference between the fitness of the best composite operator and the population indicates that the diversity of the population is always maintained during the GP search, which is very helpful in preventing premature convergence.

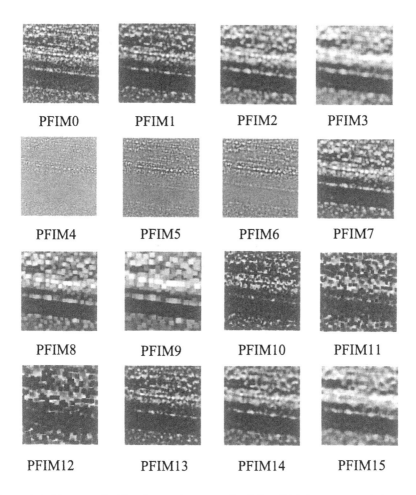

Figure 2.4. Sixteen primitive feature images of training SAR image containing road.

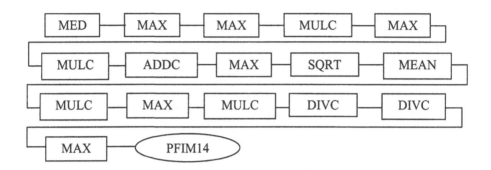

Figure 2.5. Learned composite operator tree.

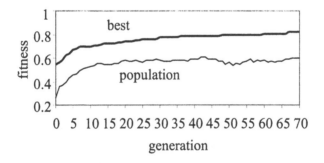

generation

Figure 2.6. Fitness versus generation (road vs. field).

Ten best composite operators are learned in ten runs. After computing the percentage of each primitive operator and primitive feature image among the total number of internal nodes (representing primitive operators) and the total number of leaf nodes (representing primitive feature images) of these ten best compsite operators, we get the utility (frequency of occurence) of primitive operators and primitive feature images, which is shown in Figure 2.7(a) and (b). MED (primitive operator 15) and PFIM5 (5×5 deviation image) have the highest frequency of utility. Figure 2.8 shows the output image of each node of the best composite operator shown in Figure 2.5. From left to right and top to bottom, the images correspond to nodes sorted in the pre-order traversal of the binary tree representing the best composite operator. The output of the root node is shown in Figure 2.3(c), and Figure 2.8 shows the outputs of other nodes. The primitive operators in Figure 2.8 are connected by arrow. The operator at the tail of an arrow provides input to the operator at the head of the arrow. After segmenting the output image of a node, we get the ROI (shown as the white region) extracted by the corresponding subtree rooted at the node. The extracted ROIs and their fitness values are shown in Figure 2.9. If an output image of a node has no positive pixel (for example, the output of MEAN primitive operator), nothing is extracted and the fitness value is 0; if an output image has positive pixels only (for example, PFIM14 has positive pixels only), everything is extracted and the fitness is 0.25. The output of the root node storing primitive operator MED is shown in Figure 2.3(d).

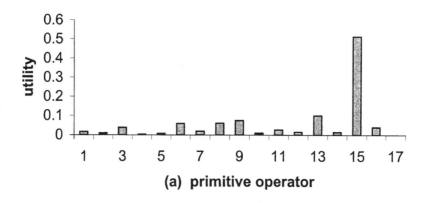

(a) primitive operator

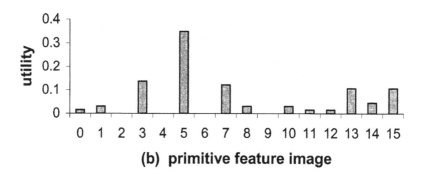

(b) primitive feature image

Figure 2.7. Utility of primitive operators and primitive feature images.

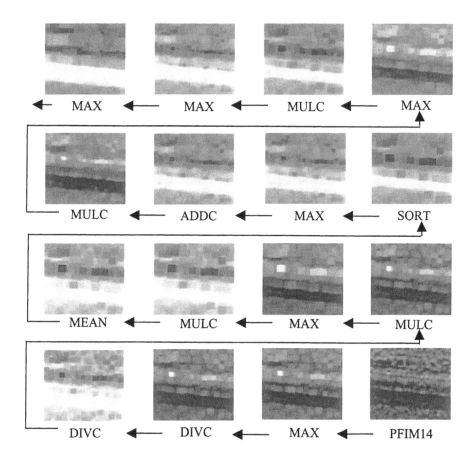

MAX ← MAX ← MULC ← MAX

MULC ← ADDC ← MAX ← SORT

MEAN ← MULC ← MAX ← MULC

DIVC ← DIVC ← MAX ← PFIM14

Figure 2.8. Feature images output by the nodes of the best composite operator. The ouput of the root node is shown Figure 2.3(c).

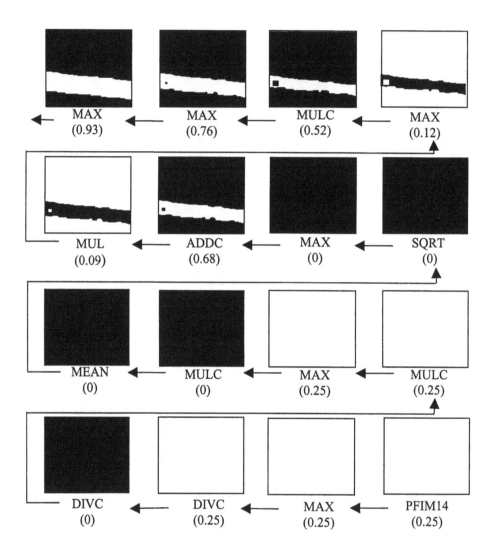

Figure 2.9. ROIs extracted from the output images of the nodes of the best composite operator. The fitness value is shown for the entire image. The ouput of the root node is shown Figure 2.3(d).

We applied the composite operator obtained in the above training to the other two real SAR images shown in Figure 2.10 (a) and Figure 2.10 (d). Figure 2.10 (b) and Figure 2.10 (e) show the output of the composite operator and Figure 2.10 (c) shows the region extracted from Figure 2.10 (a). The fitness value of the region is 0.90. Figure 2.10 (f) shows the region extracted from Figure 2.10(d). The fitness value of the region is 0.93.

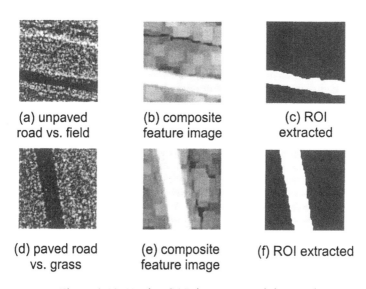

(a) unpaved road vs. field

(b) composite feature image

(c) ROI extracted

(d) paved road vs. grass

(e) composite feature image

(f) ROI extracted

Figure 2.10. Testing SAR images containing road.

Example 2 — Lake Extraction: Two SAR images contain lake (Figure 2.11(a), Figure 2.12(a)), the first one contains a lake and field, and the second one contains a lake and grass. Figure 2.11(a) shows the original training image containing lake and field and the training region from (85, 85) to (127, 127). Figure 2.11(b) shows the ground-truth provided by the user. The white region corresponds to the lake to be extracted. Figure 2.12 (a) shows the image containing lake and grass used only in testing.

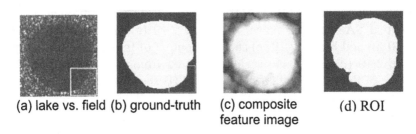

(a) lake vs. field (b) ground-truth   (c) composite
                                        feature image   (d) ROI

Figure 2.11. Training SAR image containing lake.

The steady-state GP is used to generate the composite operator and the results of the best of ten runs (ninth run) are shown. The fitness value of the best composite operator in the initial population is 0.56 and the population fitness value is 0.32. The fitness value of the best composite operator in the final population is 0.97 and the population fitness value is 0.93. Figure 2.11(c) shows the output image of the best composite operator on the whole training image and Figure 2.11(d) shows the binary image after segmentation. The fitness value of the extracted ROI is 0.93.

We apply the composite operator to the testing image containing lake and grass. Figure 2.12(b) shows the output of the composite operator and Figure 2.12(c) shows the region extracted from Figure 2.12(a). The fitness of the region is 0.98.

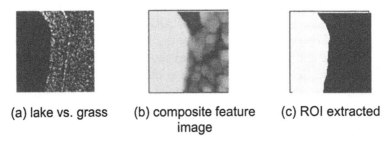

(a) lake vs. grass   (b) composite feature   (c) ROI extracted
                           image

Figure 2.12. Testing SAR image containing lake.

Example 3 — River Extraction: Two SAR images contain river and field. Figure 2.13(a) and Figure 2.13(b) show the original training image and the ground-truth provided by the user. The white region in Figure 2.13(b) corresponds to the river to be extracted. The training regions are from (68, 31) to (126, 103) and from (2, 8) to (28, 74). The testing SAR image is shown in Figure 2.16(a).

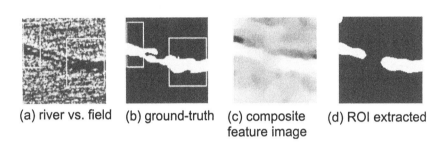

(a) river vs. field   (b) ground-truth   (c) composite feature image   (d) ROI extracted

Figure 2.13. Training SAR image containing river.

The steady-state GP was used to generate the composite operator and the results from the best of ten runs (fourth run) are reported. The fitness value of the best composite operator in the initial population is 0.65 and the population fitness value is 0.18. The fitness value of the best composite operator in the final population is 0.90 and the population fitness value is 0.85. Figure 2.13(c) shows the output image of the best composite operator on the whole training image and Figure 2.13(d) shows the binary image after segmentation. The fitness value of the extracted ROI is 0.71. The best composite operator has 29 nodes and a depth of 19. It has five leaf nodes that all contain 7×7 median image shown in Figure 2.14. There are 17 MED operators that are very useful in eliminating speckle noise. Figure 2.15 shows how the average fitness of the best composite operator and average fitness of population over all 10 runs change as GP explores the composite operator space.

(MED (MED (MED (ADD (MED (STDV (MED
PFIM15))) (MED (MED (MED (MED (MED
(MIN2 (MED PFIM15) (MED (MED (MED
(MIN2 (MED PFIM15) (MED (MED (MIN2
PFIM15 (SUBC (DIVC PFIM15)))))))))))))))))))

Figure 2.14. Learned composite operator tree.

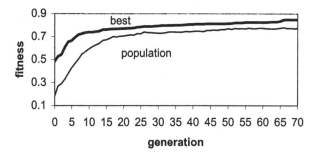

Figure 2.15. Fitness versus generation (river vs. field).

(a) river vs. field   (b) composite feature image   (c) ROI extracted

Figure 2.16. Testing SAR image containing river.

We apply the composite operator to the testing image containing a river and field. Figure 2.16(b) shows the output of the composite operator and Figure 2.16(c) shows the region extracted from Figure 2.16(a) and the fitness value of the region is 0.83. There are some islands in the river and these islands along with part of the river around them are not extracted.

Example 4 — Field Extraction: Two SAR images contain field and grass. Figure 2.17(a) and (b) show the original training image and the ground-truth. The training regions are from (17, 3) to (75, 61) and from (79, 62) to (124, 122). Extracting field from a SAR image containing field and grass is the most difficult task among the five experiments, since the grass and field are similar to each other and some small regions between grassy areas are actually field pixels.

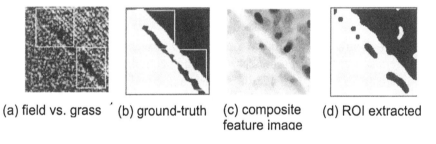

(a) field vs. grass ´ (b) ground-truth   (c) composite   (d) ROI extracted
                                           feature imaqe

Figure 2.17. Training SAR image containing field.

The generational GP was used to generate the composite operator and the results from the best of ten runs (second run) are reported. The fitness value of the best composite operator in the initial population is 0.53 and the population fitness value is 0.39. The fitness value of the best composite operator in the final population is 0.78 and the population fitness value is 0.64. Figure 2.17(c) shows the output image of the best composite operator on the whole training image and Figure 2.17(d) shows the binary image after segmentation. The fitness value of the extracted ROI is 0.89.

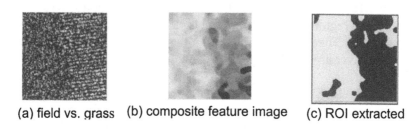

(a) field vs. grass   (b) composite feature image   (c) ROI extracted

Figure 2.18. Testing SAR image containing field.

We apply the composite operator to the testing image containing field and grass shown in Figure 2.18(a). Figure 2.18(b) shows the output of the composite operator and Figure 2.18(c) shows the region extracted from Figure 2.18(a). The fitness value of the region is 0.80.

Example 5 — Tank Extraction: We use 80×80 size SAR images of a T72 tank that are taken under different depression and azimuth angles. The training image contains a T72 tank at a 17° depression angle and 135° azimuth angle, which is shown in Figure 2.19(a). The training region is from (19, 17) to (68, 66). The testing SAR image contains a T72 tank at a 20° depression angle and 225° azimuth angle, which is shown in Figure 2.22(a). The ground-truth is shown in Figure 2.19(b).

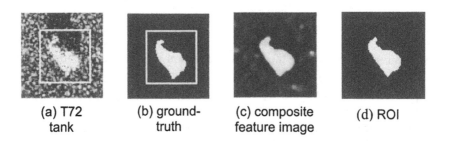

(a) T72 tank   (b) ground-truth   (c) composite feature image   (d) ROI

Figure 2.19. Training SAR image containing tank.

The generational GP is applied to synthesize composite operators for tank detection and the results from the best of ten runs (first run) are reported. The fitness value of the best composite operator in the initial population is 0.51 and the population fitness value is 0.16. The fitness value of the best composite operator in the final population is 0.88 and the population fitness value is 0.80. Figure 2.19(c) shows the output image of the best composite operator on the whole training image and Figure 2.19 (d) shows the binary image after segmentation. The fitness value of the extracted ROI is 0.88. The best composite operator, shown in Figure 2.20, has 10 nodes and its depth is 9. It has only one leaf node, which contains the 5×5 mean image. Figure 2.21 shows how the average fitness of the best composite operator and average fitness of population over all 10 runs change as GP proceeds.

(MED (SQRT (MULC (MULC (SUBC (MULC
(SQRT (SUBC (SQRT PFIM2)))))))))

Figure 2.20. Learned composite operator tree in LISP notation.

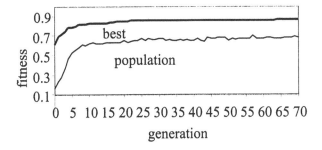

Figure 2.21. Fitness versus generation (T72 tank).

We apply the composite operator to the testing image containing T72 tank under depression angle 20° and azimuth angle 225°. Figure 2.22(b) shows the output of the composite operator and Figure 2.22(c) shows the region corresponding to the tank. The fitness of the extracted ROI is 0.84.

(a) T72 tank   (b) composite feature image (c) ROI extracted

Figure 2.22. Testing SAR image containing tank.

Our results show that GP is very much capable of synthesizing composite operators for target detection. With more and more SAR images collected by satellites and airplanes, it is impractical for human experts to scan each SAR image to find targets. Applying the synthesized composite operators on these images, regions containing potential targets can be quickly detected and passed on to automatic target recognition systems or to human experts for further examination. Concentrating on the regions of interest, the human experts and recognition systems can perform recognition task more effectively and more efficiently.

Note that composite operators shown in Figure 2.5 and Figure 2.20 may be called as "processing chains," which is a simpler binary tree in which each internal node has only one child. Most of the composite operators learned by GP in our experiments are not processing chains.

2.4.2   Infrared and color images

One experiment is performed with infrared (IR) images and two are performed with RGB color images. The experimental results from one run and the average performance of ten runs are shown in Table 2.4. As we did in chapter 2.4.1, we select the run in which GP finds the best composite operator among the composite operators found in all the ten runs. The regions extracted during the training and testing by the best composite operator from the selected run are shown in the following examples.

Table 2.4. The performance results on IR and RGB color images.

	Training performance					
	IR image - people		RGB image - car		RGB image - SUV	
	f_{op}	f_p	f_{op}	f_p	f_{op}	f_p
Ave. $f_{initial}$	0.59	0.21	0.47	0.18	0.34	0.21
Ave. f_{final}	0.85	0.65	0.72	0.67	0.61	0.56
$f_{initial}$	0.56	0.23	0.35	0.18	0.33	0.22
f_{final}	0.93 0.85*	0.79	0.84 0.82*	0.79	0.69 0.69*	0.65
	Testing performance					
	IR image - people		RGB image - car		RGB image - SUV	
f_{test}	0.84, 0.81, 0.86		0.76		0.58	

f_{op}:   fitness of the best composite operator on selected region(s),
f_p :   fitness of population on selected region(s),
*:   indicate finess on the *entire* training images,
$f_{initial}$: fitness of the initial generation on selected region(s),
f_{final}: fitness of the final population on selected region(s),
f_{test}: fitness of the best composite operator on the *entire* testing images.

People extraction in IR images: In IR images, pixel values correspond to the temperature in the scene. We have four IR images with one used in training and the other three used in testing. Figure 2.23(a) and (b) show the training image and the ground-truth. Two training regions are from (59, 9) to (106, 88) and from (2, 3) to (21, 82), respectively. The left training region contains no pixel belonging to the person. The reason for selecting it during the training is that there are major pixel intensity changes among the pixels in this region. Nothing in this region should be detected. The fitness of composite operator on this region is defined as one minus the percentage of pixels detected in the region. If nothing is detected, the fitness value is 1.0. Averaging the fitness values of the two training regions, we get the fitness during the training. When the learned composite operator is applied to the whole training image, the fitness is computed as a measurement of the overlap between the ground-truth and the extracted ROI, as we did in the previous experiments. Three testing IR images are shown in Figure 2.26(a), (d) and (g).

| (a) person | (b) ground-truth | (c) composite feature image | (d) ROI extracted |

Figure 2.23. Training IR image containing a person.

The generational GP is applied to synthesize composite operators for person detection and the results from the best of ten runs (third run) are reported. The fitness value of the best composite operator in the initial population is 0.56 and the population fitness value is 0.23. The fitness value of the best composite operator in the final population is 0.93 and the population fitness value is 0.79. Figure 2.23(c) shows the output image of the best composite operator on the whole training image and Figure 2.23(d) shows the binary image after segmentation. The fitness value of the extracted ROI is 0.85. The best composite operator (shown in Figure 2.24) has 28 nodes and a depth of 13 with 9 leaf nodes. Figure 2.25 shows how the average fitness of the best composite operator and average fitness of population over all the 10 runs change as GP proceeds.

(SQRT (SQRT (SUBC (SQRT (MAX2 (MAX2 PFIM1 (SUB (MAX2 PFIM14 PFIM15) (DIV (MULC (SQRT (MAX (MAX (ADD PFIM12 PFIM15))))) PFIM9))) (DIV (MULC (SQRT (MAX (ADD PFIM12 PFIM9)))) PFIM9))))))

Figure 2.24. Learned composite operator tree in LISP notation.

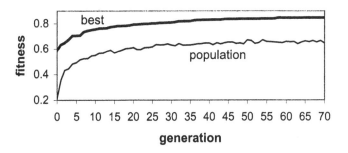

Figure 2.25. Fitness versus generation (person).

We apply the composite operator to the testing images shown in Figure 2.26. Figure 2.26(b), (e) and (h) show the output of the composite operator and Figure 2.26(c), (f) and (i) show the ROI extracted. Their fitness values are 0.84, 0.81 and 0.86 respectively.

Car extraction in RGB color images: GP is applied to learn features to detect a car in RGB color images. Unlike previous experiments, the primitive feature images in this experiment are RED, GREEN and BLUE planes of a RGB color image. Figure 2.27(a), (b) and (c) show the RED, GREEN and BLUE planes of the training image. The ground-truth is shown in Figure 2.27(d). The training region is from (21, 3) to (91, 46).

The steady-state GP is applied to synthesize composite operators for car detection and the results from best of ten runs (fourth run) are reported. The fitness value of the best composite operator in the initial population is 0.35 and the population fitness value is 0.18. The fitness value of the best composite operator in the final population is 0.84 and the population fitness value is 0.79. Figure 2.27(e) shows the output image of the best composite operator on the whole training image and Figure 2.27(f) shows the binary image after segmentation. The fitness value of the extracted ROI is 0.82. The best composite operator has 44 nodes and its depth is 21. It has ten leaf nodes with one containing GREEN plane and the others containing BLUE plane. It is shown in Figure 2.28, where PFG means GREEN plane and PFB means BLUE plane. Note that only green and blue planes are used by the composite operator. Figure 2.29 shows how the average fitness of the best composite operator and average fitness of population over all 10 runs change as GP runs.

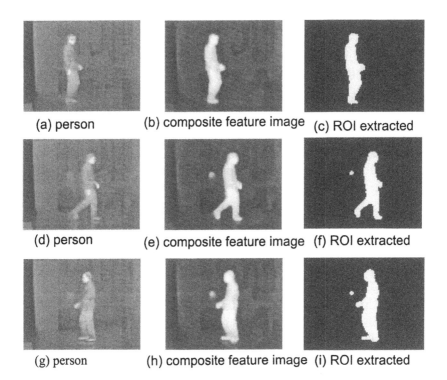

(a) person   (b) composite feature image   (c) ROI extracted

(d) person   (e) composite feature image   (f) ROI extracted

(g) person   (h) composite feature image   (i) ROI extracted

Figure 2.26. Testing IR images containing a person.

(a) RED plane   (b) GREEN plane   (c) BLUE plane

(d) ground-truth   (e) composite feature   (f) ROI extracted
                           image

Figure 2.27. Training RGB color image containing car.

(MED (MED (MED (MULC (MUL (SUB (MIN
(MEAN (MAX2 (MED (ADDC (MAX2 (ADDC
(ADDC (MED (MAX2 (MED (MED (MAX2 (MED
(ADDC PFB)) PFB))) PFB)))) PFB))) (MED PFG))))
(ADDC (MAX2 (ADDC (ADDC (MED (MAX2 (MED
(MED (MAX2 (MED (ADDC PFB)) PFB))) PFB))))
PFB))) (ADDC PFB))))))

Figure 2.28. Learned composite operator tree in LISP notation.

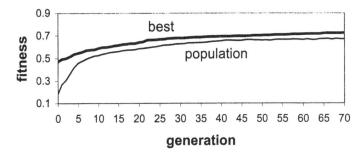

Figure 2.29. Fitness versus generation (car).

We apply the composite operator to the testing image whose RED plane is shown in Figure 2.30(a). Figure 2.30 (b) shows the output of the composite operator and Figure 2.30(c) shows the ROI extracted. The fitness value of extracted ROI is 0.76.

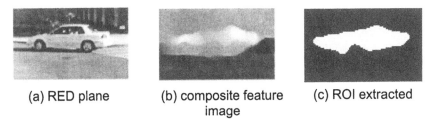

(a) RED plane   (b) composite feature   (c) ROI extracted
                           image

Figure 2.30. Testing RGB color image containing car.

SUV extraction in RGB color images: In this subsection, GP is applied to learn features to detect SUV (sports utility vehicle) in RGB color images. The images containing a SUV have more complicated background than the images containing the car, increasing the difficulty in SUV detection. This will be a difficult example for any segmentation technique in computer vision and pattern recognition. Figure 2.31(a), (b) and (c) show the RED, GREEN and BLUE planes of the training image and Figure 2.31(d) shows the ground-truth. The training region is from (20, 21) to (139, 100). Figure 2.31(f) and (g) show the RED plane and the ground-truth of the testing image.

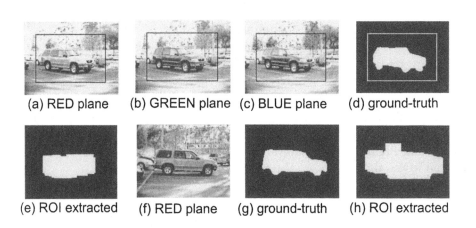

(a) RED plane   (b) GREEN plane (c) BLUE plane   (d) ground-truth

(e) ROI extracted   (f) RED plane   (g) ground-truth   (h) ROI extracted

Figure 2.31. Training and testing RGB color image containing SUV.

The steady-state GP is applied to synthesize composite operators for SUV detection and the results from the best of ten runs (fourth run) are reported. The fitness value of the best composite operator in the initial population is 0.33 and the population fitness value is 0.22. The fitness value of the best composite operator in the final population is 0.69 and the population fitness value is 0.65. Figure 2.31(e) and (h) show the ROI extracted by the best composite operator from training and testing images. The fitness values of the extracted ROIs are 0.69 and 0.58, respectively. The extracted ROIs are not very satisfactory, since the shapes of ROIs differ from the shapes of vehicles in images. However, the extracted ROIs contain SUVs in the training and testing images, which means the locations of the vehicle are correctly detected.

2.4.3   Comparison with GP with hard limit on composite operator size

As stated in chapter 2.3, GP has a well-known code bloat problem in that the size of individuals becomes larger and larger as GP proceeds if no measure is taken to control the size. Large individuals cause problems such as reducing the speed of GP, taking up a lot of computer memory, and overfitting the training data. To resolve this problem, a simple way is to set a limit on the size of individuals. If crossover or mutation produces an individual above the size limit, the individual is discarded and crossover or mutation is performed again.

In this section, the performance of a *hard-size GP* (GP with hard limit on composite operator size = 30) is compared with the *soft-size GP* (GP with soft limit on composite operator size) whose performance is reported before. The major difference between the soft-size GP and the hard-size GP, as stated in chapter 2.3, is that in the soft-size GP, a composite operator with size above the size limit is kept in the population if its fitness value is the highest (used in this chapter) or above a certain threshold value. All the other parameters of these two GPs are the same.

Table 2.5 shows the performance of the hard-size GP. In the following, the results from the best composite operator found in ten runs are shown. The average performance of hard-size GP over ten runs is compared with that of a MDL-based GP with smart operators in chapter 3.

Table 2.5. The performance results on various examples of SAR images. The hard limit on composite operator size is used.

	Training Performance									
	Road		Lake		River		Field		Tank	
	f_{op}	f_p	f_{op}	f_p	f_{op}	f_p	f_{op}	f_p	f_{op}	f_p
Ave. $f_{initial}$	0.47	0.26	0.64	0.32	0.49	0.18	0.53	0.38	0.49	0.16
Ave. f_{final}	0.82	0.81	0.93	0.92	0.82	0.77	0.73	0.72	0.85	0.83
$f_{initial}$	0.60	0.27	0.62	0.30	0.59	0.19	0.52	0.38	0.65	0.17
f_{final}	0.94 0.90*	0.93	0.99 0.95*	0.95	0.89 0.72*	0.86	0.78 0.88*	0.77	0.88 0.88*	0.87
	Testing Performance									
	Road		Lake		River		Field		Tank	
f_{test}	0.90, 0.93		0.97		0.83		0.81		0.84	

f_{op}:   fitness of the best composite operator on selected region(s),
f_p :   fitness of population on selected region(s),
*:   indicate finess on the *entire* training images,
$f_{initial}$: fitness of the initial generation on selected region(s),
f_{final}: fitness of the final population on selected region(s),
f_{test}: fitness of the best composite operator on the *entire* testing images.

• **Road extraction:** Figure 2.3(a) shows the training image and Figure 2.10(a), (d) show the testing images. The generational GP is used to generate a composite operator to extract the road and the best composite operator is found in the seventh run. The fitness value of the best composite operator in the initial population is 0.60 and the population fitness value is 0.27. The fitness value of the best composite operator in the final population is 0.94 and the population fitness value is 0.93. The fitness of the extracted ROI is 0.90. Figure 2.32(a) shows the output image of the best composite operator in the final population and Figure 2.32(b) shows the extracted ROI. We apply the composite operator obtained in the above training to the two testing SAR images. Figure 2.32(c) and (d) show the output image of the composite operator and the ROI extracted from Figure 2.10(a), respectively. The fitness value of the extracted ROI is 0.90. Figure 2.32 (e) and (f) show the output image of the composite operator and the ROI extracted from Figure 2.10(d), respectively. The fitness value of the extracted ROI is 0.93.

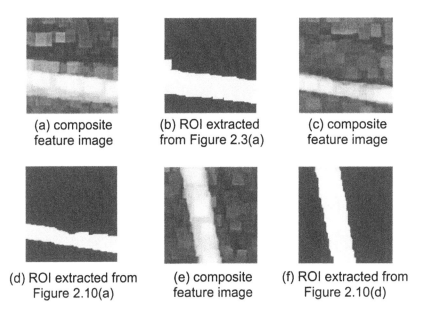

(a) composite feature image   (b) ROI extracted from Figure 2.3(a)   (c) composite feature image

(d) ROI extracted from Figure 2.10(a)   (e) composite feature image   (f) ROI extracted from Figure 2.10(d)

Figure 2.32. Results on SAR images containing road.

The best composite operator has 27 nodes and its depth is 16. It has five leaf nodes, three contain 5×5 median image and the other two contain 7×7 median image. It is shown in Figure 2.33, where PFIM14 and PFIM15 are 5×5 and 7×7 median images, respectively. The median images have less speckle noise, since median filtering is effective in eliminating speckle noise. Figure 2.34 shows the change in the average fitness of the best composite operators and the average fitness of the populations over all the 10 runs as GP explores the composite operator space. GP gradually shifts the population to the regions of space containing good composite operators.

```
(MAX (MAX (MIN (DIVC (DIV (ADDC
(ADD (ADDC (ADD (SUBC (ADDC (ADD
(SUBC (STDV (MAX (SUBC PFIM15))))
(MAX (SUBC PFIM14))))) (MAX (SUBC
PFIM14))))  (MAX  (SUBC  PFIM14))))
PFIM15)))))
```

Figure 2.33. Learned composite operator tree in LISP notation.

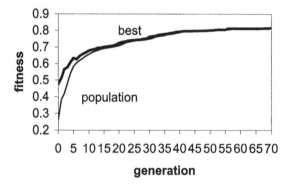

Figure 2.34. Fitness versus generation (road vs. field).

• **Lake extraction:** Figure 2.11(a) shows the training image and Figure 2.12(a) shows the testing image. The steady-state GP is used to generate the composite operator and the best composite operator is found in the 4th run. The fitness value of the best composite operator in the initial population is 0.62 and the population fitness value is 0.30. The fitness value of the best composite operator in the final population is 0.99 and the population fitness value is 0.95. The fitness of the extracted ROI is 0.95. Figure 2.35(a) shows the output image of the best composite operator in the final population and Figure 2.35(b) shows the extracted ROI. We apply the composite operator to the testing SAR image. Figure 2.35(c) and (d) show the output image of the composite operator and the extracted ROI with fitness value 0.97, respectively. In Figure 2.35(a) and (c), pixels in the small dark regions have very low pixel values (negative values with very large absolute value), thus making many pixels appear bright, although some of them have negative pixel values.

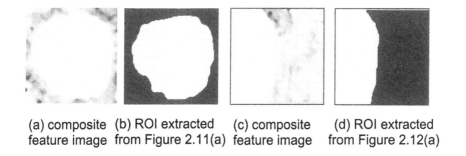

(a) composite   (b) ROI extracted   (c) composite   (d) ROI extracted
feature image from Figure 2.11(a) feature image   from Figure 2.12(a)

Figure 2.35. Results on SAR images containing lake.

- **River extraction:** Figure 2.13(a) shows the training image and Figure 2.16(a) shows the testing image. The steady-state GP is used to generate the composite operator and the results from the first run are reported. The fitness value of the best composite operator in the initial population is 0.59 and the population fitness value is 0.19. The fitness value of the best composite operator in the final population is 0.89 and the population fitness value is 0.86. The fitness of the extracted ROI is 0.72. Figure 2.36(a) shows the output image of the best composite operator in the final population and Figure 2.36(b) shows the extracted ROI. We apply the composite operator to the testing image. Figure 2.36(c) and (d) show the output image of the composite operator and the extracted ROI with fitness value 0.83.

The best composite operator has 30 nodes and its depth is 23. It has four leaf nodes, three contain 5×5 mean image and the other one contains 3×3 mean image. There are more than ten MED operators that are very useful in eliminating speckle noise. It is shown in Figure 2.37. Figure 2.38 shows how the average fitness of the best composite operators and the average fitness of the populations over all the 10 runs change as GP explores the composite operator space.

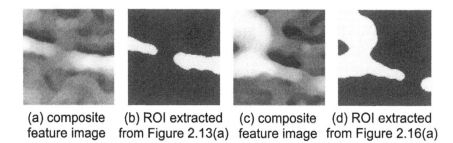

| (a) composite | (b) ROI extracted | (c) composite | (d) ROI extracted |
| feature image | from Figure 2.13(a) | feature image | from Figure 2.16(a) |

Figure 2.36. Results on SAR images containing river.

```
(MULC (MED (MED (MED (MED (MED
(MED (MED (MED (MED (MED (MIN
(ADDC (LOG (ADD (MAX (MIN (MULC
PFIM2))) (DIV (MIN (MULC (MED (MIN
(MAX (SUB PFIM2 (MULC PFIM2)))))))
PFIM1))))))))))))))))
```

Figure 2.37. Learned composite operator tree in LISP notation.

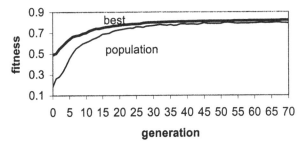

Figure 2.38. Fitness versus generation (river vs. field).

• **Field extraction:** Figure 2.17(a) shows the training image and Figure 2.18(a) shows the testing image. The generational GP is used to generate the composite operator and the results from the 7th run are reported The fitness value of the best composite operator in the initial population is 0.52 and the population fitness value is 0.38. The fitness value of the best composite operator in the final population is 0.78 and the population fitness value is 0.77. The fitness of the extracted ROI is 0.88. Figure 2.39(a) shows the output image of the best composite operator in the final population and Figure 2.39(b) shows the extracted ROI. We apply the composite operator to the testing image. Figure 2.39(c) and (d) show the output image of the composite operator and the extracted ROI with fitness value 0.81.

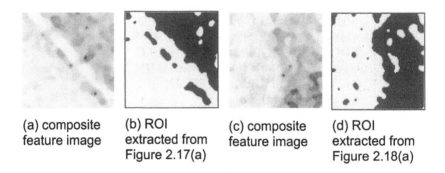

(a) composite
feature image

(b) ROI
extracted from
Figure 2.17(a)

(c) composite
feature image

(d) ROI
extracted from
Figure 2.18(a)

Figure 2.39. Results on SAR images containing field.

- **Tank extraction:** Figure 2.19(a) shows the training image and Figure 2.22(a) shows the testing image. The generational GP is used to generate the composite operator and the results from the 6th run are reported. The fitness value of the best composite operator in the initial population is 0.65 and the population fitness value is 0.17. The fitness value of the best composite operator in the final population is 0.88 and the population fitness value is 0.87. The fitness of the extracted ROI is 0.88. Figure 2.40(a) shows the output image of the best composite operator in the final population and Figure 2.40(b) shows the extracted ROI. We apply the composite operator to the testing image. Figure 2.40(c) and (d) show the output image of the composite operator and the extracted ROI with fitness value 0.84.

The best composite operator has 28 nodes and its depth is 17. It has four leaf nodes with two containing a 3×3 minimum image, one containing a 7×7 maximum image and one containing a 7×7 minimum image. It is shown in Figure 2.41. Figure 2.42 shows how the average fitness of the best composite operators and the average fitness of the populations over all the 10 runs change as GP proceeds.

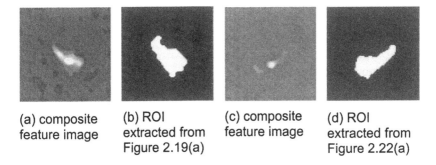

(a) composite feature image

(b) ROI extracted from Figure 2.19(a)

(c) composite feature image

(d) ROI extracted from Figure 2.22(a)

Figure 2.40. Results on SAR images containing tank.

(MED (MED (MUL (MIN PFIM10) (MUL (MAX PFIM12) (MIN2 (MAX (SUBC (DIVC (MIN (MEAN PFIM9))))) (SUBC (MED (SUBC (MAX (MAX (SUBC (MAX (MAX (SUBC (MAX (MAX (SUBC PFIM10)))))))))))))))))

Figure 2.41. Learned composite operator tree in LISP notation.

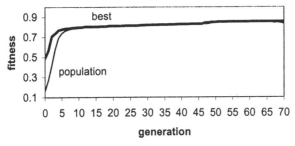

Figure 2.42. Fitness versus generation (T72 tank).

Comparing Table 2.3 and Table 2.5, we find that there is not much difference between the soft and hard size limits since both use a limit of 30 as the size of a composite operator. The only difference between them is that in the case of the soft size limit an exception is allowed if the fitness of an individual is the highest in the population.

2.4.4   Comparison with image-based GP

This subchapter is an advancement to our previous work in [17], where we also applied genetic programming to learn composite operators for object detection. The three major differences between the method presented here and that in [17] are:

1. Unlike [17] where a whole training image is used during training (Image-based GP), here GP runs on carefully selected region(s) (Region-based GP) to reduce the training time.

2. The hard size limit on the composite operator is replaced by the soft size limit in this chapter. This removes the restriction on the selection of crossover point in the parent composite operators to improve the search efficiency of GP, as stated in chapter 2.3.2.

3. Only the first mutation type in chapter 2.3.2 and only the first seven primitive feature images are used in [17]. With more mutation types and more primitive feature images used, the diversity of the composite operator population can be further increased.

We summarize the experimental results on SAR images in [17] for the purpose of comparison. The parameters are: the same population size (100), 100 generations (vs. 70), the same fitness threshold value (1.0), the same crossover rate (0.6), 0.1 mutation rate (vs. 0.05), a hard limit of 30 on the maximum size (number of internal nodes) of composite operators (vs. soft limit of 30), and the same segmentation threshold (0). In each experiment, GP is invoked ten times with the same parameters. The experimental results from the run in which GP finds the best composite operator among the composite operators found in all ten runs and the average performance of ten runs are shown in Table 2.6.

• **Road extraction:** In this case, the entire training image (shown in Figure 2.3(a)) is used and the same testing images in Figure 2.10(a), (d) are used. The generational GP was used to generate a composite operator to extract the road. The fitness value of the best composite operator in the initial population is 0.47 and the population fitness value is 0.19. The fitness value of the best composite operator in the final population is 0.92 and the population fitness value is 0.89. Figure 2.43(a) shows the output image of the best composite operator in the final population and Figure 2.43(b) shows the extracted ROI. We applied the composite operator obtained in the above training to the two testing SAR images. Figure 2.43(c) and (d) show the output image of the composite operator and the ROI extracted from Figure 2.10(a). The fitness value of the extracted ROI is 0.89. Figure 2.43(e) and (f) show the output image of the composite operator and the ROI extracted from Figure 2.10(d). The fitness value of the extracted ROI is 0.92.

• **Lake extraction:** The entire training image in Figure 2.11(a) is used and Figure 2.12(a) shows the testing image. The steady-state GP was used to generate the composite operator. The fitness value of the best composite operator in the initial population is 0.65 and the population fitness value is 0.42. The fitness value of the best composite operator in the final population is 0.93 and the population fitness value is 0.92. Figure 2.44(a) shows the output image of the best composite operator in the final population and Figure 2.44(b) shows the extracted ROI. We applied the composite operator to the testing SAR image. Figure 2.44(c) and (d) show the output image of the composite operator and the extracted ROI with fitness value 0.92. In Figure 2.44(a) and (c), pixels in the small dark regions have very low pixel values (negative values with very large absolute values), thus making many pixels appear bright, although some of them have negative pixel values.

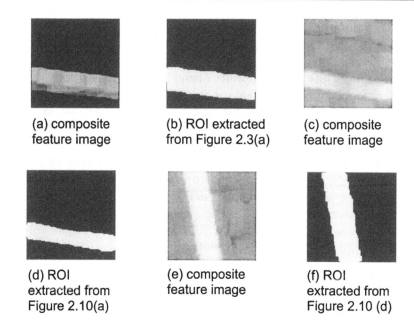

(a) composite
feature image

(b) ROI extracted
from Figure 2.3(a)

(c) composite
feature image

(d) ROI
extracted from
Figure 2.10(a)

(e) composite
feature image

(f) ROI
extracted from
Figure 2.10 (d)

Figure 2.43. Results on SAR images containing road.

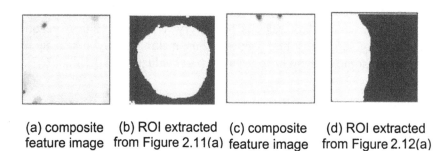

(a) composite
feature image

(b) ROI extracted
from Figure 2.11(a)

(c) composite
feature image

(d) ROI extracted
from Figure 2.12(a)

Figure 2.44. Results on SAR images containing lake.

Table 2.6. The performance results of image-based GP on various SAR images.

	Training performance							
	Road		Lake		River		Field	
	f_{op}	f_p	f_{op}	f_p	f_{op}	f_p	f_{op}	f_p
Ave. $f_{initial}$	0.47	0.18	0.73	0.39	0.37	0.11	0.65	0.41
Ave. f_{final}	0.81	0.76	0.92	0.87	0.68	0.58	0.84	0.77
$f_{initial}$	0.47	0.19	0.65	0.42	0.43	0.21	0.62	0.44
f_{final}	0.92*	0.89	0.93*	0.92	0.74*	0.68	0.87*	0.86
	Testing performance							
	Road		Lake		River		Field	
f_{test}	0.89, 0.92		0.92		0.84		0.68	

f_{op}: fitness of the best composite operator on selected region(s),
f_p : fitness of population on selected region(s),
*: indicate finess on the *entire* training images,
$f_{initial}$: fitness of the initial generation on selected region(s),
f_{final}: fitness of the final population on selected region(s),
f_{test}: fitness of the best composite operator on the *entire* testing images.

- **River extraction:** The entire training image in Figure 2.13(a) is used and Figure 2.16(a) shows the testing image. The steady-state GP was used to generate the composite operator. The fitness value of the best composite operator in the initial population is 0.43 and the population fitness value is 0.21. The fitness value of the best composite operator in the final population is 0.74 and the population fitness value is 0.68. Figure 2.5(a) shows the output image of the best composite operator in the final population and Figure 2.5(b) shows the extracted ROI. We applied the composite operator to the testing image. Figure 2.5(c) and (d) show the output image of the composite operator and the extracted ROI with fitness value 0.84. Like Figure 2.44(c), pixels in the small dark region have very low pixel values, thus making many pixels with negative pixel values appear bright.

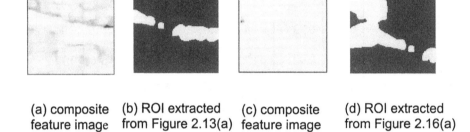

(a) composite   (b) ROI extracted   (c) composite   (d) ROI extracted
feature image   from Figure 2.13(a)   feature image   from Figure 2.16(a)

Figure 2.45. Results on SAR images containing river.

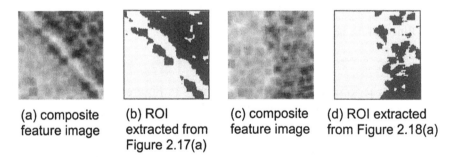

(a) composite   (b) ROI   (c) composite   (d) ROI extracted
feature image   extracted from   feature image   from Figure 2.18(a)
                    Figure 2.17(a)

Figure 2.46. Results on SAR images containing field.

• **Field extraction:** In this case, the entire training image in Figure 2.17(a) is used and Figure 2.18(a) shows the testing image. The generational GP was used to generate the composite operator. The fitness value of the best composite operator in the initial population is 0.62 and the population fitness value is 0.44. The fitness value of the best composite operator in the final population is 0.87 and the population fitness value is 0.86. Figure 2.46(a) shows the output image of the best composite operator in the final population and Figure 2.46(b) shows the extracted ROI. We applied the composite operator to the testing image. Figure 2.46(c) and (d) show the output image of the composite operator and the extracted ROI with fitness value 0.68.

Table 2.7. Average training time of region GP and image GP (in seconds).

	Road	Lake	River	Field
Region GP	12876	2263	6560	9685
Image GP	23608	9120	66476	21485

From Table 2.3 and associated figures, it can be seen that if the carefully selected training regions represent the characteristics of training images, the composite operators learned by GP running on training regions are effective in extracting the ROIs containing the object and their performance is comparable to the performance of composite operators learned by GP running on whole training images. By running on the selected regions, the training time is greatly reduced. Table 2.7 shows the average training time of GP running on selected regions (Region GP) and GP running on the whole training images (Image GP) over all ten runs. Since the number of generations in [17] is 100 and the number of generations in this chapter is 70, the training time of "Image GP" stated in Table 2.7 is normalized as the actual training time of "Image GP" times 0.7. It can be seen that the training time using selected training regions is much shorter than that using the whole image.

2.4.5   Comparison with a traditional ROI extraction algorithm

To show the effectiveness of composite operators in ROI extraction, they are compared with a traditional ROI extraction algorithm. The *traditional* ROI extraction algorithm uses a threshold value to segment the image into foreground and background. The region consisting of pixels with value greater than the threshold value is called the bright region and its complement is called the dark region. If the bright region has a higher fitness than the dark region, the bright region is the foreground. Otherwise, the dark region is the foreground. The foreground is the ROI extracted by this traditional algorithm. The threshold value plays a vital role in the ROI extraction and selecting an appropriate threshold value is the key to the success of this traditional ROI extraction algorithm. The performance of composite operators is compared with that of the traditional ROI extraction algorithm when the best threshold value is used. To find the best threshold value, every possible threshold value is tried by the algorithm and its performance is recorded. In order to show the effectiveness of composite features over that of primitive features, the traditional ROI extraction algorithm is applied to all the 16 primitive feature images (for SAR and IR images) or the 3 primitive feature images (RED, GREEN AND BLUE planes of RGB color images), and the best result from the 16 or 3 primitive feature images is recorded in Table 2.8 and Figure 2.47.

The Traditional ROI Extraction Algorithm

1. *find the maximum and minimum pixel values of the image.*
2. *if the maximum pixel value is greater than 1000*
3.   *normalize the pixel values into the range of 0 to 1000. The pixel values are changed according to the following equation.*

    new_pixval = (org_pixval – min_pixval) / (max_pixval – min_pixval) * 1000

    where new_pixval and org_pixval are the new and original pixel values, respectively and min_pixval and max_pixval are the minimum and maximum pixel values in the original image. After normalization, the minimum and maximum pixel values are 0 and 1000, respectively.
        else
4.   *do not normalize the image.*
        endif
5. *each integer value between the minimum and maximum pixel values is used as the threshold value and its performance in ROI extraction is recorded.*
6. *select the best threshold value and output its corresponding ROI.*

The fitness values of the extracted ROIs and their corresponding threshold values are shown in Table 2.8. Figure 2.47 shows the ROIs extracted by the traditional ROI extraction algorithm corresponding to the best threshold value. For the purpose of comparison, Figure 2.48 shows the corresponding performance of the GP-learned composite operators on the same images. From Figure 2.47, Figure 2.48 and Table 2.8, it is clear that the composite operators learned by GP are more effective in ROI extraction. Actually, its performance is better than the best performance of the traditional ROI extraction algorithm in all the examples except a couple of them where there is a minor difference. Table 2.9 shows the average running time of the composite operators and the traditional ROI extraction algorithm in extracting ROIs from training and testing images. From Table 2.9, it is obvious that the composite operators are more efficient.

Table 2.8. Comparison of the performance of traditional ROI extraction algorithm and composite operators generated by GP.

Examples	Traditional techiniue				GP-based technique	
	Thresold value	Primitive feature	Fig. No.	Fitness	Fitness	Fig. No.
paved road vs. field	31	PFIM15	2.47(a)	0.68	0.93	2.48(a)
unpaved road vs. field	32	PFIM15	2.47(b)	0.72	0.90	2.48(b)
paved road vs. grass	31	PFIM15	2.47(c)	0.82	0.93	2.48(c)
lake vs. field	32.9	PFIM3	2.47(d)	0.92	0.93	2.48(d)
lake vs. grass	30	PFIM15	2.47(e)	0.95	0.98	2.48(e)
river vs. field	45	PFIM15	2.47(f)	0.62	0.71	2.48(f)
river vs. field	45.5	PFIM15	2.47(g)	0.84	0.83	2.48(g)
field vs. grass	72.3	PFIM3	2.47(h)	0.82	0.89	2.48(h)
field vs. grass	196	PFIM9	2.47(i)	0.71	0.80	2.48(i)
T72 tank	99.6	PFIM2	2.47(j)	0.86	0.88	2.48(j)
T72 tank	82.2	PFIM2	2.47(k)	0.86	0.84	2.48(k)
person	96	PFIM1	2.47(l)	0.84	0.85	2.48(l)
person	94	PFIM13	2.47(m)	0.83	0.84	2.48(m)
person	99	PFIM7	2.47(n)	0.81	0.81	2.48(n)
person	95	PFIM1	2.47(o)	0.84	0.86	2.48(o)
car	101	PFIM2	2.47(p)	0.45	0.82	2.48(p)
car	107	PFIM2	2.47(q)	0.41	0.76	2.48(q)
SUV	68	PFIM1	2.47(r)	0.30	0.69	2.48(r)
SUV	106	PFIM1	2.47(s)	0.44	0.58	2.48(s)

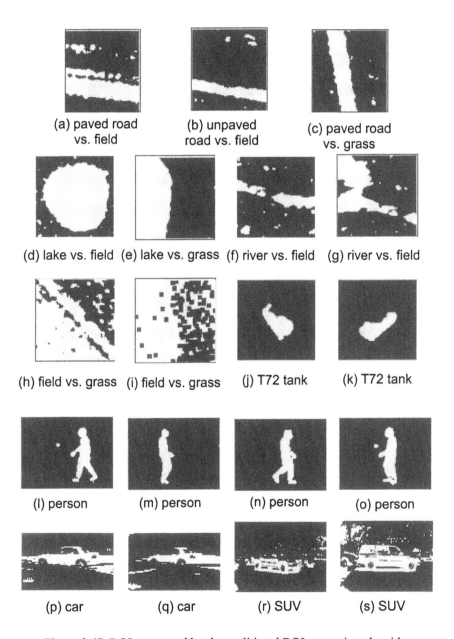

(a) paved road vs. field (b) unpaved road vs. field (c) paved road vs. grass

(d) lake vs. field (e) lake vs. grass (f) river vs. field (g) river vs. field

(h) field vs. grass (i) field vs. grass (j) T72 tank (k) T72 tank

(l) person (m) person (n) person (o) person

(p) car (q) car (r) SUV (s) SUV

Figure 2.47. ROIs extracted by the traditional ROI extraction algorithm.

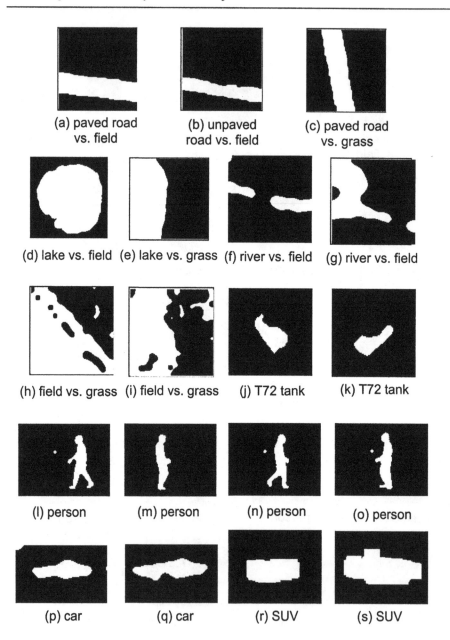

(a) paved road
vs. field

(b) unpaved
road vs. field

(c) paved road
vs. grass

(d) lake vs. field   (e) lake vs. grass   (f) river vs. field   (g) river vs. field

(h) field vs. grass   (i) field vs. grass   (j) T72 tank   (k) T72 tank

(l) person   (m) person   (n) person   (o) person

(p) car   (q) car   (r) SUV   (s) SUV

Figure 2.48. ROIs extracted by the GP-evolved composite operators.

Table 2.9. Average running time (in seconds) of the composite operators and the traditional ROI extraction algorithm.

	Road	Lake	River	Field	Tank	Person	Car	SUV
Composite operator	5	15	33	8	3	1	2	6
Traditional ROI exaction algorithm	12.3	10	50.5	32	23	3.4	5.5	20.5

2.4.6 A multi-class example

In the above examples, we showed the effectiveness and efficiency of composite operators learned by GP in ROI extraction. In this section, a complicated SAR image (shown in Figure 2.49(a)) containing lake, road, field, tree and shadow is used as a testing image. Note that shadow is an unknown region (reject class, not considered in this chapter) in this example. Figure 2.49(b), (c) and (d) show the ground-truth for lake, road and field.

We apply the composite operators for lake, road and field learned in Examples 2, 1 and 4, respectively, to the above testing image. The lake operator is applied first; then the road operator is applied to the rest of the image excluding the lake ROIs; finally, the field operator is applied to the rest of the image excluding both lake and road ROIs. The ROIs extracted are shown in Figure 2.50. The fitness values are 0.85, 0 and 0.75, respectively. These results are not promising. Since the pixel values of road and lake regions are quite similar (see Figure 2.53, many pixels in the road and lake regions have values between 0 and 20), the lake composite operator extracts part of the road and the road composite operator extracts no road pixel. In order to force GP to learn composite operators that can distinguish the subtle difference between the lake and road pixels, a SAR image (shown in Figure

2.52) containing both lake and road is used as a training image. Figure 2.52(a) shows the original image with the training regions from (4, 96) to (124, 119) and from (2, 25) to (127, 86) used by GP to learn composite operators for the lake extraction. To learn composite operators for the road extraction, the same image with the training region from (90, 30) to (135, 117) shown in Figure 2.52(c) and the training image used in Example 1 are used for training. Figure 2.52(b) and (d) show the ground-truth for the lake and road, respectively. Note that the images in Figure 2.49(a) and Figure 2.52(a) are quite different.

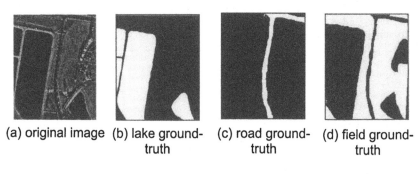

(a) original image   (b) lake ground-   (c) road ground-   (d) field ground-
                           truth   truth   truth

Figure 2.49. SAR image containing lake, road, field, tree and shadow.

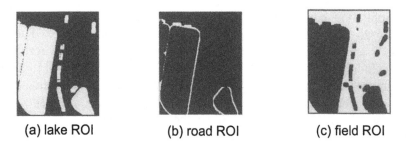

(a) lake ROI   (b) road ROI   (c) field ROI

Figure 2.50. Lake, road and field ROIs extracted by the composite operators learned in Examples 1, 2 and 4.

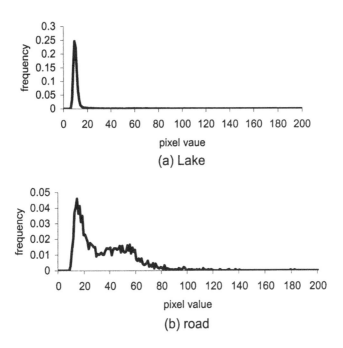

Figure 2.51. Histogram of pixel values (range 0 to 200) within lake and road regions.

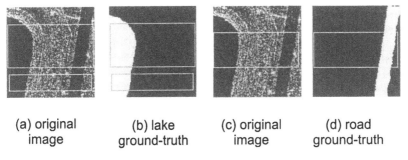

Figure 2.52. SAR image containing lake and road.

(a) lake ROI extracted   (b) road ROI extracted   (c) road ROI extracted

Figure 2.53. lake and road ROIs extracted from training images.

The steady-state GP is applied to synthesize composite operators for lake detection and the ROI extracted by the learned composite operator from the training image is shown in Figure 2.53(a). The fitness value of the extracted ROI is 0.95. The generational GP is applied to synthesize composite operators for road detection. The ROIs extracted by the learned composite operator from the training images (Figure 2.3(a) and Figure 2.52(c)) are shown in Figure 2.53(b) and (c). The fitness values are 0.78 and 0.90, respectively.

We apply the newly learned lake and road composite operators to the testing image in Figure 2.49(a). The extracted lake and road ROIs are shown in Figure 2.54(a) and (b). The fitness values of the extracted ROIs are 0.93 and 0.46, respectively. After extracting the lake and road from the image, we exclude the regions corresponding to the extracted lake and road ROIs and apply the field composite operator learned in Example 4 to the rest of the image. The extracted ROI is shown in Figure 2.54(c) and its fitness value is 0.81. The running times are 53, 127 and 26 seconds, respectively for the results shown in Figure 2.54.

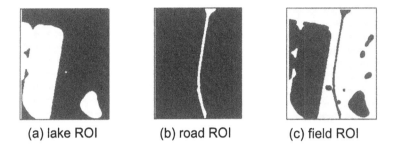

(a) lake ROI	(b) road ROI	(c) field ROI

Figure 2.54. Lake, road and field ROIs extracted from the testing image.

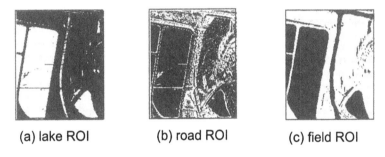

(a) lake ROI	(b) road ROI	(c) field ROI

Figure 2.55. Lake, road and field ROIs extracted by the traditional algorithm.

Finally, the traditional ROI extraction algorithm is applied to the above testing image. The extracted ROIs, corresponding to the best threshold values, of the lake, road and field are shown in Figure 2.55(a), (b) and (c), respectively. To extract road, the regions corresponding to the extracted lake ROIs are removed and the algorithm is applied to the rest of the image. Figure 2.55(b) demonstrates that it is very difficult for the traditional ROI extraction algorithm to distinguish road from field in SAR images. To extract field, the regions corresponding to the ground-truth of the lake and road (not the ROIs corresponding to the lake and road) are excluded. The reason that we do not use extracted ROIs is that the extracted road ROIs are very bad. The fitness values of the extracted lake, road and field ROIs are 0.86, 0.15 and 0.79, respectively. The best threshold values are 16, 55 and 28.5, and the running times are 192, 176 and 195 seconds, respectively. It can be seen that the GP learned composite operators are more effective in the lake, road and field detection, compared to the traditional ROI extraction algorithm.

2.5   Conclusions

In this chapter, we use genetic programming to synthesize composite operators and composite features to detect potential objects in images. We use a soft composite operator size limit to avoid code-bloating and severe restrictions on GP search. We also compare it with the hard limit on composite operator size. Our experimental results show that the primitive operators and primitive features defined by us are effective. GP can synthesize effective composite operators for object detection by running on the carefully selected training regions of images and the synthesized composite operators can be applied to the whole training images and other similar testing images. We do not find significant difference between generational and steady-state genetic programming algorithms.

As discussed, GP has code bloat problem. Controlling code bloat due to the limited computational resources inevitably restricts the search efficiency of GP. How to reach the balance between the two conflicting factors (size of the composite operator and performance) is critical in the implementation of GP. In the next chapter, we address this problem by designing a new fitness function based on the minimum description length (MDL) principle to incorporate the size of composite operators into the fitness evaluation process.

Chapter 3

MDL-BASED EFFICIENT GENETIC PROGRAMMING FOR OBJECT DETECTION

3.1   Introduction

In chapter 2, the efficacy of genetic programming in learning composite features for object detection is demonstrated. The motivation for using GP is to overcome the human experts' limitation of considering only a very limited number of conventional combinations of primitive features. Chapter 2 shows that GP is an effective way of synthesizing composite features from primitive ones for object detection. However, genetic programming is computationally expensive. In the traditional GP with hard limit on the individual size (also called a *normal GP*), crossover and mutation locations are randomly selected, leading to the disruption of the effective components (subtree in this approach) of composite operators especially at the later stage of the GP search. This greatly reduces the efficiency of GP. It is very important for GP to identify and keep the effective components of composite operators to improve the efficiency. In this chapter, smart crossover and smart mutation are proposed to better choose crossover and mutation points to prevent effective components of a composite operator from being disrupted. Also, a public library is established to save the effective components of composite operators for later reuse. Finally, a fitness function based on the minimum description length (MDL) principle is designed to incorporate the size of a composite operator into the fitness evaluation to address the well-known code bloat problem of GP without imposing severe restrictions on the GP search. The GP with smart crossover, smart mutation and MDL-based fitness function is called a *smart GP*.

3.2   Motivation and Related Research

Crossover and mutation are two major mechanisms employed by GP to search the composite operator space (also called feature combination space). As GP proceeds, effective components are generated. The power of crossover lies in the fact that by swapping sub-trees between two effective composite operators (parents), the effective components (sub-trees) in these two parents can be assembled together into child composite operators (offspring) and the new offspring may be better than both parents. However, although crossover can assemble good components to yield better offspring, it is also a destructive force in the sense that it can disrupt good components due to the random selection of crossover points. When the search begins, since the initial population is randomly generated, it is unlikely that a composite operator contains large good components and the probability of crossover breaking up a good component is small. At this time, crossover is a constructive force and the fitness of a composite operator is increased. As search proceeds, small good components are generated and assembled into larger and larger good components. When more and more composite operators contain large good components to achieve high fitness, the good component accounts for a large portion of a composite operator and the composite operator becomes more and more fragile because the good components are more prone to being broken up by subsequent crossover due to the random selection of crossover points. The crossover can damage the fitness of a composite operator in ways other than disrupting good components. Sometimes, a good component is moved into an inhospitable context, that is, the crossover inserts a good component into a composite operator that does not use the good component in any useful way or other nodes of the composite operator cancel out the effect of the good component. According to [82], crossover has an overwhelmingly negative effect on the fitness of the offspring from crossover, especially in the later stage of GP search.

Mutation is introduced to maintain the diversity of a population, since a serious weakness of evolutionary algorithms is that the population recombined repeatedly will develop uniformity sooner or later [82]. However, in the later stage of GP search when more and more composite operators contain large good components, the random selection of mutation points leads to a high probability of disrupting good components and makes mutation a destructive force. When both crossover and mutation become negative factors in the GP search, it is very unlikely that better composite operators will be generated. To improve the efficiency and effectiveness of GP, it is highly beneficial if good components can be identified and kept from destructive crossover and mutation operations and stored in a public library for later reuse. These components are treated as atomic terminals and are directly inserted into composite operators as a whole when the mutations are performed or during initialization.

GP has a well-known code bloat problem in which the sizes of individuals become larger and larger. In normal GP with individuals represented by tree structures, a crossover operation is performed by swapping sub-trees rooted at the randomly selected nodes called crossover points, and one of the mutation operations is performed by substituting a randomly selected sub-tree with another randomly generated tree. It is easy to see that the size of one offspring (i.e., the number of nodes in the binary tree representing the offspring) may be greater than both parents if crossover and mutation are performed in this simple way. If we do not control the sizes of composite operators, they will become larger and larger as GP proceeds, as stated in chapter 2. When the size becomes too large, it takes a long time to execute a composite operator, greatly reducing the speed of GP. Also, large-size composite operators may overfit training data by approximating the noise in images. Although the result on the training image is very good, the performance on unseen testing images may be bad. Finally, large composite operators take up a lot of computer memory.

Usually in normal GP, a limit on the size of composite operators is established when performing crossover or mutation. If the size of an offspring exceeds the size limit, the crossover or mutation operation is performed again until the sizes of both offspring are within the limit. Although this simple method prevents the code bloat, the size limit may greatly restrict the search performed by GP [17], since after randomly selecting a crossover point in one composite operator, GP cannot select some nodes of the other composite operator as crossover point in order to guarantee that both offspring do not exceed the size limit. Also, the size limit restricts the size of trees used to replace sub-trees in mutation. However, the composite operator space is huge [17], and to find effective composite operators, GP must search extensively. Restricting the search greatly reduces the efficiency of GP, making it less likely to find good composite operators. To allieviate the restrictions, in chapter 2, the soft limit on the composite operator size is proposed. With a soft size limit, GP allows the generation of large compsite operators above the size limit and keeps those large composite operators only when they are the best, or with performance very close the best composite operator(s) in the population, thus taking off the restrictions on the selection of crossover and mutation points without causing code bloat. However, with little knowledge on the composite operator space and the object characteristics, it is very difficult, if not impossible, to determine the appropriate hard or soft size limit to prevent code bloat and overfitting while allowing the resulted composite operators to capture the characteristics of objects. How to avoid restricting the GP search without causing code bloat is the key to the success of GP search. Also, with little knowledge on the objects to be detected, it is critical for GP to automatically determine the appropriate size of composite operators that are needed to capture the characteristics of objects. In this chapter, a fitness function is designed based on the minimum description length (MDL) principle [100] to take the size of a composite operator into the fitness evaluation process. According to the MDL principle, large composite operators effective on training regions may not have good fitness and will be culled out by selection. Thus, we can take off the restriction on crossover and mutation while preventing composite operators from growing too large.

To improve the efficiency of GP, Tackett [116] devises a method called brood recombination to reduce the destructive effect of crossover. In this method, when crossover is performed, many offspring are generated from two parents and only the best two offspring are kept. D'haeseleer [24] devises strong context preserving crossover (SCPC) to preserve the context. SCPC only permits crossover between nodes that occupied exactly the same position in the two parents. He finds modest improvement in results by mixing regular crossover and SCPC. Smith [111] proposes a conjugation operator for GP to transfer genetic information from one individual to another. In his conjugation method, the parent with higher fitness becomes the donor and the other with lower fitness becomes the recipient. The conjugation operator is different from crossover and it simulates one of the ways in which individuals exchange genetic materials in nature. Ito et al. [48] propose a depth-dependent crossover for GP in which the depth selection ratio is varied according to the depth of a node. A node closer to the root node of a tree has a better chance of being selected as a crossover point to lower the chance of disrupting small good components near leaves. Their experimental results show the superiority of the depth-dependent crossover to the random crossover in which crossover points are randomly selected. Bhanu and Lin [16], [69] propose smart crossover and mutation operators to identify and keep the good components of composite operators. Their initial experiments show that with smart GP operators, GP can search the composite operator space more efficiently.

Unlike the work of Ito [48] that used only the syntax of a tree (the depth of a node), the smart crossover and smart mutation proposed in this chapter evaluate the performance of each node to determine the interactions among them and use the fitness values of the nodes to determine crossover and mutation points. Also, unlike our previous work [16], a public library is introduced to keep the good components for later reuse and more types of mutations are added to increase the population diversity. Nine more primitive feature images are included to build composite operators. To reduce the training time, the training in this chapter is performed on the selected regions of training images, not the whole images as in the previous work. More importantly, a new MDL-based fitness function is designed to reach a balance point between the conflicting factors of code bloat and less restriction on the GP search.

Quinlan and Rivest [97] explore the use of the minimum description length principle for the construction of decision trees. The MDL defines the best decision tree to be the one that yields the minimum combined length of the decision tree itself plus the description of the misclassified data items. Their experimental results show that the MDL provides a unified framework for both growing and pruning the decision tree, and these trees seem to compare favorably with those created by other techniques such as C4.5 algorithm. Gao et al. [34] use the MDL principle to determine the best model granularity such as the sampling interval between the adjacent sampled points along the curve of Chinese characters or the number of nodes in the hidden layer of a three layer feed-forward neural network. Their experiments show that in these two quite different settings the theoretical value determined by the MDL principle coincides with the best value found experimentally. The key point of their work is that using the MDL principle, the optimal granularity of the model parameters can be computed automatically rather than being tuned manually. In this chapter, a fitness function is designed based on the MDL principle to incorporate the size of composite operators into the fitness evaluation to address the code-bloat problem without imposing severe restrictions on the GP search.

3.3   Improving the Efficiency of GP

The primitive feature images and primitive operators are the same as those used in chapter 2. There are 16 primitive feature images: the original image (0), mean (1–3), deviation (4–6), maximum (7–9), minimum (10–12) and median (13–15) images obtained by applying templates of sizes 3×3, 5×5 and 7×7. 17 primitive operators are ADD, SUB, MUL, DIV, MAX2, MIN2, ADDC, SUBC, MULC, DIVC, SQRT, LOG, MAX, MIN, MED, MEAN and STDV. The key parameters are the population size M, the number of generation N, the crossover rate, the mutation rate and the goodness threshold (defined in chapter 3.3.1). The GP stops whenever it finishes the pre-specified number of generations or whenever the best composite operator in the population has goodness value greater than the goodness threshold.

3.3.1   MDL principle-based fitness function

To address the code bloat problem and prevent severe restriction on the GP search, we design a MDL-based fitness function to incorporate the composite operator size into the fitness evaluation process. The fitness of a composite operator is defined as the sum of the description length of the composite operator and the description length of the segmented training regions with respect to this composite operator as a predictor for the label (object or background) of each pixel in the training regions. Here, both lengths are measured in bits and the details of the coding techniques are relevant. The trade-off between the simplicity and complexity of composite operators is that if the size of the composite operators is too small, it may not capture the characteristics of objects to be detected, on the other hand, if the size is too large, the composite operator may overfit the training image, thus performing poorly on the unseen testing images. With the MDL-based fitness function, the composite operator with the minimum combined description lengths of both the operator itself and image-to-operator error is the best composite operator and may perform best on the unseen testing images. Based on minimum description length principle, we propose the following fitness function for GP to maximize:

$$F(CO_i) = - (r \times \log (N_{po}) \times Size(CO_i) +$$

$$(1 - r) \times (n_o + n_b) \times (\log(W_{im}) + \log(H_{im}))) \qquad (3.1)$$

where CO_i is the ith composite operator in the population, N_{po} is the number of primitive operators (including primitive feature images) available for GP to synthesize composite operators, $Size(CO_i)$ is the size of the composite operator which is the number of nodes in the binary tree representing it, n_o and n_b are the number of object and background pixels misclassified, W_{im} and H_{im} are the width and height of the training image and r is a parameter determining the relative importance of the composite operator size and the detection rate, which is 0.7 in this chapter. The value r = 0.7 is selected experimentally. In our experiments, we find 0.7 is an appropriate value to balance the composite operator size and its performance. Note that the first term of the fitness function is the description length of the composite operator. The description length is the number of bits needed to encode a composite operator and it is not the size of a composite operator (the number of nodes in the composite operator). However, the description length is closely related to the size of a composite operator. The larger the size of a composite operator, the longer is its description length.

We now give a brief explanation of this fitness function. Suppose a sender and a receiver both have the training image and the training regions and they agree in advance that composite operators can be used to locate the object in the image, that is, to determine the label (object or background) of each pixel in the training regions. But only the sender knows the ground-truth (the label of each pixel). Now, the sender wants to tell the receiver which pixels belong to the object and which pixels belong to the background. One simple approach to do this is to send a bit sequence of n (n is the number of pixels in the training regions) bits where 1 represents the object and 0 represents background, provided that both the sender and the receiver know the order of the training regions and they agree that the pixels are scanned in the top-to-bottom and left-to-right fashion. However, n is usually very large, thus the communication burden is heavy. To reduce the number of bits to be transmitted, the sender can send the composite operator to the receiver. Then the receiver applies the composite operator on the training regions to get segmented training regions. When sending the composite operator, the sender can send its nodes in a preorder traversal. Given N_{po} primitive operators (including primitive features), $\log(N_{po})$ bits are needed to encode each node. Thus, the cost of sending composite operator is $\log(N_{po}) \times Size(CO_i)$. However, some pixels may be misclassified by the composite operator. In order for the receiver to get the truth, the sender needs to tell the receiver which pixels are misclassified. Each pixel is represented by its coordinate in the image. If the width and height of the image are W_{im} and H_{im} respectively, then $\log(W_{im})+\log(H_{im})$ bits are needed to encode each pixel. Thus, the cost of sending the misclassified pixels is $(n_o + n_b) \times(\log(W_{im})+\log(H_{im}))$. If the composite operator is very effective and its size is not too large, then only few pixels are misclassified and the number of bits to send is much smaller than n.

In chapter 2, the fitness function is defined as $n(G \cap G') / n(G \cup G')$, where G and G' are foregrounds in the ground-truth image and the resultant image of a composite operator respectively and $n(X)$ denote the number of pixels within the intersection of region X and the training region. It measures how the ground-truth and the detection results are overlapped. In this chapter, this measure is called the *goodness* of a composite operator. It is not used to drive smart GP, but only used to measure the effectiveness of a composite operator.

3.3.2   Genetic programming with smart crossover and smart mutation

The selection operation selects composite operators from the current population. In this chapter, as before, we use tournament selection with a tournament size equal to five.

In the normal GP, to perform crossover, two composite operators are selected on the basis of their fitness values. The higher the fitness value, the more likely the composite operator is selected for crossover. These two composite operators are called parents. One internal node in each of these two parents is randomly selected, and the two subtrees rooted at these two nodes are exchanged between the parents to generate two new composite operators, called offspring. The crossover is called random crossover due to the random selection of the crossover point. Usually, at the later stage of GP search, effective composite operators contain large effective components. These components are prone to be disrupted by random crossover, leading to a reduction in the efficiency of genetic programming.

To avoid this problem, we propose a smart crossover that can identify and keep the effective components. To define smart crossover, the output image of each node, not just the resultant image from the root node, is evaluated and its fitness value is recorded. Based on the node fitness values, we define the fitness of an edge as the fitness difference between the parent node and the child node linked by the edge. If the fitness value of a node is smaller than that of its parent node, the edge linking them is a good edge. Otherwise, the edge is labeled as a bad edge. During crossover, all the bad edges are identified and one of them is selected by random selection or roulette selection (based on the fitness of the bad edges) invoked with equal probability. The child node of the selected edge is the crossover point and the subtrees rooted at the crossover points are swapped between parents. If a composite operator has no bad edge, the crossover point is randomly selected.

Since GP evaluates the fitness of each node, GP knows the fitness of each component (subtree) of a composite operator. A public library is established to store effective components for later reuse by smart mutation. The larger the library, the more effective components can be kept for later reuse, but the likelihood of each effective component being reused is reduced. In this chapter, the size of the public library is 100. After the library is full, a new effective component replaces the worst one in the library if it is better than the replaced one.

To avoid premature convergence, mutation is introduced to randomly change the structure of some individuals to maintain the diversity of the populationComposite operators are randomly selected for mutation. In a normal GP, there are three types of random mutation, invoked with equal probability, that involve randomly selecting mutation points as described in chapter 2.3.2.

In the smart mutation, however, the mutation point is the parent or child node of a bad edge or a bad node whose goodness is below the average goodness of all the nodes in the tree. The mutation point is selected from those qualified nodes randomly or by roulette selection based on the goodness of bad edges or bad nodes. There are four smart mutations invoked with equal probability:

1. Select the parent node of a bad edge as the mutation point. If the parent node has only one child, it is deleted and the child node is linked to the grandparent node (parent node of the parent node). If no grand parent node exists, the child becomes the root node; if the parent node has two children, the parent node and the sub-tree rooted at the child with smaller goodness value are deleted and the other child is linked directly to the grand parent node. If no grand parent node exists, the child becomes the root node.

2. Select the parent node of a bad edge as the mutation point and replace the primitive operator stored in the node with another primitive operator of the same number of input as the replaced one.

3. Select two subtrees whose roots are child nodes of two bad edges within the composite operator and swap them. Neither of the two sub-trees can be the sub-tree of the other.

4. Select a bad node as the mutation point. Delete the subtree rooted at the node and replace it with another randomly generated tree or a randomly selected effective component from the public library.

The first two mutations delete a node that cancels the effect of its child or children; the third mutation moves two components away from unfriendly contexts that cancel their effects and inserts them into new contexts to see if the new contexts are appropriate to them; the fourth mutation deletes a bad component and replaces it with a new component or a good one stored in the public library.

We use an ε-greedy policy to determine whether a smart operator (smart crossover or mutation) or a random operator (random crossover or mutation) is used. With probability ε, the smart operator is invoked; with probability 1 - ε, the random operator is invoked. In this chapter, ε is a variable that is adjusted by the following formula:

$$\varepsilon = \varepsilon_{min} + (\varepsilon_{max} - \varepsilon_{min}) \times Good_{popu} \qquad (3.2)$$

where ε_{min} is 0.5 and ε_{max} is 0.9, $Good_{popu}$ is population goodness (the average goodness of the composite operators in the current population). The reason for using the random operators is that smart operators bias the selection of crossover and mutation points. They avoid disrupting effective components, but at the same time they restrict the GP search. According to our experiments, restricting the search reduces the efficiency of GP. At the beginning when the population is just initialized, few composite operators contain effective components. At this time, GP should search extensively to generate effective components and assemble them together. It is harmful to apply smart operators at the early stage of GP search since they just restrict the search. Only after some time when the effective components are gathered in composite operators, smart operators should be applied to identify the effective components to avoid disrupting them and keep them in a public library for later reuse. So, in this chapter, smart operators are not used in the first 20 generations. In the last 50 generations, smart operators are applied with higher and higher probability as the population goodness becomes larger and larger. Here, the number 20 is experimentally determined, since in our experiments, it is observed that the population fitness (the average fitness of all the composite operators in the population) increases significantly in the first 20 generations, which means after 20 generations, some effective components are generated and assembled together.

3.3.3   Steady-state and generational genetic programming

As in chapter 2, steady-state genetic programming and generational genetic programming are used to synthesize composite operators. The major difference is that in generational GP, the offspring from crossover are kept aside and do not participate in the crossover operation on the current population. The current population is not changed during crossover. But in steady-state GP, the offspring from crossover are evaluated and replace the worst individuals in the population immediately, and they participate in the crossover operations on the current population. In smart GP, a MDL-based fitness function is used, smart GP crossover and smart mutation are invoked with probability determined by ε-greedy policy and a public library is set up to store the effective components of composite operators. Similarly, we adopt an elitism replacement method to keep the best composite operator from generation to generation. At the end of each generation, GP checks each composite operator and replaces it with the subtree whose root node has the highest goodness value among all the nodes of the composite operator. This is helpful to further control the size of composite operators and avoid overfitting. Figure 3.1 and Figure 3.2 show the pseudo code for modified steady-state and generational genetic programming algorithms, respectively.

Modified Steady-state Genetic Programming Algorithm:

0. randomly generate population P of size M and evaluate composite operators in P.
1.   for gen = 1 to N do   // N is the number of generation
2.   keep the best composite operator in P.
3.   repeat
4.   select 2 composite operators from P based on their fitness values for crossover.
5.   select 2 composite operators with the lowest fitness values in P for replacement.
6.   if gen < 20 then
7. ·   perform random crossover and let the 2 offspring replace the 2 composite operators selected for replacement.
*   else*
8.   perform smart or random crossover and let the 2 offspring replace the 2 composite operators selected for replacement.
*   endif*
9.   execute the 2 offspring and evaluate their fitness values.
10.   until crossover rate is met.
11.   if gen < 20 then
12.   perform random mutation on each composite operator with probability of mutation rate.
*   else*
13.   perform smart or random mutation on each composite operator with probability of mutation rate.
*   endif*
14.   execute and evaluate mutated composite operators.
*   // after crossover and mutation, a new populationP' is generated.*
15.   perform elitism mechanism. let the best composite operator of P replace the worst composite operator in P' and let P = P'.
16.   update the value of ε according to equation (3.2).
17.   store good components of composite operators in the public library.
18.   if the goodness of the best composite operator in P is above goodness threshold value, then
19.   stop.
*   endif*
20.   check each composite operator in P and use its best component to replace it.
*   endfor // loop*

Figure 3.1. Modified Steady-state genetic programming.

Modified Generational Genetic Programming Algorithm:

0. *randomly generate population P of size M and evaluate each composite operator in P.*
1. *for gen = 1 to N do   // N is the number of generation*
2. *keep the best composite operator in P.*
3. *if gen < 20 then*
4.   *perform random crossover on the composite operators in P until crossover rate is satisfied and keep all the offspring from crossover.*
5. *perform mutation on the composite operators in P and the offspring from crossover with the probability of mutation rate.*
    else
6. *perform smart or random crossover on the composite operators in P until crossover rate is satisfied and keep all the offspring from crossover.*
7. *perform smart or random mutation on the composite operators in P and the offspring from crossover with the probability of mutation rate.*
    endif
8. *perform selection on P to select some composite operators and combine them with the composite operators from crossover to get a new population P' of the same size as P.*
9. *evaluate offspring from crossover and the mutated composite operators.*
10. *perform elitism mechanism. let the best composite operator from P replace the worst composite operator in P' and let P = P'.*
11. *update the value of ε according to equation (3.2).*
12. *store good components of composite operators in the public library.*
13. *if the goodness of the best composite operator in P is above the goodness threshold, then*
14. *stop.*
    endif
15.   *check each composite operator in P and use its best component to replace it.*
    endfor // loop 1

Figure 3.2. Modified Generational genetic programming.

3.4   Experiments

Various experiments are performed to test the efficacy of genetic programming in extracting regions of interest from real synthetic aperture radar (SAR) images. The SAR images are the same as used in chapter 2.4.1. As in chapter 2 (except chapter 2.4.4), here, GP is not applied to the whole training image, but only to a region or regions carefully selected from the training image, to generate the composite operators. The generated composite operator is then applied to the whole training image and some other testing images to evaluate it. In each experiment in this chapter, both normal genetic programming (GP with random crossover, random mutation and hard limit on the composite operator size) and smart genetic programming (GP with smart crossover, smart mutation and a MDL-based fitness function) are applied. For the purpose of objective comparison, we invoke normal GP and smart GP with the same set of parameters and training regions. The parameters in the experiments are: populationsize (100), the number of generations (70), the goodness threshold value (1.0), the crossover rate (0.6), the mutation rate (0.05), and the segmentation threshold (0). For normal GP, the hard size limit of a composite operator is 30. These are the same parameters as used before in chapter 2.

Five experiments (chapters 3.4.1 to 3.4.5) that are comparable to chapter 2.4.1 are performed with the same SAR images. In each experiment, GP is invoked ten times with the same parameters and the same training region(s). In this chapter, we present the results from the run in which GP finds the best composite operator among the best composite operators found in all ten runs. The comparison between normal GP and smart GP is provided in chapter 3.4.6. There is much randomness involved in GP, so for the purpose of objective comparison, only the average performance over all ten runs is used in comparison. Note that the fitness and goodness of composite operators are the same in our previous work [17] and the definition of goodness in this chapter is the same as the definition of fitness in [17] and in chapter 2, so the comparison is based on the goodness of composite operators. Table 3.1 shows the performance of the best composite operators learned by normal GP and smart GP on various SAR images used in the experiments.

Table 3.1. The performance of the best composite operators from normal and smart GPs.

Normal GP					
	Road	Lake	River	Field	Tank
GP	G	S	S	G	G
G_{BI}	0.60	0.62	0.59	0.52	0.65
G_{BF}	0.94	0.99	0.89	0.78	0.88
PF	0.90*, 0.90, 0.93	0.95*, 0.97	0.72*, 0.83	0.88*, 0.81	0.88*, 0.84
Size	18	28	30	9	28
Time	5	15	33	8	3
Smart GP					
	Road	Lake	River	Field	Tank
GP	G	S	S	G	G
F_{BI}	-2303.6	-1585.5	-2480.8	-7936.2	-807.2
F_{BF}	-325.4	-158.9	-404.6	-1999.4	-190.8
G_{BI}	0.45	0.55	0.23	0.39	0.54
G_{BF}	0.94	0.97	0.90	0.79	0.89
PF	0.91*, 0.91, 0.93	0.94*, 0.98	0.71*, 0.86	0.90*, 0.84	0.89*, 0.84
Size	27	13	13	15	5
Time	2.6	1	19	12	2

GP – the type of GP used to synthesize composite operators. G: generational GP, S: steady-state GP.

F_{BI} – fitness of the best composite operator in the initial population (on training region).

F_{BF} – fitness of the best composite operator in the final population (on training region).

G_{BI} – goodness of the best composite operator in the initial population (on training region).

G_{BF} – goodness of the best composite operator in the final population (on training region).

PF – performance, the goodness of the ROI extracted by the best composite operator from training and testing images. * indicates the goodness of ROI extracted from the training image.

Size – size of the best composite operator.

Time – average running time (in seconds) of the best composite operator on the training and testing images.

3.4.1   Road extraction

The training image contains horizontal paved road and field, as shown in Figure 3.3(a); two testing images contain unpaved road vs. field and vertical paved road vs. grass, as shown in Figure 3.9(a) and Figure 3.9 (f), respectively. Two training regions (Figure 3.3(a)) are located from (5, 19) to (50, 119) and from (82, 48) to (126, 124). Figure 3.3(b) shows the ground-truth. The white region corresponds to the road and only the portion of ground-truth in the training regions is used in the fitness evaluation. These testing and training images (and regions) are the same as those previously used in chapter 2, Figure 2.3(a) and (b) and Figure 2.10(a) and (b), respectively.

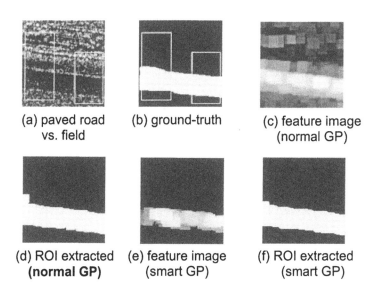

(a) paved road   (b) ground-truth   (c) feature image
vs. field   (normal GP)

(d) ROI extracted   (e) feature image   (f) ROI extracted
(normal GP)   (smart GP)   (smart GP)

Figure 3.3. Training SAR image containing road.

The generational GP is used to synthesize a composite operator to detect the road. For normal GP, the goodness value of the best composite operator in the initial population is 0.60 and the goodness value of the best composite operator in the final population is 0.94. Figure 3.3(c) shows the output image of the best composite operator on the whole training image and Figure 3.3(d) shows the binary image after segmentation. The goodness value of the extracted ROI is 0.90. For smart GP, the fitness and goodness of the best composite operator in the initial population are −2303.6 and 0.45, respectively. The corresponding values in the final population are −325.4 and 0.94, respectively. Figure 3.3(e) shows the output image of the best composite operator on the whole training image and Figure 3.3(f) shows the binary image after segmentation. The goodness value of the extracted ROI is 0.91. The best composite operator has 18 nodes and a depth of 13. It has three leaf nodes all containing 7×7 median image, which contains less speckles due to the median filter's effectiveness in eliminating speckle noise. It is shown in Figure 3.4 where PFIM15 represents 7×7 median image. Compared to smart GP, the best composite operator from normal GP has 27 nodes and a depth of 16.

(MAX (MAX (MAX (MAX (MAX (SUBC (MUL (DIVC (ADDC (MAX (MAX (MAX (ADDC PFIM15)))))) (DIV PFIM15 (STDV PFIM15)))))))))

Figure 3.4. Learned composite operator tree in LISP notation.

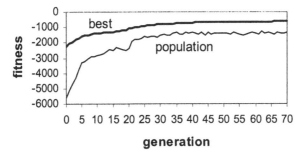

Figure 3.5. Fitness versus generation (road vs. field).

Figure 3.5 shows how the average fitness of the best composite operators and the average fitness of the populations over all 10 runs change as GP proceeds. In Figure 3.5, the population fitness is much lower than that of the best composite operator even at the end of GP search. It is reasonable, since the selection of crossover points is not restricted by a hard size limit on composite operators. The difference between the sizes of the composite operators in the population is large and so are their fitness values. The population fitness is not important since only the best composite operator is used in testing. If GP finds one effective composite operator, the GP learning is successful. That's why we do not compare the population fitness between normal GP and smart GP. The large difference between the fitness of the best composite operator and that of the population indicates that the diversity of the population is maintained during GP search, which is very helpful in preventing premature convergence.

Ten best composite operators are obtained in the initial and final generations of 10 runs, respectively. Figure 3.6 shows the frequency of primitive operators and primitive feature images appearing in the best composite operators of initial and final generations. To compute frequency, we first compute the total number of each primitive operator and the total number of each primitive feature image in the 10 best composite operators, then divide them by the total number of internal nodes and leaf nodes of these 10 best composite operators, respectively. From Figure 3.6(b), it can be seen that MED operator has the most frequent occurrence in the best composite operators learned by GP. This is similar to the results in chapter 2, Figure 2.7.

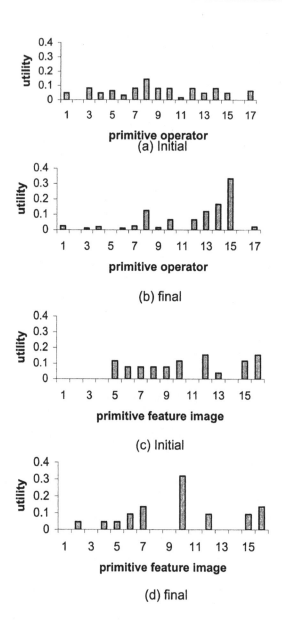

Figure 3.6. Frequency of primitive operators and primitive feature images.

Figure 3.7 shows the output image at each node of the best composite operator shown in Figure 3.4. The primitive operators in Figure 3.7 are connected by arrow. The operator at the tail of an arrow provides input to the operator at the head of the arrow. After segmenting the output image of a node, we get the ROI (shown as the white region) extracted by the corresponding subtree rooted at the node. The extracted ROIs and their goodness values are shown in Figure 3.8. If an output image has positive pixels only (for example, PFIM15 has positive pixels only), everything is extracted and the goodness is 0.25. From Figure 3.8, it can be seen that since the feature image from subtree (DIV PFIM15 (STDV PFIM15)) has no pixel with negative value, it does not affect the ROI extracted from the feature image output by its parent node MUL. This branch of the composite operator is a redundant code. Note that the best composite operator shown in Figure 3.7 does not use primitive operator MED. MED is very effective in speckle noise elimination, so it is frequently selected by GP to build effective composite operators as shown in Figure 3.6, but Figure 3.7 shows that without it, GP may still generate effective composite operators. The interaction among primitive operators and primitive features is very complicated, indicating the high complexity of the search space structure and the difficulty of the feature synthesis process. Also, some combinations of other primitive operators and primitive feature images may approximate the function of primitive operator MED.

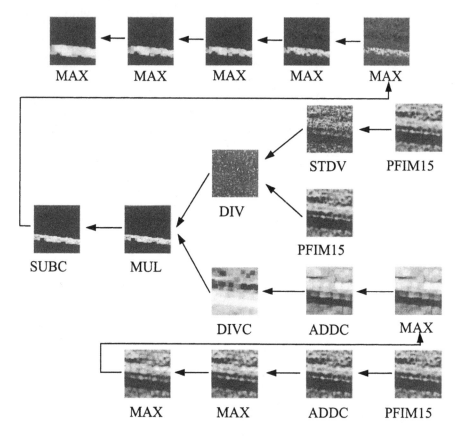

Figure 3.7. Feature images output at the nodes of the best composite operator learned by smart GP.

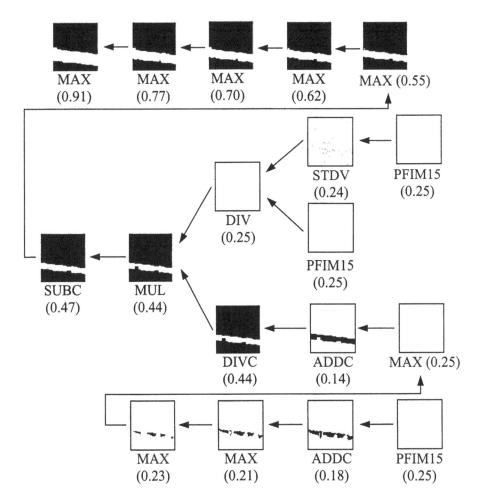

Figure 3.8. ROIs extracted from the output images at the nodes of the best composite operator from smart GP. The goodness value is shown for the entire image.

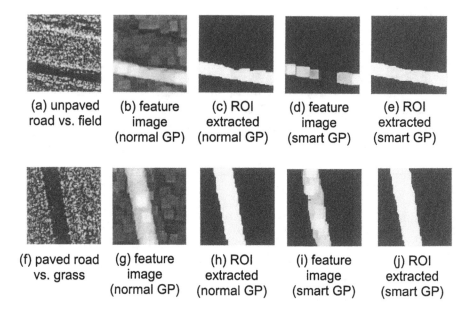

(a) unpaved road vs. field

(b) feature image (normal GP)

(c) ROI extracted (normal GP)

(d) feature image (smart GP)

(e) ROI extracted (smart GP)

(f) paved road vs. grass

(g) feature image (normal GP)

(h) ROI extracted (normal GP)

(i) feature image (smart GP)

(j) ROI extracted (smart GP)

Figure 3.9. Testing SAR images containing road.

The composite operator obtained in the above training is applied to the other two real SAR images shown in Figure 3.9(a) and Figure 3.9(f). Figure 3.9(b) and Figure 3.9(g) show the output of the composite operator from normal GP and Figure 3.9(c) and Figure 3.9(h) show the regions extracted from Figure 3.9(a) and Figure 3.9(f), respectively. The goodness values of the extracted regions are 0.90 and 0.93. Figure 3.9(d) and Figure 3.9(i) show the output of the composite operator from smart GP and Figure 3.9(e) and Figure 3.9(j) show the regions extracted from Figure 3.9(a) and Figure 3.9(f), respectively. The goodness values of the extracted regions are 0.91 and 0.93. The average running time of the best composite operators from normal GP on training and testing images is 5 seconds; the corresponding time of that from smart GP is 2.6 seconds.

3.4.2   Lake extraction

Two SAR images contain lake. The training image, shown in Figure 3.10(a), contains a lake and field, and the testing image, shown in Figure 3.11(a) contains a lake and grass. The training region is from (85, 85) to (127, 127). Figure 3.10(b) shows the ground-truth. These testing and training images (and regions) are the same as those previously used in chapter 2, Figure 2.11(a) and Figure 2.12(a).

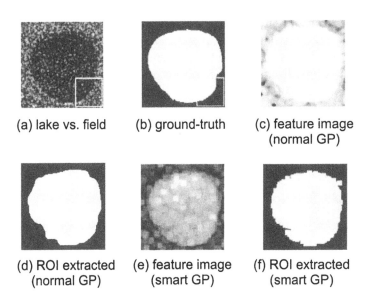

(a) lake vs. field   (b) ground-truth   (c) feature image
(normal GP)

(d) ROI extracted   (e) feature image   (f) ROI extracted
(normal GP)   (smart GP)   (smart GP)

Figure 3.10. Training SAR image containing lake.

The steady-state GP is used to generate composite operators. For the normal GP, the goodness value of the best composite operator in the initial population is 0.62 and the goodness value of the best composite operator in the final population is 0.99. Figure 3.10(c) shows the output image of the best composite operator on the whole training image and Figure 3.10(d) shows the binary image after segmentation. The goodness value of the extracted ROI is 0.95. For the smart GP, the fitness and goodness of the best composite operator in the initial population are −1585.5 and 0.55, respectively. The corresponding values in the final population are −158.9 and 0.97, respectively. Figure 3.10(e) shows the output image of the best composite operator on the whole training image and Figure 3.10(f) shows the binary image after segmentation. The goodness value of the extracted ROI is 0.94.

The composite operator is applied to the testing image containing a lake and grass. Figure 3.11(b) shows the output of the composite operator from normal GP and Figure 3.11(c) shows the region extracted. The goodness value of the region is 0.97. Figure 3.11(d) shows the output of the composite operator from the smart GP and Figure 3.11(e) shows the region extracted. The goodness value of the region is 0.98. The average running time of the best composite operators from the normal GP on training and testing images is 15 seconds; the corresponding time from smart GP is 1 second. The size of the best composite operator from normal GP is 28. The best composite operator from smart GP has size 13 and it is shown in Figure 3.12.

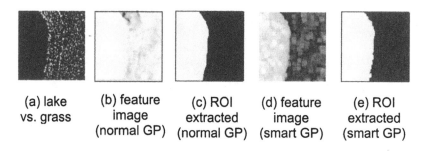

(a) lake vs. grass   (b) feature image (normal GP)   (c) ROI extracted (normal GP)   (d) feature image (smart GP)   (e) ROI extracted (smart GP)

Figure 3.11. Testing SAR image containing lake.

(MAX (ADDC (MIN2 (LOG (SUB (DIV
PFIM10 (LOG PFIM2)) (ADDC (ADDC
PFIM2)))) PFIM4)))

Figure 3.12. Learned composite operator tree in LISP notation.

3.4.3   River extraction

Two SAR images contain river and field. Figure 3.13(a) and Figure 3.13(b) show the original training image and the ground-truth provided by the user. The white region in Figure 3.13(b) corresponds to the river to be extracted. The training regions are from (68, 31) to (126, 103) and from (2, 8) to (28, 74). The testing SAR image is shown in Figure 3.16(a). Note that Figure 3.13(a), Figure 3.13(b) and Figure 3.16(a) are the same as those previously used in chapter 2, Figure 2.13(a) and (b) and Figure 2.16(a), respectively.

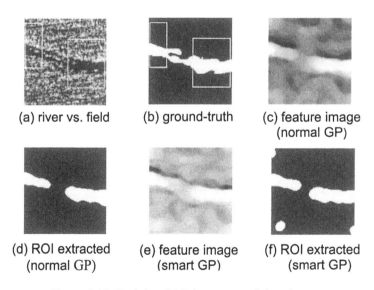

(a) river vs. field   (b) ground-truth   (c) feature image
                                            (normal GP)

(d) ROI extracted   (e) feature image   (f) ROI extracted
    (normal GP)   (smart GP)   (smart GP)

Figure 3.13. Training SAR image containing river.

The steady-state GP is used to generate a composite operator. For normal GP, the goodness values of the best composite operator in the initial and final populations are 0.59 and 0.89, respectively. Figure 3.13(c) shows the output image of the best composite operator on the whole training image and Figure 3.13(d) shows the binary image after segmentation. The goodness of the extracted ROI is 0.72. For smart GP, the fitness and goodness of the best composite operator in the initial population are −2480.8 and 0.23. The corresponding values in the final population are −404.6 and 0.90. Figure 3.13(e) shows the output image of the best composite operator on the whole training image and Figure 3.13(f) shows the binary image after segmentation. The goodness of the extracted ROI is 0.71. The best composite operator has 13 nodes and a depth of 12. It has one leaf node containing 3×3 mean image. Among 13 nodes, seven of them are MED operators effective in eliminating speckle noise. It is shown in Figure 3.14. Compared to smart GP, the best composite operator from normal GP has 30 nodes with a depth of 23. Figure 3.15 shows how the average fitness of the best composite operators and the average fitness of the populations over all 10 runs change as GP searches the composite operator space.

```
(DIVC (SUBC (SUBC (MED (MED
(MIN (MED (MED (MED (MED (MED
(SUBC PFIM1)))))))))))))
```

Figure 3.14. Learned composite operator tree in LISP notation.

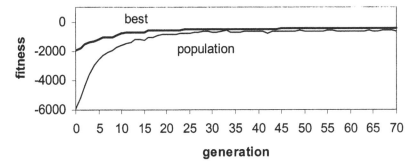

Figure 3.15. Fitness versus generation (river vs. field)

The composite operator is applied to the testing image containing a river and field. Figure 3.16(b) shows the output of the composite operator from the normal GP and Figure 3.16(c) shows the region extracted from Figure 3.16(a). The goodness of the region is 0.83. Figure 3.16(d) shows the output of the composite operator from the smart GP and Figure 3.16(e) shows the region extracted. The goodness of the region is 0.86. There are some islands along with the river around them that are not extracted, since these islands look similar to the field. The average running time of the best composite operators from normal GP on training and testing images is 33 seconds; the corresponding time of that from smart GP is 19 seconds.

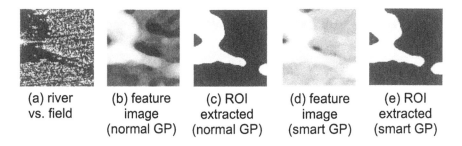

| (a) river vs. field | (b) feature image (normal GP) | (c) ROI extracted (normal GP) | (d) feature image (smart GP) | (e) ROI extracted (smart GP) |

Figure 3.16. Testing SAR image containing river.

3.4.4   Field extraction

Two SAR images contain field and grass. Figure 3.17(a) and Figure 3.17(b) show the original training image and the ground-truth. The training regions are from (17, 3) to (75, 61) and from (79, 62) to (124, 122). Extracting field from a SAR image containing field and grass is considered as the most difficult task among the five experiments, since the grass and field are similar to each other and some small regions in the grass area are actually fields. The testing image is shown in Figure 3.18(a). Note that Figure 3.17(a) and Figure 3.17(b) and Figure 3.18(a) are the same as those in chapter 2, Figure 2.17(a) and (b) and Figure 2.18(a), respectively.

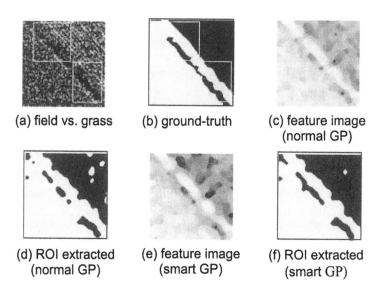

(a) field vs. grass   (b) ground-truth   (c) feature image
                                                   (normal GP)

(d) ROI extracted   (e) feature image   (f) ROI extracted
    (normal GP)   (smart GP)   (smart GP)

Figure 3.17. Training SAR image containing field.

The generational GP is used to generate composite operators. For the normal GP, the goodness values of the best composite operators in the initial and finally populations are 0.52 and 0.78, respectively. Figure 3.17(c) shows the output image of the best composite operator on the whole training image and Figure 3.17(d) shows the binary image after segmentation. The goodness value of the extracted ROI is 0.88. For the smart GP, the fitness and goodness of the best composite operator in the initial population are −7936.2 and 0.39. The corresponding values in the final population are −1999.4 and 0.79. Figure 3.17(e) shows the output image of the best composite operator on the whole training image and Figure 3.17(f) shows the binary image after segmentation. The goodness value of the extracted ROI is 0.90.

The composite operator is applied to the testing image containing field and grass shown in Figure 3.18(a). Figure 3.18(b) shows the output of the composite operator from normal GP and Figure 3.18(c) shows the extracted region with goodness value 0.81. Figure 3.18(d) shows the output of the composite operator from the smart GP and Figure 3.18(e) shows the extracted region with goodness value 0.84. The average running time of the best composite operators from normal GP on training and testing images is 8 seconds; the corresponding time of that from smart GP is 12 seconds. The size of the best composite operator from normal GP is 9, and the size of best composite operator from smart GP is 15 and it has 7 MED primitive operators. It is shown in Figure 3.19. In this experiment, the best composite operator learned by the smart GP has larger size and it takes a longer time to execute than that learned by the normal GP. However, the time it takes a composite operator to run on a particular image is not only determined by its size. It is also related to the type of primitive operators it contains. For example, it takes a longer time for primitive operator MED than primitive operator ADDC to execute.

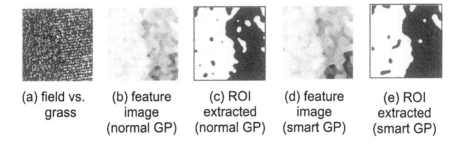

(a) field vs. grass   (b) feature image (normal GP)   (c) ROI extracted (normal GP)   (d) feature image (smart GP)   (e) ROI extracted (smart GP)

Figure 3.18. Testing SAR image containing field.

From the experiment on the field extraction, we can see that the proposed algorithm has difficulties in dealing with textures and objects with great variations, and the reason lies in the fact that only domain-independent primitive operators and primitive features are used in the feature synthesis. The predefined primitive operators and primitive features have significant impact on the performance of the learned composite operators. If texture-specific primitive operators and primitive features are included for the synthesis of composite operators, GP may learn composite operators that are effective in dealing with textures.

(ADDC (ADDC (MED (MAX (MED (ADDC (MED (MED (MED (MED (MED (MAX (DIVC (MAX PFIM9)))))))))))))))

Figure 3.19. Learned composite operator tree in LISP notation.

3.4.5   Tank extraction

GP is applied to synthesize features for the detection of T72 tanks. Their SAR images are taken under different depression and azimuth angles and the size of the images is 80×80. The training image contains T72 tank under depression angle 17° and azimuth angle 135°, which is shown in Figure 3.20(a). The training region is from (19, 17) to (68, 66). The testing SAR image contains a T72 tank under depression angle 20° and azimuth angle 225°, which is shown in Figure 3.23(a). The ground-truth is shown in Figure 3.20(b). These testing and training images (and regions) are the same images (under the same depression and azimuth angles) as those previously used in chapter 2, Figure 2.19(a) and (b) and 2.22(a), respectively.

The generational GP is applied to synthesize composite operators for tank detection. For the normal GP, the goodness value of the best composite operator in the initial population is 0.65 and the goodness value of the best composite operator in the final population is 0.88. Figure 3.20(c) shows the output image of the best composite operator on the whole training image and

Figure 3.20(d) shows the binary image after segmentation. The goodness value of the extracted ROI is 0.88. For the smart GP, the fitness and goodness of the best composite operator in the initial population are −807.2 and 0.54, respectively. The corresponding values in the final population are -190.8 and 0.89, respectively. Figure 3.20(e) shows the output image of the best composite operator on the whole training image and Figure 3.20(f) shows the binary image after segmentation. The goodness value of the extracted ROI is 0.89. The best composite operator has 5 nodes and a depth of 4. It has one leaf node containing 3×3 maximum image. Two internal nodes are primitive operator MED, which is useful in eliminating speckle noises in SAR image. It is shown in Figure 3.21. Compared to the smart GP, the best composite operator from normal GP has 28 nodes and a depth of 17. Figure 3.22 shows how the average fitness of the best composite operators and the average fitness of the populations over all 10 runs change as GP proceeds.

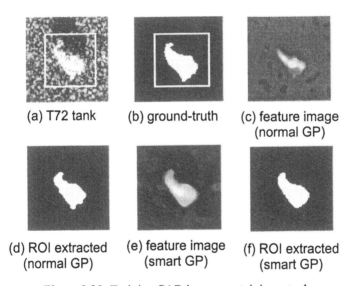

(a) T72 tank   (b) ground-truth   (c) feature image
                                          (normal GP)

(d) ROI extracted   (e) feature image   (f) ROI extracted
    (normal GP)   (smart GP)   (smart GP)

Figure 3.20. Training SAR image containing a tank.

(MED   (MED   (SUBC
(DIVC PFIM7))))

Figure 3.21. Learned composite operator tree in LISP notation.

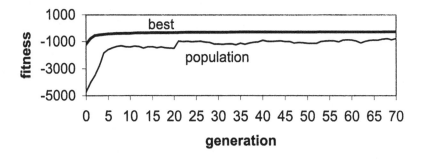

Figure 3.22. Fitness versus generation (T72 tank).

The composite operator is applied to the testing image containing T72 tank under depression angle 20° and azimuth angle 225°. Figure 3.23(b) shows the output of the composite operator from normal GP and Figure 3.23(c) shows the region corresponding to the tank. The goodness of the extracted ROI is 0.84. Figure 3.23(d) shows the output of the composite operator from smart GP and Figure 3.23(e) shows the region corresponding to the tank. The goodness of the extracted ROI is 0.84. The average running time of the best composite operators from normal GP on training and testing images is 3 seconds; the corresponding time from smart GP is 2 seconds.

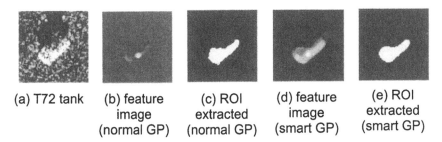

| (a) T72 tank | (b) feature image (normal GP) | (c) ROI extracted (normal GP) | (d) feature image (smart GP) | (e) ROI extracted (smart GP) |

Figure 3.23. Testing SAR image containing tank.

3.4.6 Comparison of smart GP with normal GP

This subchapter compares the performance of the smart GP with that of the normal GP. For objective comparison, only the average performance over all ten runs is used in comparison. The comparison is based on the goodness of composite operators synthesized by normal and smart GPs. The reason for using goodness as the comparison metric is that a composite operator having higher fitness than another composite operator does not mean it always has a higher performance than the composite operator with lower fitness, since its size may be much smaller. Comparing the goodness values, it can be clearly shown that on the average, composite operators from smart GP have a smaller size and better or at least comparable performance with that from normal GP.

Figure 3.24 shows how the average goodness of the best composite operators improves as normal GP and smart GP proceed. The thick line represents the goodness of smart GP and the thin line represents the goodness of normal GP. It shows that if normal GP already achieves very good performance such as in the lake and tank cases, then it is difficult for smart GP to significantly improve the performance, since there is not much room for improvement. At this time, smart GP may achieve similar or a little better performance than normal GP.

If primitive operators and primitive features are not suitable to the tasks to be solved, both normal and smart GP may not generate effective composite operators such as in the field case, since primitive operators and primitive features have significant impact on the effectiveness of learned composite operators.

The smart GP operators have a bad side effect of restricting the GP search by biasing the selection of crossover and mutation points to keep the effective components generated during GP search. If effective components are generated and assembled together in some composite operators in the first 20 generations, then it is beneficial to apply the smart GP operators in the remaining generations to keep effective composite operators. Otherwise, it may be harmful to apply smart GP. Note that even when smart operators are not applied in the first 20 generations, smart GP and normal GP are different, since the fitness functions used to drive smart GP and normal GP are different. From Figure 3.24, it can be seen that on the average, smart GP finds good composite operators more quickly.

Table 3.2 shows the average goodness and standard deviation of the best composite operator in the initial and final populations. Table 3.3 shows the average size of the best composite operators from normal GP and smart GP. It also shows the average performance of the best composite operators on the whole training image and other testing image(s). The standard deviation values of size and performance are also provided. It can be seen that although smart GP does not always generate composite operators with better performance, on the average, the best composite operators learned by smart GP have better performance and smaller size than those from normal GP, reducing the computational expense during testing.

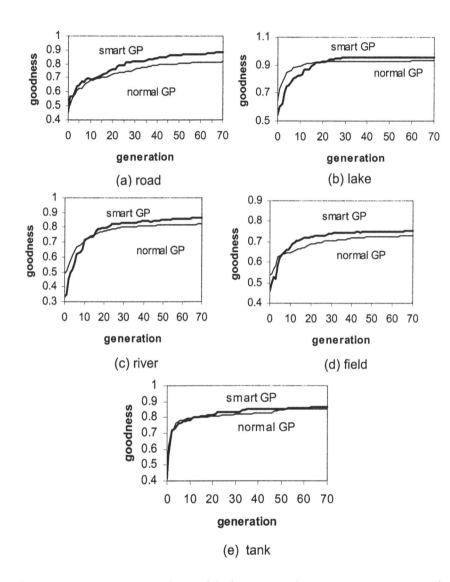

Figure 3.24. The average goodness of the best composite operators versus generation.

Table 3.2. The average goodness of the best composite operators from normal and smart GPs.

		Normal GP				
		Road	Lake	River	Field	Tank
Initial	mean	0.473	0.645	0.490	0.539	0.490
	stdv	0.086	0.138	0.178	0.028	0.166
Final	mean	0.817	0.933	0.822	0.729	0.850
	stdv	0.078	0.091	0.040	0.070	0.024
		Smart GP				
		Road	Lake	River	Field	Tank
Initial	mean	0.467	0.544	0.337	0.459	0.411
	stdv	0.139	0.194	0.198	0.096	0.229
Final	mean	0.881	0.955	0.864	0.752	0.865
	stdv	0.042	0.017	0.029	0.031	0.009

Table 3.4 shows the average and standard deviation of training time (in seconds) of normal GP and smart GP. By intuition, the training time of smart GP should be much longer than that of normal GP, since in normal GP, only the output image of the root node is evaluated and smart GP evaluates the output image of each node of a composite operator. From Table 3.4, it can be seen that the difference between the training times is not as much as expected. In the experiments with lake and tank images, the training time of smart GP is much shorter. The reason lies in the code bloat problem of GP. In normal GP, a size limit of composite operator (in this chapter, it is 30) is specified. At the later stage of the GP search, most of the composite operators have size equal or close to the size limit. In smart GP, the MDL-based fitness function takes the size of composite operators into the fitness evaluation. The difference between the sizes of composite operators is large, even at the later stage of the GP search. Although a few composite operators have a size larger than the size limit in normal GP, many of them have a size smaller than the size limit. If the size limit set in normal GP is large, it can be expected that the training time of the normal GP will be longer than that of smart GP. Also, in the above experiments, the goodness threshold value is set at 1.0 to force GP to finish the pre-specified number of generations. If the goodness threshold value is smaller than 1.0, the smart GP may run fewer generations, since it finds effective composite operators more quickly, thus reducing its training time.

Table 3.3. The average size and performance of the best composite operators from normal and smart GPs.

		Normal GP				
		Road	Lake	River	Field	Tank
Size	mean	29.4	28.4	27.6	20.2	24.6
	stdv	1.07	1.74	4.43	8.93	6.17
Training	mean	0.789	0.891	0.583	0.794	0.829
	stdv	0.080	0.128	0.112	0.101	0.035
Testing	mean	0.620, 0.797	0.913	0.754	0.675	0.766
	stdv	0.274, 0.151	0.161	0.129	0.124	0.042
		Smart GP				
		Road	Lake	River	Field	Tank
Size	mean	24.6	11.8	16.8	14.9	5.7
	stdv	4.58	5.65	7.19	9.98	1.9
Training	mean	0.860	0.916	0.650	0.839	0.849
	stdv	0.038	0.021	0.049	0.039	0.025
Testing	mean	0.831, 0.914	0.972	0.836	0.784	0.821
	stdv	0.115, 0.025	0.009	0.023	0.033	0.012

Table 3.4. Average training time of Normal GP and Smart GP.

		Road	Lake	River	Field	Tank
Normal GP	mean	6915	2577	7951	3606	2686
	stdv	5348	1213	8006	2679	2163
Smart GP	mean	10249	770	11035	5251	649
	stdv	8893	724	10310	5506	589

Table 3.5 shows the average performance of the best composite operators (over 10 runs) from smart GP with and without the public library on training and testing images containing road and tank images. From Table 3.5, it can be seen that with the public library to keep the effective components for later reuse, GP can generate more effective composite operators.

Table 3.6 shows the average running time of the composite operators from normal and smart GPs on road, lake, river, field, and tank SAR images. The time is measured in seconds. From Table 3.6 it can be seen that on average, the composite operators from smart GP are more efficient.

Table 3.5. The average performance of the best composite operators from smart GPs with and without the public library.

		Smart GP (Lib Size 100)		Smart GP (No Lib)	
		Road	Tank	Road	Tank
Training image	mean	0.860	0.849	0.800	0.820
	stdv	0.038	0.025	0.106	0.052
Testing image	mean	0.831, 0.914	0.821	0.640, 0.812	0.782
	stdv	0.115, 0.025	0.012	0.113, 0.083	0.050

Table 3.6. Average running time (in seconds) of the composite operators from normal and smart GPs.

	Road	Lake	River	Field	Tank
Smart GP	2.6	1	19	12	2
Normal GP	5	15	33	8	3

3.5   Conclusions

In this chapter, we use genetic programming to evolve composite operators for object detection. To improve the efficiency of genetic programming, we design smart crossover and smart mutation that can identify and prevent the effective components of composite operators from being disrupted and use a public library to keep them for later reuse. To address the well-known code bloat problem of GP, we design a new fitness function based on the minimum description length to take the size of a composite operator into the fitness evaluation process. The new fitness function prevents composite operators from growing too large, while at the same time imposes relatively less severe restrictions on the GP search. Our experimental results with real SAR images show that with the MDL-based fitness function and the smart search operators, the smart GP can learn better composite operators more quickly than the traditional normal GP, improving the efficiency of GP. Compared to the normal GP, the composite operators learned by smart GP have better performance on the training and testing images and have smaller sizes, reducing the computational expense and the running time during testing. Currently, in order to get the goodness at each node, its output image has to be evaluated against the ground-truth, which is a time consuming and inefficient process. To further improve the efficiency of GP, it is important to find a way to estimate the goodness of internal nodes based on the goodness of the root node.

Chapter 4

FEATURE SELECTION FOR OBJECT DETECTION

4.1   Introduction

The goal of feature selection is to find the subset of features that produces the best object detection and recognition performance and requires the least computational effort. Feature selection is important to object detection and recognition systems mainly for three reasons:

First, using more features can increase system complexity, yet it may not always lead to higher detection/recognition accuracy. Sometimes, many features are available to a detection/recognition system. However, these features are not independent and may be correlated. A bad feature may greatly degrade the performance of the system. Thus, selecting a subset of good features is important.

Second, features are selected by a learning algorithm during the training phase. The selected features are used as a model to describe the training data. Selecting many features means a complicated model is used to approximate the training data. According to the minimum description length (MDL) principle, a simple model is better than a complex model [100]. Since the training data may be corrupted with a variety of noises, a complex model may overfit the training data. Thus, a complex model may be sensitive to noise in the training data and its performance on unseen test data may be bad.

Third, using fewer features can reduce the computational cost, which is important for real-time applications. Also it may lead to better classification accuracy due to the finite sample size effect.

In this chapter, we use genetic algorithm (GA) [41], [42], [77] to select as few features as possible to describe the training data effectively. The specific application we focus on is the detection of targets in SAR images. Automatic detection of potential targets in SAR imagery is an important problem [7], [65]. A constant false alarm rate (CFAR) detector is commonly used to "prescreen" the image to localize the possible targets [65]. Generally, targets correspond to bright spots caused by strong radar return from natural or man-made objects. Parts of the imagery that are not selected are rejected from further consideration. In the next stage of processing, regions of interest are further examined to distinguish man-made objects from natural clutter. Finally, a classifier such as a Bayesian classifier, a template matcher or a model-based recognizer is used to reject man-made clutter.

GAs are widely used in image processing, pattern recognition and computer vision [7], [13], [23]. They are used to evolve morphological probes that sample the multi-resolution images [101], to generate image filters for target detection [53], to select good parameters of partial shape matching for occluded object recognition [89], to perform pattern clustering and classification [113], etc. GAs are also used to automatically determine the relative importance of many different features and to select a good subset of features available to the system [95].

The problem we address is to select a minimal set of features to distinguish targets from natural clutter. The approach is based on a closed loop system involving GA based feature selection and a Bayesian classifier. GA uses a MDL-based fitness function that combines the number of features to be used and the error rate of the classifier. The results are presented using real SAR images. The experimental results show that the MDL-based fitness function is the most effective in selecting a minimal set of features to describe the data accurately compared to other three fitness functions, and the subset of features selected by GA can greatly reduce the computational cost while at the same time maintaining the desired detection accuracy.

Chapter 4.2 presents the motivation and related research. Chapter 4.3 describes the approach, feature evaluation criteria, fitness functions, the prescreener used to detect potential target regions, the features for target discrimination and the application of GAs to feature selection. Experimental results are presented in chapter 4.4 and chapter 4.5 provides the conclusions of the chapter.

4.2   Motivation and Related Research

Bhanu and Lee [12] present a closed loop image segmentation system which incorporates a genetic algorithm to adapt the segmentation process to changes in image characteristics caused by various environmental conditions such as time of day, time of year, clouds, etc. The segmentation problem is formulated as an optimization problem and the genetic algorithm efficiently searches the hyperspace of segmentation parameter combinations to determine the parameter set which maximizes the segmentation quality criteria in terms of edge-border coincidence, boundary consistency, pixel classification, object overlap and object contrast. Their experimental results demonstrate that genetic algorithm can continuously adapt the segmentation process to normal environmental variations to provide robust performance when interacting with a dynamic environment. Emmanouilidis et al. [30] discuss the use of multi-criteria genetic algorithms for feature selection. With multi-criteria fitness functions, genetic algorithm tries to minimize the number of features selected while maintaining the high classification accuracy. The algorithm is shown to yield a diverse population of alternative feature subsets with various accuracy and complexity trade-off. It is applied to select features for performing classification with fuzzy models and is evaluated on real-world data sets such as a cancer data set in which each data point has 9 input features and one output label (malignant or benign). Estevez and Caballero [31] propose a genetic algorithm to select features for neural network classifiers. Their algorithm is based on a niching method to find and maintain multiple optima. They also introduce a new mutation operator to speed up the convergence of the genetic algorithm. Rhee and Lee [99] present an unsupervised feature selection method using a fuzzy-genetic approach. The method minimizes a feature evaluation index which incorporates a weighted distance between a pair of patterns used to rank the importance of the individual features. A pattern is represented by a set of features and the task of genetic algorithm is to determine the weight coefficients of features in the calculation of weighted distance. Matsui et al. [74] use genetic algorithm to select the optimal combination of features to improve the performance of tissue classification neural networks and apply their method to problems of brain MRI segmentation to classify gray matter/white matter regions. MDL related prior work is described in chapter 3.2.

In this chapter, we use genetic algorithm to select a good subset of features used for target detection in SAR images. The target detection task involves the selection of a subset of features to discriminate SAR images containing targets from those containing clutter. Our method is a novel combination of genetic algorithm based optimization of a criterion function that involves classification error and the number of features that are used for the discrimination of targets from natural clutter in SAR images. The criterion (fitness) function we propose in this chapter is based on the minimum description length principle and it compares favorably with other three fitness functions. We assume the joint distribution of features follows a Gaussian distribution. The criterion function is optimized in a closed-loop with a Bayesian classifier evaluating the performance of each set of features. The GA used in feature selection is adaptive in the sense that it can automatically adapt the parameters, such as crossover rate and mutation rate, based on the efficiency of GA search in the feature space. As compared to this work, the feature selection presented in [65], [84] for target vs. natural clutter discrimination measures exhaustively the performance of each combination of the features by the P_d (probability of detection) versus P_{fa} (probability of false alarm) plot produced by it. The higher the P_d and the lower the P_{fa}, the better the combination of features.

4.3   Feature Evaluations and Selection

The purpose of the genetic algorithm based feature selection approach presented in this chapter is to select a set of features to discriminate the targets from the natural clutter false alarms in SAR images. The approach includes four stages: rough target detection, feature extraction from the potential target regions, feature selection based on the training data and the final discrimination. The first stage is based on the Lincoln Lab ATR system and the second stage uses some of features (first 10 of the 20 features) used in their system [65], [84], [85]. In the feature selection stage, we use GA to select a best feature subset, defined as a particular set of features that is the best in discriminating the target from the natural clutter. The diagram for feature selection is given in Figure 4.1.

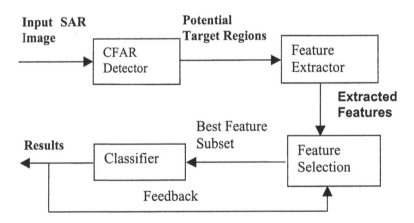

Figure 4.1. System diagram for feature selection.

4.3.1   Feature selection

Adding more features does not necessarily improve discrimination performance. An important goal is to choose the best set of features from the discriminating features that are available. Before we do the feature selection, it is appropriate to give a set of feature evaluation criteria, which measure the discrimination capability of each feature or a combination of several features

- **Divergence:** Divergence is basically a form of the Kulback-Liebler distance measure between density functions. If we assume that the target as well as the natural clutter feature vectors follow Gaussian distributions, that is, $N(\mathbf{u}_1, \Sigma_1)$ and $N(\mathbf{u}_2, \Sigma_2)$, where $\mathbf{u}_1$ and $\mathbf{u}_2$ are mean values and Σ_1 and Σ_2 are covariance matrices, respectively, the divergence can be computed as follows

$$d_{12} = \frac{1}{2} \ trace\ \left\{ \Sigma_1^{-1} \Sigma_2 + \Sigma_2^{-1} \Sigma_1 - 2\ I \right\} + \frac{1}{2}(\mathbf{u}_1 - \mathbf{u}_2)^T \left(\Sigma_1^{-1} + \Sigma_2^{-1} \right) (\mathbf{u}_1 - \mathbf{u}_2) \qquad (4.1)$$

One major drawback of the divergence d_{12} is that it is not easily computed, unless the Gaussian assumption is employed. For SAR imagery, the Gaussian assumption itself is in question.

- **Scatter matrices:** These criteria are based upon the information related to the way feature vector samples are scattered in the l-dimensional feature space. We define two kinds of scatter matrices, that is, within-class scatter matrix and between-class scatter matrix. Within-class scatter matrix for M classes is, $S_w = \sum_{i=1}^{M} P_i S_i$, where S_i is the covariance matrix for class ω_i and P_i is the a priori probability of class ω_i. S_w matrix measures how feature vector samples are scattered within each class. Between-class scatter matrix S_b, is defined as follows: $S_b = \sum_{i=1}^{M} P_i (\mathbf{u}_i - \mathbf{u}_0)(\mathbf{u}_i - \mathbf{u}_0)^T$, where $\mathbf{u}_0$ is the global mean vector and $\mathbf{u}_i$ is the mean for each class, $i = 1, ..., M$. The between-class scatter matrix measures how the feature vector samples are scattered between different classes. Based on the different combinations of these two scatter matrices, a set of class separability criteria can be derived; one such measure can be defined as: $J = \dfrac{|S_b|}{|S_w|}$. If the feature vector samples within each class are scattered compactly and the feature vector samples from different classes are far away from one another, we expect the value for J would be high. This also implies that the features we choose have high discrimination.

- **Feature vector evaluation using a classifier:** Another method for feature evaluation depends on the specific classifier. The task of feature selection is to select or determine a set of features that, when fed into the classifier, will let the classifier achieve the high performance. So it makes sense to relate the feature selection procedure with the particular classifier used. During the training time, we have all the features extracted from the training data. What we can do is to select a subset of features and feed them into the classifier and see the classification result. Then the goodness of each feature subset is indicated by its classification error rate.

4.3.2   Various criteria for fitness function

We use GA to seek the smallest (or the least costly) subset of features for which the classifier's performance does not deteriorate below a certain specified level [95], [109]. The basic system framework is shown in Figure 4.1.

When the error of a classifier is used to measure the performance, a subset of features is defined as feasible if the classifier's error rate is below the so-called *feasibility threshold*. We search for the smallest subset of features among all feasible subsets. During the search, each subset can be coded as a d-element bit string (d is the total number of features). The ith element of the bit string assumes 0 if the ith feature is excluded from the subset and 1 if it is present in the subset.

In order for the GA to select a subset of features, a fitness function must be defined to evaluate the performance of each subset of features. GA explores the space of subset of features to try to find a minimum subset of features with good classification performance.

- **Fitness function based on MDL**

In our system, the classifier is a fixed Bayesian classifier, but the set of features that is input into the classifier is a variable. In order to apply MDL to feature selection, we view the features selected by GA as the model used to describe the training data. Selecting more features means that a more complex model is used to approximate the data. Although a complex model may have perfect performance on the training data, it may not be a good model, since it may be overly sensitive to statistical irregularities and idiosyncrasies of the data and causes accidental noise to be modeled as well, leading to the poor performance on the unseen test data.

To fix the above problem, we use an MDL principle to prevent the overfitting of the training data. Roughly speaking, the MDL principle states that among all the models approximating the data to or above certain accuracy, the simplest one is the best one. To restrict the model from growing too complex while maintaining the description accuracy, the cost of describing a set of data with respect to a particular model is defined as the sum of the length of the model and the length of the data when encoded using the model as a predictor for the data. The description length of data-to-model error is defined as the combined length of all data items failed to be described by the model. GA is used to select the subset of features minimizing the above cost. Here, both description lengths are measured in bits and the details of the coding techniques are relevant. The trade-off between simplicity and complexity of both lengths is that if a model is too simple, it may not capture the characteristics of the data and lead to increased error coding length; if a model is too complicated, it may model the noise and become too sensitive to minor irregularities to give accurate prediction of the unseen data. MDL states that among the given set of models, the one with the minimum combined description lengths of both the model and data-to-model error is the best approximation and can perform best on the unseen test data.

Based on MDL, we propose the following fitness function for GA to maximize:

$$F(c_i) = -[k\log(f) + n_e\log(n)] \tag{4.2}$$

where c_i is a chromosome coding the selected set of features, f is the total number of features extracted from each training data, k is the number of features selected (c_i has k bits of 1 and $f - k$ bits of 0), n is the total number of data items in the training set and n_e is the number of data items misclassified. It is easy to see that the fewer the number of features selected and smaller the number of data items misclassified, the larger the value of the fitness function.

Chapter 3.2 provided an explanation of an MDL-based fitness function. In the following, we give a brief simpler explanation of the above (equation 4.2) fitness function. Suppose a sender and a receiver both know all the data items and their order in the training set and also they agree in advance on the feature extractor used to extract the f features from each data item and the classifier used to classify each data based on the features extracted. But only the sender knows the label (target or clutter) of each data item. Now, the sender wants to tell the receiver the label of each data item. One simple approach to do this is to send a bit sequence of n bits where 1 represents the target and 0 represents the clutter. If n is large, then the communication burden will be heavy. In order to reduce the number of bits to be transmitted, in an alternative approach, the sender can tell the receiver which features can be used to classify the data, since the receiver can extract the features and apply the classifier on the features extracted to get the label of each data item. There are a total of f features and $log(f)$ bits are needed to encode the index of each feature. If k features are selected, $k \, log(f)$ bits are needed in order to inform the receiver which features should be extracted. However, some data items may be misclassified, so the sender needs to tell the receiver which data items are misclassified so that the receiver can get the correct labels of all the data in the training set. Since there are a total of n data items, $log(n)$ bits are needed to encode the index of each data item. If n_e data items are misclassified, then $n_e \, log(n)$ bits are needed to convey to the receiver the indices of these misclassified data items. If the set of features selected is effective in discriminating targets from clutter, n_e may be very small, thus the number of bits needs to be transmitted is much smaller than n.

- **Other fitness functions**

We have three other additional fitness functions to drive GA and compare their performance with that of the MDL-based fitness function.

In order to define two other fitness functions, we first define the following penalty function [109]:

$$p(e) = \frac{\exp^{(e-t)/m} - 1}{\exp(1) - 1} \tag{4.3}$$

where e is the error rate (the number of misclassified data item divided by the total number of data items in the training set) of the classifier, t is the feasibility threshold and m is called the "tolerance margin". In this chapter, t = 0.01 and m = 0.005. We can see easily that if e < t, p(e) is negative and as e approaches zero, p(e) slowly approaches its minimal value. Note also that $p(t)$ = 0 and $p(t + m) = 1$. For greater values of the error rate, this penalty function rises quickly toward infinity.

The *second* fitness function is defined as follows:

$$F(c_i) = -p(e) \tag{4.4}$$

This fitness function considers only the error rate of the classifier and does not care about how many features are selected. It can be predicted that this fitness function may lead to the selection of many features.

The *third* fitness function takes the complexity of the model, that is the number of features selected, into consideration. It combines the complexity of the model and its performance on the training data and is defined as follow:

$$F(c_i) = -(\gamma \cdot k + (1-\gamma)p(e)) \tag{4.5}$$

where k is the number of features selected by GA. The variable γ ranges from 0 to 1 and it determines the relative importance of the number of features selected and the error rate of the classifier. If we want to use fewer features, we can assign a large value to γ; if we think lower error rate is more important, we can assign a small value to γ. In our experiments, γ takes value 0.1, 0.3 and 0.5.

The *fourth* fitness function is defined as follows:

$$F(c_i) = -(\gamma \frac{k}{20} + (1 - \gamma)e) \tag{4.6}$$

where k is the number of features as defined in (4.5) and γ ranges from 0 to 1 and is a parameter that determines the relative importance of the number of feature selected and the error rate of the classifier.

GA tries to maximize these three fitness functions in order to find an optimal set of features for discriminating targets from clutter.

4.4   System Description

The system has four major elements as shown in Figure 4.1: a CFAR detector, feature extractor, feature selector, and a typical Bayesian Classifier.

4.4.1   CFAR detector

A two-parameter CFAR detector is used as a prescreener to identify potential targets in the image on the basis of radar amplitude. A guard area around a potential target pixel is used for the estimation of clutter statistics. The amplitude of the test pixel is compared with the mean and standard deviation of the clutter according to the following rule:

$$X_{CFAR} = \frac{X_t - \hat{u}_c}{\hat{\sigma}_c} > K_{CFAR} \Rightarrow \text{target, otherwise clutter} \tag{4.7}$$

where X_t is the amplitude of the test pixel, $\hat{u}_c$ is the estimated mean of the clutter amplitude, $\hat{\sigma}_c$ is the estimated standard deviation of the clutter amplitude, and K_{CFAR} is a constant threshold value that defines the false-alarm rate. In this chapter, the value of K_{CFAR} is 4.0.

Only those test pixels whose amplitude is much higher than that of the surrounding pixels are declared to be targets. The higher we set the threshold value of K_{CFAR}, the more a test pixel must stand out from its background for it to be declared as a target. Because a single target can produce multiple CFAR detections, the detected pixels are grouped together if they are within a target-sized neighborhood. The CFAR detection threshold in the prescreener is set relatively low to obtain a high initial probability of detection for the target data. It is the responsibility of the discriminator to capture and reject those escaping clutter false alarms from the prescreener stage. An example SAR image and corresponding detection results are shown in Figure 4.2.

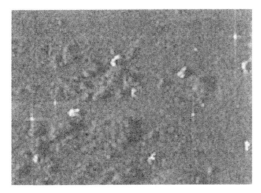

(a) Example SAR image.

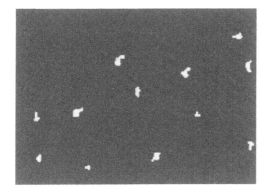

(b) Detection result.

Figure 4.2. SAR image and CFAR detection result.

4.4.2   Feature extractor

First, we use a target-sized rectangular template to determine the position and orientation of the detected target [38]. The algorithm slides and rotates the template until the energy within the template is maximized. Then we extract a set of features from the target-sized template or the region of interest. By using this set of 20 features, we attempt to discriminate the targets from the natural clutter. The first ten features are the same as those used in [65]. The features from eleven to twenty are general features used in pattern recognition and object recognition

- **The standard-deviation feature (feature 1):** The standard deviation of the data within the template is a statistical measurement of the fluctuation of the pixel intensities. If we use $P(r,a)$ to represent the radar intensity in power from range r and azimuth a, the standard deviation can be calculated as follows:

$$\sigma = \sqrt{\frac{S_2 - \frac{S_1^2}{N}}{N-1}} \text{ where} \qquad \begin{aligned} S_1 &= \sum_{r,\,a \in region} 10 \log_{10} P(r,a) \\ S_2 &= \sum_{r,\,a \in region} [10 \log_{10} P(r,a)]^2 \end{aligned} \qquad (4.8)$$

and N is the number of points in the region.

Targets usually exhibit much larger standard deviation than the natural clutter, as illustrated by Figure 4.3.

(a) A typical object image with
standard deviation 5.2832

(b) A typical natural clutter image
with standard deviation 4.5187

Figure 4.3. Example of the standard deviation feature.

- **The fractal dimension feature (feature 2):** The fractal dimension of the pixels in the region of interest provides information about the spatial distribution of the brightest scatterers of the detected object. It complements the standard-deviation feature, which depends only on the intensities of the scatterers, not on their spatial locations.

The first step in applying the fractal-dimension concept to a radar image is to select an appropriately sized region of interest, and then convert the pixel values in the region of interest to binary. One method of performing this conversion is to select the N brightest pixels in the region of interest and convert their values to 1, while converting the rest of pixel values to 0. Based on these N brightest pixels, we approximate the fractal dimension by using the following formula:

$$\text{dim} = - \frac{\log M_1 - \log M_2}{\log 1 - \log 2} = \frac{\log M_1 - \log M_2}{\log 2} \tag{4.9}$$

where M_1 represents the minimum number of 1-pixel-by-1-pixel boxes that cover all N brightest pixels in the region of interest (This number is obviously equal to N) and M_2 represents the minimum number of 2-pixel-by-2-pixel boxes required to cover all N brightest pixels.

The bright pixels for a natural clutter tend to be widely separated, thus produce a low value for the fractal dimension, while the bright pixels for the target tend to be closely bunched, thus we expect a high value for the fractal dimension, which is illustrated by Figure 4.4. Figure 4.4(a) shows a target image chip. In Figure 4.4(b), the 50 brightest pixels from the target image are tightly clustered, and 22 2×2-pixel boxes are needed to cover them, which results in a high fractal dimension of 1.2. Figure 4.4(c) shows a natural clutter image chip. In Figure 4.4(d), the 50 brightest pixels from this natural clutter are relatively isolated, and 46 2×2-pixel boxes are needed to cover them, which results in a low fractal dimension of 0.29.

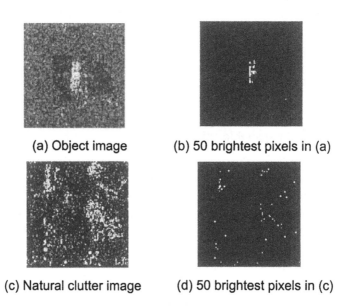

(a) Object image   (b) 50 brightest pixels in (a)

(c) Natural clutter image   (d) 50 brightest pixels in (c)

Figure 4.4. Example of the fractal dimension feature.

• **Weighted-rank fill ratio feature (feature 3):** This textural feature measures the percentage of the total energy contained in the brightest scatterers of a detected object. We define the weighted-rank fill ratio as follows:

$$\eta = \frac{\displaystyle\sum_{k\ brightest\ pixels} P(r,a)}{\displaystyle\sum_{all\ pixels} P(r,a)} \tag{4.10}$$

This feature attempts to exploit the fact that power returns from most targets tend to be concentrated in a few bright scatters, whereas power returns form natural-clutter false alarm tend to be more diffuse. The weighted-rank fill ratio values of target in Figure 4.3(a) and clutter in Figure 4.3(b) are 0.3861 and 0.2321 respectively.

• **Size-related features (feature 4 - 6):** The three size-related features utilize only the binary image created by the morphological operations on the CFAR image. The morphological operations are applied in the order of clean (remove isolated pixels), bridge (connect unconnected components if they are close to each other, at most 3 pixels apart) and close (dilation followed by erosion). The resulting largest component is called morphological blob.

1. The mass (feature 4) is computed by counting the number of pixels in the morphological blob.

2. The diameter (feature 5) is the length of the diagonal of the smallest rectangle that encloses the blob.

3. The square-normalized rotational inertia (feature 6) is the second mechanical moment of the blob around its center of mass, normalized by the inertia of an equal mass square.

In our experiments, we found the size features are not effective in scenarios where the targets are partially occluded or hidden. After the prescreener stage, the size and the shape of the detected morphological blob can be arbitrary. For the clutter, there is also no ground to assert that the resulting morphological blob will exhibit a certain amount of coherence. The experimental results in Figure 4.5 show the arbitrariness of the morphological blobs for the targets as well as the clutter.

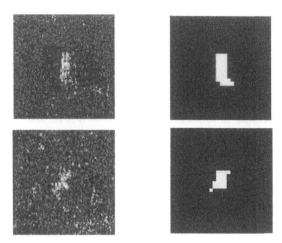

(a) The left-hand side figures represent the object images and the right-hand figures represent their corresponding morphological blobs.

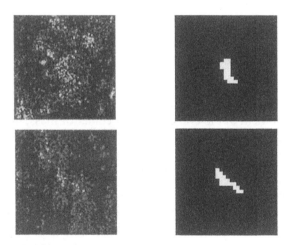

(b) The left-hand side figures represent the clutter images and the right-hand figures represent their corresponding morphological blobs.

Figure 4.5. Examples of images used to compute size features (4-6) for (a) object and (b) clutter.

- **The contrast-based features (features 7 - 9):** The CFAR statistic is computed for each pixel in the target-shaped blob to create a CFAR image. Then the three features can be derived as follows:

1. The maximum CFAR (feature 7) is the maximum value in the CFAR image contained within the target-sized blob.

2. The mean CFAR (feature 8) is the average of the CFAR image taken over the target-shaped blob.

3. The percent bright CFAR (feature 9) is the percentage of pixels within the target-sized blob that exceed a certain CFAR value.

The maximum CFAR feature, the mean CFAR feature and the percent bright CFAR feature values of target in Figure 4.3(a) are 55.69, 5.53 and 0.15, respectively, and these feature values of clutter in Figure 4.3(b) are 10.32, 2.37 and 0.042, respectively. We can see that CFAR feature values for the target are much larger than those for the natural clutter false alarm.

- **The count feature (feature 10):** The count feature is very simple; it counts the number of pixels that exceeded the threshold T and normalizes this value by the total possible number of pixels in a target blob. The threshold T is set to the quantity corresponding to the $98th$ percentile of the surrounding clutter. The count feature values of target in Figure 4.3(a) and clutter in Figure 4.3(b) are 0.6 and 0.1376, respectively. We can see that the count feature value for the target is much larger than that for the natural clutter false alarm. This is reasonable because the intensity values of the pixels belonging to the target stand out from the surrounding clutter, while the natural clutter false alarms do not have this property.

The following ten features: four projection features; three distance features and three moment features, are common features used in image processing and object recognition. They are extracted from binary image resulting from CFAR detection. In these images, foreground pixels (pixels with value 1) are potential target pixels.

- **Projection features (features 11 – 14):** Four projection features are extracted from each binary image:

1. *horizontal projection (feature 11):* Project the foreground pixels on a horizontal line (x axis of image) and compute the distance between the leftmost point and the rightmost point.

2. *vertical projection (feature 12):* Project the foreground pixels on a vertical line (y axis of image) and compute the distance between the uppermost point and the lowermost point.

3. *major diagonal projection (feature 13):* Project the foreground pixels on the major diagonal line and compute the distance between the upper leftmost point and the lower rightmost point.

4. *minor diagonal projection (feature 14):* Project the foreground pixels on the minor diagonal line and compute the distance between the lower leftmost point and the upper rightmost point.

The average values of horizontal, vertical, major and minor diagonal projection features of all the clutter images, we collected, are approximately 60.0, 60.0, 90.0 and 90.0, respectively. Their corresponding values for target images are 34.5, 29.5, 46.7 and 47.8, respectively. It can be seen that the feature values for the clutter are larger than those for the target. This result is reasonable, since the bright pixels of a natural clutter tend to be widely separated. This has already been shown by the fractal dimension feature value.

- **Distance features (features 15 – 17):** Three distance features are extracted from each binary image. Before computing distance features, we first compute the centroid of all the foreground pixels in the binary image.

1. *minimum distance (feature 15):* Compute the distance from each foreground pixel to the centroid and select the minimum one.

2. *maximum distance (featire 16):* Compute the distance from each foreground pixel to the centroid and select the maximum one.

3. *average distance (feature 17):* Compute the distance from each foreground pixel to the centroid and get the average value of all these distances.

The average values of minimum, maximum and average distance features of all the clutter images we collected are approximately 40.0, 70.0 and 60.0, respectively. Their corresponding values of target images are 3.8, 26.7 and 11.5, respectively. It can be seen that the feature values for the clutter are larger than those for the target. This result is reasonable, since the bright pixels of a natural clutter tend to be widely separated.

• **Moment features (features 18 – 20):** Three moment features are extracted from each binary image. All three moments are central moments, so before computing moment features, we first compute the centroid of all the foreground pixels in the binary image.

The central moments can be expressed as:

$$\mu_{pq} = \int_{-\infty}^{\infty} \int_{-\infty}^{\infty} (x - \overline{x})^p (y - \overline{y})^q \, dx \, dy \qquad (4.11)$$

where $(\overline{x}, \overline{y})$ is the centroid and p and q are integers.

We compute μ_{20}, μ_{02} *and* μ_{22} from each binary image and these are the horizontal, vertical and diagonal second-order moments (features 18, 19, 20) respectively.

The average values of horizontal, vertical and diagonal second-order moment features of all the clutter images we collected are approximately 910.0, 910.0 and 374020.0, respectively. Their corresponding values of target images are 80.5, 46.7 and 4021.6, respectively. It can be seen that the feature values for the clutter are larger than those for the target. This result is reasonable, since the bright pixels of a natural clutter tend to be widely separated.

4.4.3   GA for feature selection

The genetic algorithm is an optimization procedure that operates in binary search spaces (the search space consists of binary strings). A point in the search space is represented by a finite sequence of 0's and 1's, called a *chromosome*. The algorithm manipulates a finite set of chromosomes, the *population,* in a manner resembling the mechanism of natural evolution. Each chromosome is evaluated to determine its "fitness," which determines how likely the chromosome is to survive and breed into the next generation. The probability of survival is proportional to the chromosome's fitness value. Those chromosomes which have higher fitness values are given more chances to "reproduce" by the processes of *crossover* and *mutation*. The function of crossover is to mate two parental chromosomes to produce a pair of offspring chromosomes. In particular, if a chromosome is represented by a binary string, crossover can be implemented by randomly choosing a point, called the crossover point, at which two chromosomes exchange their parts to create two new chromosomes. Mutation randomly perturbs the bits of a single parent to create a child. This procedure can increase the diversity of the population. Mutations can be performed by flipping randomly one or more bits in chromosomes. In this chapter, we implement an adaptive genetic algorithm that can automatically adapt the parameters such as crossover rate and mutation rate based on the performance of GA. To be specific, if the fitness value of the best individual is not improved for 3 or 5 generations in a row, GA will automatically raise the mutation rate to increase the diversity of the population. Also, elitism mechanism is adopted such that the best individual (set of features selected) is copied from generation to generation when performing reproduction.

In this research, there are 20 features as described earlier. Each feature is represented as a bit in the genetic algorithm. There are 2^{20} possible combinations of these features.

4.5   Experiments

We use SAR images from MSTAR public data (target and clutter data) [104] and generate 1008 target chips (small SAR images containing target) and 1008 clutter chips (small SAR images containing clutter) of size 120×120. We also use SAR images that are downloaded from the website of MIT Lincoln Lab. From these SAR images, 40 target chips and 40 clutter chips of size 120×120 are generated. By adding these two sets of images, we have 1048 target chips and 1048 clutter chips. Some of the chips are used in training and the rest are used in testing. The chips used in training are randomly selected. The GA selects a good subset of features from the 20 features described previously to classify a SAR image chip into either a target or clutter. We use the CFAR detector in the prescreener stage to detect the potential target regions. Since we know the ground-truth, we know which one is the real target and which one is the clutter false alarm among the potential target regions detected. This allows us to construct a set of training data (training target data and training natural clutter false alarm data) for feature selection. Then we extract a set of 20 features from each potential target region and do the feature selection. Finally in the testing stage we use the selected features to discriminate the targets from the natural clutter false alarms.

For our GA-based feature selection framework, we adopt a Bayesian classifier to classify the training data and the resulting error rate is used as the feedback into the feature selection algorithm. The size of the population is 100, the initial crossover rate is 0.8 and the initial mutation rate is 0.01. If the fitness value of the best individual is not improved for 3 generations in a row, GA increases the mutation rate by 0.02. In order to reduce the training time, we set an error rate threshold ε. The GA stops when either the error rate of the best set of features selected is below the specified threshold ε or the mutation rate is increased above 0.09.

We carried out a series of experiments to test the efficacy of GA in feature selection. First, we use the MDL-based fitness function. Then we use the other three fitness functions. Finally, we compare and analyze the performance of these fitness functions. In order to have an objective comparison of various experiments, the GA is invoked ten times for each experiment with the same set of parameters and the same set of training chips. Only the average performance is used for comparison.

4.5.1   MDL principle-based fitness function

We performed four experiments with this fitness function. In the first experiment, 300 target chips and 300 clutter chips are used in training and 748 target chips and 748 clutter chips are used in testing, the error rate threshold value ε is 0.002; in the second experiment, 500 target chips and 500 clutter chips are used in training and 548 target chips and 548 clutter chips are used in testing, the error rate threshold value ε is 0.0015; in the third and fourth experiments, 700 target chips and 700 clutter chips are used in training and 348 target chips and 348 clutter chips are used in testing, the error rate threshold values ε are 0.0015 and 0.0011, respectively. The features selected during training are used for classification during testing. It is worth noting that the training chip set in the third and fourth experiments is the superset of that in the second experiment and the training chip set in the second experiment is the superset of that in the first experiment. The target and clutter chips used during training are selected at random.

Table 4.1 shows the experimental results where 300 target and 300 clutter chips are used in training. GA is invoked 10 times and each row records the experimental results from the corresponding invocation. The last row records the average results of 10 runs. The column "Best generation" records the generation number in which the best set of features is found and the column "Total generation" shows the total number of generations GA runs. Note that Bg is often much less than Tg, which indicates that the termination criteria are somewhat loose and, thus, we are somewhat inefficient in training time. It can be seen that although the training error rate is 0.003 in each run, different features are selected. In some runs, the same number of testing clutter chips are misclassified, but the clutter chips that are misclassified in each run are different. From the testing results, we can observe that sometimes clutter chips are misclassified as target chips. The testing results show that GA finds an effective set of features to discriminate target from clutter.

Table 4.2 and Table 4.3 show the experimental results when 500 target and clutter chips and 700 target and clutter chips are used in training, respectively.

The results in Table 4.2 are very good. On the average, 5.1 features are selected and both the training and testing error rate are very low. However, the results in Table 4.3 are not good. Although the training and testing error rates are low, 9.2 features are selected on the average. From Table 4.3, we can see that GA runs 4.9 generations on the average. It is clear that GA stops prematurely. The reason for the premature termination is that the error rate threshold value 0.0015 is high in this case, since there are 700 target chips and 700 clutter chips. In order to force GA to explore the search space, we lower the error rate threshold value to 0.0011 and get the results shown in Table 4.4. These results are much better than those in Table 4.3. Only 5.3 features are selected on the average, although the average testing error rate is almost doubled. Considering both the test error rate and the number of features selected, the first run in Table 4.1 and Table 4.4, and the sixth run in Figure 4.2 yield the best results. Figure 4.6 shows how fitness values change as GA searches the feature subset space during these runs; Figure 4.7 shows how training error rate changes and Figure 4.8 shows how the number of features selected changes.

From the above experiments, we can see that the MDL-based fitness function and adaptive GA are very efficient in feature selection. Only 4 to 6 features are selected on the average while the detection accuracy is kept high.

Table 4.1. Experimental results with 300 training target and clutter chips (MDL, equation (4.2); $\varepsilon = 0.002$).

Runs	B_g	T_g	F_n	Features selected	Training error rate	Number of errors T	Number of errors C	Testing error rate	Number of errors T	Number of errors C
1	29	47	4	0100101001 0000000000	0.003	1	1	0.001	0	2
2	9	27	6	0110001011 0000100000	0.003	1	1	0.011	0	116
3	10	28	4	0100001001 0100000000	0.003	1	1	0.011	0	116
4	43	61	4	0000001001 0100100000	0.003	1	1	0.005	0	7
5	19	37	4	0101001001 0000000000	0.003	1	1	0.017	0	225
6	13	31	4	0100001001 1000000000	0.003	1	1	0.007	0	110
7	23	41	4	0100001001 0010000000	0.003	1	1	0.011	0	116
8	6	24	6	0010011011 0000100000	0.003	1	1	0.011	0	116
9	17	35	5	0100001001 0011000000	0.003	1	1	0.003	0	5
10	11	29	5	0100001001 0010100000	0.003	1	1	0.005	0	7
Ave.	18	36	4.6		0.003	1	1	0.0082	0	12

B_g: best generation. T_g: total generation. F_n: number of features selected. T: target. C: clutter.

Table 4.2. Experimental results with 500 training target and clutter chips (MDL, equation (4.2); $\varepsilon = 0.0015$).

Run	B_g	T_g	F_n	Features selected	Training error rate	Number of errors T	Number of errors C	Testing error rate	Number of errors T	Number of errors C
1	17	35	5	0100001001 1000100000	0.002	1	1	0.006	0	7
2	13	31	5	0100001001 0000001001	0.002	1	1	0.006	0	7
3	19	38	5	0100001001 0000011000	0.002	1	1	0.006	0	7
4	20	38	5	0100001001 0000011000	0.002	1	1	0.006	0	7
5	10	28	5	0100001001 0010100000	0.002	1	1	0.006	0	7
6	26	44	5	0100001001 1100000000	0.002	1	1	0.003	0	3
7	25	43	5	0100001001 0000010100	0.002	1	1	0.007	0	8
8	9	27	6	0000001011 0000011010	0.002	1	1	0.007	0	8
9	8	26	5	0100001001 0000011000	0.002	1	1	0.006	0	7
10	17	35	5	0001001001 0011000000	0.002	1	1	0.004	0	4
Ave.	16.4	34.5	5.1		0.002	1	1	0.0057	0	6.5

B_g: best generation. T_g: total generation. F_n: number of features selected.
T: target. C: clutter.

Table 4.3. Experimental results with 700 training target and clutter chips (MDL, equation (4.2); $\varepsilon = 0.0015$).

Run	B_g	T_g	F_n	Features selected	Training error rate	Number of errors T	Number of errors C	Testing error rate	Number of errors T	Number of errors C
1	8	8	9	0101101001 1010001001	0.0014	1	1	0.006	0	4
2	9	9	10	1101001001 1010101010	0.0014	1	1	0.001	0	1
3	7	7	7	0000001011 0100101010	0.0014	1	1	0.012	0	8
4	2	2	10	1101001001 0110011010	0.0014	1	1	0.001	0	1
5	5	5	8	0100001001 0011111000	0.0014	1	1	0.007	0	5
6	2	2	7	1000011011 0100001000	0.0014	1	1	0.012	0	8
7	5	5	10	1101001001 0110101100	0.0014	1	1	0.001	0	1
8	3	3	10	1100101011 0101010001	0.0014	1	1	0.003	0	2
9	4	4	11	1101011001 1010111000	0.0014	1	1	0.001	0	1
10	4	4	10	1101001001 0011111000	0.0014	1	1	0.001	0	1
Ave.	4.9	4.9	9.2		0.0014	1	1	0.0045	0	3.2

B_g: best generation. T_g: total generation. F_n: number of features selected.
T: target. C: clutter.

Table 4.4. Experimental results with 700 training target and clutter chips (MDL, equation (4.2); $\varepsilon = 0.0011$).

Run	B_g	T_g	F_n	Features selected	Training error rate	Number of errors T	Number of errors C	Testing error rate	Number of errors T	Number of errors C
1	10	28	6	0001001001 1000001010	0.0014	1	1	0.004	0	3
2	19	37	5	0100001001 0000001010	0.0014	1	1	0.012	0	8
3	17	35	5	0100001001 0010100000	0.0014	1	1	0.01	0	7
4	16	34	6	0001011001 0010001000	0.0014	1	1	0.006	0	4
5	16	34	5	0100001001 0000011000	0.0014	1	1	0.01	0	7
6	19	37	5	0100001001 0010100000	0.0014	1	1	0.01	0	7
7	10	28	5	0100001001 0000010100	0.0014	1	1	0.01	0	7
8	15	33	5	0100001001 0000011000	0.0014	1	1	0.01	0	7
9	10	28	6	0100011001 1000010000	0.0014	1	1	0.007	0	5
10	23	41	5	0100001001 0000001001	0.0014	1	1	0.01	0	7
Ave.	15.5	33.5	5.3		0.0014	1	1	0.0089	0	6.1

B_g: best generation. T_g: total generation. F_n: number of features selected.
T: target. C: clutter.

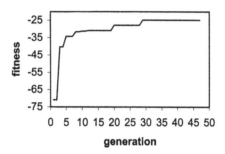

(a) 700 training target and clutter chips.

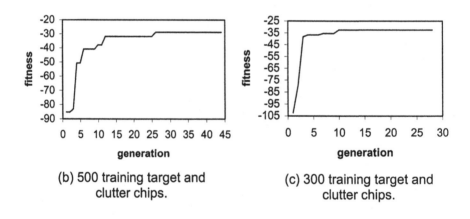

(b) 500 training target and
clutter chips.

(c) 300 training target and
clutter chips.

Figure 4.6. Fitness values vs. generation number.

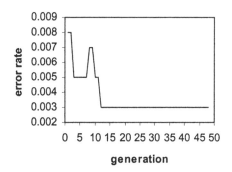

(a) 300 training target and clutter chips.

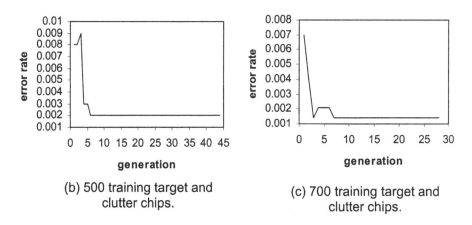

(b) 500 training target and
clutter chips.

(c) 700 training target and
clutter chips.

Figure 4.7. Training error rates vs. generation number.

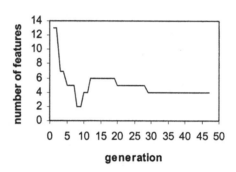

(a) 300 training target and clutter chips.

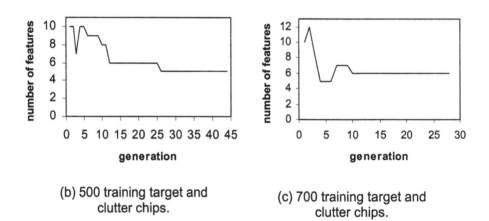

(b) 500 training target and
clutter chips.

(c) 700 training target and
clutter chips.

Figure 4.8. The number of features selected vs. generation number.

4.5.2   Other fitness functions

For the purpose of objective comparison, the training chip set in the following experiments is the same as that in the second experiment above, that is, 500 target chips and 500 clutter chips are used in training and 548 target chips and 548 clutter chips are used in testing.

First, we use (4.4) as the fitness function and invoke GA 10 times. The error rate threshold value is 0.0015. Table 4.5 shows the experimental results. This function is only dependent on the error rate, so GA found a set of features with very low error rate quickly. The selected features are shown by the "Number of features" and "Features selected" columns. However, since the number of features is not taken into consideration by the fitness function, many features are selected. More than 10 features are selected on the average in 10 runs.

Next, we use (4.5) as the fitness function. We performed three experiments with this function, and the values of γ are 0.1, 0.3 and 0.5 in these three experiments, respectively. The error rate threshold is 0.0015. Since this function considers the number of features selected, only a few features will be selected.   Table 4.6, Table 4.7 and Table 4.8 show the corresponding experimental results when γ is 0.1, 0.3 and 0.5.

From Table 4.6, we can see that since the training error rate is low, the number of features selected accounts for a large percentage of the value of the fitness function, forcing GA to select only 2 features in each run. However, the error rate for testing results is not encouraging. It is more than 0.02 on the average.

When γ is 0.3, the number of features account for a larger part of the value of the fitness function than when γ is 0.1, forcing GA to select almost only one feature. Actually, in 8 of the 10 runs shown in Table 4.7, GA selects the best feature (feature 7) among all the 20 features (see Table 4.12) to discriminate the target from clutter. When γ is 0.5, the number of features almost dominates the value of fitness function. The same phenomenon occurs and the experimental results are shown in Table 4.8.

Finally, we use (4.6) as the fitness function. We did three experiments with this function, and the values of γ are 0.1, 0.3 and 0.5 in these three experiments, respectively. The error rate threshold is 0.0015. Like (4.5), this function considers both the number of features selected and the error rate. When γ is large, this function forces GA to select one feature. Usually, the best feature (feature 7) is selected (see Table 4.12). Table 4.9, Table 4.10 and Table 4.11 show the corresponding experimental results when γ is 0.1, 0.3 and 0.5, respectively.

In order to show that GA selects the best feature when the number of features dominates the fitness function, we examine the efficacy of each feature in discriminating the targets from clutter. The data used in examination are 500 target chips and 500 clutter chips used in the above training. The results are shown in Table 4.12. From this table, it can be seen that the best feature (feature 7, the maximum CFAR feature) is selected by GA.

4.5.3   Comparison and analysis

Figure 4.9 shows the average performance of each of the above experiments pictorially. The X-axis is the average number of features selected and the Y-axis is the average training error rate. We use the average number of features selected and the average training error rate to form a performance point and evaluate the performance according to the location of performance point. A good performance point should have lower values of both the average number of features and the training error. The three points (shown as circles) are the performance points when the MDL-based fitness function is used and the rest are the performance points corresponding to other fitness functions.

From the above experimental results, we can see that GA is capable of selecting a good set of features to discriminate the target from clutter. The MDL-based fitness function is the best fitness function compared to the three other functions. Fitness function (4.4) doesn't include the number of features. Although GA can find a good set of features quickly driven by this function, many features are selected. This greatly increases the computational complexity in the testing phase. Fitness functions (4.5) and (4.6) take the number of features selected into consideration. However, the number of features dominates the fitness function value, forcing GA to select only one or two features, leading to the unsatisfactory training and testing error rates. In order to balance the number of features selected and the error rate, parameter γ must be finely tuned. This is not an easy task and it usually takes a lot of time. The MDL-based fitness function is based on a sound theory and it balances these two terms very well. Only a few features are selected while the training and testing error rates are kept low.

Table 4.5. Experimental results with 500 training target and clutter chips (penalty function, equation (4.4); $\varepsilon = 0.0015$).

Run	B_g	T_g	F_n	Features selected	Training error rate	Number of errors		Testing error rate	Number of errors	
						T	C		T	C
1	4	22	13	0111111011 1100111000	0.002	1	1	0.004	0	4
2	11	11	10	1011011011 0001100100	0.001	1	0	0.005	0	5
3	2	20	9	0101101001 1011000100	0.002	1	1	0.005	0	5
4	4	22	11	1010011011 0101011100	0.002	1	1	0.004	0	4
5	3	21	10	1110001011 1010010100	0.002	1	1	0.003	0	3
6	10	10	9	0011011011 0000110100	0.001	1	0	0.005	0	5
7	8	26	10	1101101001 0011010010	0.002	1	1	0.001	0	1
8	2	20	11	1110101011 0001001110	0.002	1	1	0.003	0	3
9	3	21	10	0110011011 1101100000	0.002	1	1	0.005	0	5
10	3	21	9	1110011011 0000110000	0.002	1	1	0.008	0	9
Ave.	5	19.4	10.2		0.0018	1	1	0.0043	0	4.4

B_g: best generation. T_g: total generation. F_n: number of features selected.
T: target. C: clutter.

Table 4.6. Experimental results with 500 training target and clutter chips (penalty and # of features, equation (4.5); $\gamma = 0.1$; $\varepsilon = 0.0015$).

Run	B_g	T_g	F_n	Features selected	Training error rate	Number of errors T	Number of errors C	Testing error rate	Number of errors T	Number of errors C
1	18	36	2	0000001001 0000000000	0.005	2	3	0.024	0	26
2	12	30	2	0000001000 0000001000	0.007	1	6	0.007	0	8
3	17	35	2	0000001001 0000000000	0.005	2	3	0.024	0	26
4	20	38	2	0000001001 0000000000	0.005	2	3	0.024	0	26
5	16	34	2	0000001001 0000000000	0.005	2	3	0.024	0	26
6	11	29	2	0000001001 0000000000	0.005	2	3	0.024	0	26
7	15	33	2	0000001001 0000000000	0.005	2	3	0.024	0	26
8	17	35	2	0000001001 0000000000	0.005	2	3	0.024	0	26
9	14	32	2	0000001001 0000000000	0.005	2	3	0.024	0	26
10	12	30	2	0000001000 0000001000	0.007	1	6	0.007	0	8
Ave.	15.2	33.2	2		0.0054	1.8	3.6	0.0206	0	22.4

B_g: best generation. T_g: total generation. F_n: number of features selected.
T: target. C: clutter.

Table 4.7. Experimental results with 500 training target and clutter chips (penalty and # of features, equation (4.5); $\gamma = 0.3$; $\varepsilon = 0.0015$).

Run	B_g	T_g	F_n	Features selected	Training error rate	Number of errors		Testing error rate	Number of errors	
						T	C		T	C
1	23	41	1	0000001000 0000000000	0.01	1	9	0.036	0	39
2	20	38	1	0000001000 0000000000	0.01	1	9	0.036	0	39
3	11	29	2	1000001000 0000000000	0.005	1	4	0.033	0	36
4	8	26	3	0000000010 0010010000	0.008	4	4	0.005	0	5
5	30	48	1	0000001000 0000000000	0.01	1	9	0.036	0	39
6	14	32	1	0000001000 0000000000	0.01	1	9	0.036	0	39
7	25	43	1	0000001000 0000000000	0.01	1	9	0.036	0	39
8	20	38	1	0000001000 0000000000	0.01	1	9	0.036	0	39
9	22	40	1	0000001000 0000000000	0.01	1	9	0.036	0	39
10	27	45	1	0000001000 0000000000	0.01	1	9	0.036	0	39
Ave.	20	38	1.3		0.0093	1.3	8	0.0326	0	35.3

B_g: best generation. T_g: total generation. F_n: number of features selected. T: target. C: clutter.

Table 4.8. Experimental results with 500 training target and clutter chips (penalty and # of features, equation (4.5); $\gamma = 0.5$; $\varepsilon = 0.0015$).

Run	B_g	T_g	F_n	Features selected	Training error rate	Number of errors		Testing error rate	Number of errors	
						T	C		T	C
1	17	35	1	0000001000 0000000000	0.01	1	9	0.036	0	39
2	29	41	1	0000001000 0000000000	0.01	1	9	0.036	0	39
3	22	40	1	0000001000 0000000000	0.01	1	9	0.036	0	39
4	15	33	1	0000001000 0000000000	0.01	1	9	0.036	0	39
5	32	50	1	0000001000 0000000000	0.01	1	9	0.036	0	39
6	11	29	1	0000001000 0000000000	0.01	1	9	0.036	0	39
7	11	29	1	0000001000 0000000000	0.01	1	9	0.036	0	39
8	23	41	1	0000001000 0000000000	0.01	1	9	0.036	0	39
9	9	27	2	0000000010 0000001000	0.012	5	7	0.011	0	12
10	23	41	1	0000001000 0000000000	0.01	1	9	0.036	0	39
Ave.	19.2	37.2	1.1		0.01	1.5	8.8	0.0335	0	36.3

B_g: best generation. T_g: total generation. F_n: number of features selected.
T: target. C: clutter.

Table 4.9. Experimental results with 500 training target and clutter chips (error rate and # of features, equation (4.6); $\gamma = 0.1$; $\varepsilon = 0.0015$).

Run	B_g	T_g	F_n	Features selected	Training error rate	Number of errors		Testing error rate	Number of errors	
						T	C		T	C
1	21	39	1	0000001000 0000000000	0.01	1	9	0.036	0	39
2	16	34	1	0000001000 0000000000	0.01	1	9	0.036	0	39
3	14	32	2	0000100010 0000000000	0.01	7	3	0.006	0	7
4	25	43	1	0000001000 0000000000	0.01	1	9	0.036	0	39
5	13	31	1	0000001000 0000000000	0.01	1	9	0.036	0	39
6	17	35	1	0000001000 0000000000	0.01	1	9	0.036	0	39
7	17	35	2	0000100010 0000000000	0.01	7	3	0.006	0	7
8	33	51	1	0000001000 0000000000	0.01	1	9	0.036	0	39
9	22	40	1	0000001000 0000000000	0.01	1	9	0.036	0	39
10	12	30	1	0000001000 0000000000	0.01	1	9	0.036	0	39
Ave.	19	37	1.2		0.01	2.2	7.8	0.03	0	32.6

B_g: best generation. T_g: total generation. F_n: number of features selected.
T: target. C: clutter.

Table 4.10. Experimental results with 500 training target and clutter chips (penalty and # of features, equation (4.6); $\gamma = 0.3$; $\varepsilon = 0.0015$)

Run	B_g	T_g	F_n	Features selected	Training error rate	Number of errors		Testing error rate	Number of errors	
						T	C		T	C
1	11	29	1	0000001000 0000000000	0.01	1	9	0.036	0	39
2	27	45	1	0000001000 0000000000	0.01	1	9	0.036	0	39
3	17	35	1	0000001000 0000000000	0.01	1	9	0.036	0	39
4	11	29	1	0000001000 0000000000	0.01	1	9	0.036	0	39
5	11	29	1	0000001000 0000000000	0.01	1	9	0.036	0	39
6	11	29	1	0000001000 0000000000	0.019	7	12	0.028	0	31
7	20	38	1	0000000010 0000000000	0.01	1	9	0.036	0	39
8	30	48	1	0000000010 0000000000	0.019	7	12	0.028	0	31
9	7	25	1	0000000010 0000000000	0.019	7	12	0.028	0	31
10	12	30	1	0000001000 0000000000	0.01	1	9	0.036	0	39
Ave.	15.7	33.7	1		0.013	2.8	9.9	0.0336	0	36.3

B_g: best generation. T_g: total generation. F_n: number of features selected.
T: target. C: clutter.

Table 4.11. Experimental results with 500 training target and clutter chips (penalty and
# of features, equation (4.6); $\gamma = 0.5$; $\varepsilon = 0.0015$).

Run	B_g	T_g	F_n	Features selected	Training error rate	Number of errors		Testing error rate	Number of errors	
						T	C		T	C
1	25	43	1	0000000010 0000000000	0.019	7	12	0.028	0	31
2	11	29	1	0000001000 0000000000	0.01	1	9	0.036	0	39
3	8	26	1	0000000010 0000000000	0.019	7	12	0.028	0	31
4	11	29	1	0000001000 0000000000	0.01	1	9	0.036	0	39
5	8	26	1	0000001000 0000000000	0.01	1	9	0.036	0	39
6	15	33	1	0000001000 0000000000	0.01	1	9	0.036	0	39
7	9	27	1	0000001000 0000000000	0.01	1	9	0.036	0	39
8	12	30	1	0000001000 0000000000	0.01	1	9	0.036	0	39
9	29	47	1	0000001000 0000000000	0.01	1	9	0.036	0	39
10	24	42	1	0000001000 0000000000	0.01	1	9	0.036	0	39
Ave.	15.2	33.2	1		0.013	2.2	9.4	0.0344	0	37.4

B_g: best generation. T_g: total generation. F_n: number of features selected.
T: target. C: clutter.

Table 4.12. Experimental results using only one feature for discrimination (target chips = 500, clutter chips = 500).

Feature	Error rate	Number of errors		Feature	Error rate	Number of errors	
		Target	Clutter			Target	Clutter
1	0.119	17	102	11	0.118	18	100
2	0.099	16	83	12	0.111	6	105
3	0.056	7	49	13	0.126	9	117
4	0.057	17	40	14	0.131	7	124
5	0.068	13	55	15	0.09	5	85
6	0.354	0	354	16	0.069	3	66
7	0.01	1	9	17	0.075	3	72
8	0.5	480	20	18	0.209	0	209
9	0.019	7	12	19	0.2	2	198
10	0.073	15	58	20	0.244	0	244

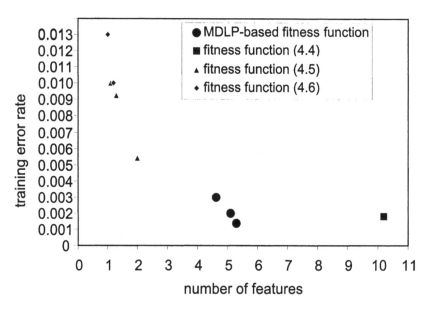

Figure 4.9. Average performance of various fitness functions

Table 4.13. The number of times each feature is selected in MDL Experiments 1, 2 and 4.

Features	Exp 1	Exp 2	Exp 4	Total
1	0	0	0	0
2*	8	8	8	24
3	2	0	0	2
4	1	1	2	4
5	1	0	0	1
6	1	0	2	3
7*	10	10	10	30
8	0	0	0	0
9	2	1	0	3
10*	10	10	10	30
11	1	2	1	4
12	2	1	0	3
13	3	2	3	8
14	1	1	0	2
15	4	2	2	8
16	0	4	4	8
17	0	5	6	11
18	0	1	1	2
19	0	1	2	3
20	0	1	1	2

In order to evaluate which features are more important than others using the MDL-based approach, we combine the results of first, second and fourth experiments. Note that in the first, second and fourth experiments (shown in Table 4.1, Table 4.2 and Table 4.4), GA is invoked for a total of 30 times. Table 4.13 shows the number of times each feature is selected in these 30 runs. It can be seen from Table 4.13 that the fractal dimension feature (feature 2), the maximum CFAR feature (feature 7) and the count feature (feature 10) are very useful in detecting targets in SAR images, while the standard deviation feature (feature 1) and the mean CFAR feature (feature 8) are not used at all. The major diagonal projection feature (feature 13), the minimum distance feature (feature 15), the maximum distance feature (feature 16) and the average distance feature (feature 17) have low utility while other features have very low utility. These results are consistent with those shown in Table 4.12. Considered individually, the maximum CFAR feature (feature 7) is the best feature (see Table 4.12) and it is selected by GA (in combination with other features) in all the 30 runs.

4.6   Conclusions

In this chapter, we introduced the GA feature selection algorithm into a specific application domain to discriminate the targets from the natural clutter false alarms in SAR images. Rough target detection, feature extraction, GA feature selection and final discrimination are successfully implemented and good results are obtained. Our experimental results show that the GA selected a good subset of features. Also, we proposed a MDL-based fitness function and compared its performance with three other fitness functions. Our experimental results show that the MDL-based fitness function balances the number of features selected and the error rate very well and it is the best fitness function compared to other three functions.

Chapter 5

EVOLUTIONARY FEATURE SYNTHESIS FOR OBJECT RECOGNITION

5.1   Introduction

In this chapter, we investigate the effectiveness of domain knowledge in improving the efficiency of the evolutionary search and the efficacy of genetic programming in synthesizing composite features for object recognition. The basic task of object recognition is to identify the kinds of objects in an image, and sometimes the task may include estimating the pose of the recognized objects. One of the key approaches to object recognition is based on features extracted from images. These features capture the characteristics of the object and are fed into a classifier to perform recognition. The quality of object recognition is heavily dependent on the effectiveness of the features. However, it is difficult to extract good features from real images due to various factors, including noise. More importantly, there are many features that can be extracted. What are the appropriate features or how to select an appropriate set of features from the available features? If it is very difficult or even impossible to extract effective features from images, then how to synthesize useful features based on the available ones? To make use of knowledge about a specific domain and improve the quality of synthesized features, the question is how to incorporate domain knowledge in the feature synthesis? The answers to these questions are largely dependent on the instinct, knowledge, experience, and the bias of human experts.

In this chapter, the effectiveness of coevolutionary genetic programming (CGP) [57], [69], [94] in generating composite operator vectors for object recognition is investigated. As presented in Chapter 2, genetic programming (GP) is an evolutionary computational paradigm that is an extension of genetic algorithm and works with a population of individuals. An individual in a population can be any complicated data structure such as linked lists, trees and graphs, etc. CGP is an extension of GP in which several populations are maintained and employed to evolve solutions cooperatively. A population maintained by CGP is called a sub-population and it is responsible for evolving a part of a solution. A complete solution is obtained by combining the partial solutions from all the sub-populations. In this chapter, individuals in sub-populations are composite operators, which are the elements of a composite operator vector. A composite operator is represented by a binary tree whose internal nodes are the pre-specified domain-independent primitive operators and leaf nodes are primitive features. It is a way of combining primitive features. The advantage of using a tree structure is that it is powerful enough in expressing the ways of combining primitive features and unlike a graph, it has no loops and this guarantees that the execution of individuals represented by trees terminate and not be trapped in an infinite loop. The primitive features can be directly extracted simple features or complicated features designed by human experts based on the characteristics of objects to be recognized in a particular kind of imagery (e.g., SAR images). The primitive features are real value attributes in this chapter. With each element evolved by a sub-population of CGP, a composite operator vector is cooperatively evolved by all the sub-populations. By applying composite operators, corresponding to each sub-population, to the primitive features extracted from images, composite feature vectors are obtained. These composite feature vectors are fed into a classifier for recognition. It is worth noting that the primitive operators and primitive features are decoupled from the CGP mechanism that generates composite features, so they can be tailored to particular recognition tasks without affecting the other parts of the system. Thus, the method and the recognition system are flexible and can be applied to a wide variety of images.

Chapter 5.2 explains the motivation for using genetic programming as a tool for learning composite features. It also surveys the related works. Chapter 5.3 provides the overall structure of the learning and recognition system and gives the technical details used in this chapter. Experimental results are presented in chapter 5.4 and chapter 5.5 summarizes the conclusions and proposes possible future research directions.

5.2   Motivation and Related Research

5.2.1   Motivation

The recognition accuracy of an automatic object recognition system is determined by the quality of the feature set used. Usually, it is the human experts who design the features to be used in recognition. Designing a set of effective features requires human ingenuity and insight into the characteristics of the objects to be recognized and in general, it is very difficult to identify a set of features that characterize a complex set of objects. Typically, many types of features are explored before a recognition system can be built to perform the desired recognition task. There are a lot of features available and these features may be correlated, making the design and selection of appropriate features a very time consuming and expensive process. Sometimes, it is very difficult to figure out and extract simple features that are effective in recognition directly from images. However, human experts generally know what kinds of features are useful for a particular kind of imagery. These simple features can be selected as primitive features. At this time, synthesizing composite features that are effective to the current recognition task from these primitive features becomes extremely important.

The process of synthesizing composite features can often be dissected into some primitive operations on the primitive features. It is usually the human experts who, replying on their knowledge and rich experience, figure out a smart way to combine these primitive operations to yield good composite features. The task of finding good composite features is equivalent to finding good points in the composite feature space. However, the ways of combining primitive features are almost infinite, leading to a huge composite feature space. It is obvious that a smart search strategy is necessary in order to find good composite features in such a huge space. The human experts can only try a very limited number of combinations due to time limits and usually only the conventional combinations are tried due to knowledge, experience and even the bias of human experts. CGP, on the other hand, may try many unconventional combinations and in some cases it is these unconventional combinations that yield exceptionally good recognition performance. Also, the inherent parallelism of CGP and the concept of sub-populations (search by many individuals) facilitate its implementation on multi-processor supercomputers to further increase the search speed and allow a much larger portion of the search space to be explored by CGP than that explored by human experts, thus greatly enhancing the chance of finding good composite features. As a result, CGP is a very useful tool in comparison to human experts in the feature design and synthesis.

5.2.2   Related research

In general, feature selection and feature synthesis are two kinds of feature transformations. In feature selection [15], original features are not changed and some original features are selected to form a subset of features to be used by classifiers. Genetic algorithm is widely used in feature selection as discussed in Chapter 4. In feature synthesis, a transformation, linear or nonlinear, is applied to the original features to generate new features. Weighted summation is a kind of linear transformation on the original features, and the weights of features can be determined by genetic algorithm. In multi-layer neural networks, each node of a neural network takes the weighted sum of the outputs of its child nodes as input[120]. The weights are determined by backpropagation algorithm during training. The output of a node is determined by the input and the activation function of the node. It can be viewed as a nonlinear transformation on the original features. The CGP-based feature synthesis is another kind of nonlinear transformation on the original features, which are the primitive features in this chapter.

Genetic programming (GP) has been used in image processing, object detection and recognition. Harris and Buxton [39] apply GP to the production of high performance edge detectors for 1D signals and image profiles. The method is also extended to the development of practical edge detectors for use in image processing and machine vision. Ebner and Zell [29] use GP to automate the process of chaining a series of well known image processing operators to perform image processing. Poli [92] uses GP to develop effective image filters to enhance and detect features of interest and to build pixel-classification-based segmentation algorithm. Bhanu and Lin [14] use GP to generate composite operators for object detection. The primitive operators and primitive features used in their system are very basic and domain-independent, so their object detection system can be applied to a wide variety of images. Their experimental results showed that GP is a viable way of synthesizing composite features from primitive features for object detection and ROI (region-of-interest) extraction. Howard et al. [44] apply GP to automatic detection of ships in low resolution SAR imagery using an approach that evolves detectors. The detectors are algebraic formulae involving the values at pixels belonging to a small region surrounding the pixel undergoing the test and the detectors evolved by GP compare favorably in accuracy to those obtained using a neural network. Roberts and Howard [103] use GP to develop automatic object detectors in infrared images. They present a multi-stage approach to address feature detection and object segregation and the detectors developed by GP do not require images to be preprocessed. Stanhope and Daida [114] use GP paradigms for the generation of rules for target/clutter classification and rules for the identification of objects. GP determines relevant features from previously defined features to form a selected feature set. It evolves logical expressions based on the comparison of the selected features to both real-valued constants and other features in the selected feature set to create a classifier. Krawiec and Bhanu [64] present a method for the automatic synthesis of recognition procedures chaining elementary operations for computer vision and pattern recognition tasks based on cooperative coevolution and linear genetic programming. Each sub-population evolves a part of the recognition procedure and all the sub-populations coevolve the whole recognition procedure by selecting the best individual from each sub-population and chaining them together. Their experimental results show that linear genetic programming is effective in synthesizing a recognition procedure from elementary image processing operations. They also show that coevolutionary linear genetic programming is superior to regular single-population linear genetic programming that is equivalent to genetic algorithms.

Unlike the work of Stanhope and Daida [114], the primitive operators in this chapter are not logical operators, but operators on real numbers and the composite operators are binary trees of primitive operators on real numbers, not binary trees of logical operators. In [114], GP is used to evolve logical expressions and the final outcome of the logical expression determines the type of the object under consideration (for example, 1 means target and 0 means clutter). In this chapter, CGP is used to evolve composite feature vectors to be used by a Bayesian classifier [120] and each sub-population is responsible for evolving a specific composite feature in the composite feature vector. The classifier evolved by GP in [114] is a logical expression represented by the binary tree with the best classification rate in the population, but the classifier evolved by CGP in this chapter is a Bayesian classifier determined by the composite feature vectors obtained from the training images. Unlike the work of Krawiec and Bhanu [64], composite operators in this chapter are binary trees of primitive operators and primitive features, whereas the recognition procedures in [64] are linked lists of simple image processing operations.

5.3   Coevolutionary GP for Feature Synthesis

In the CGP-based approach proposed in this chapter, individuals are composite operators represented by binary trees with primitive operators as internal nodes and primitive features as leaf nodes. The search space is the set of all possible composite operators. The search space is huge and it is extremely difficult to find good composite operators from this vast space unless one has a smart search strategy. The system consists of training and testing modules, which are shown in Figure 5.1(a) and 1(b), respectively. During training, CGP runs on training images and evolves composite operators to obtain composite features. Since a Bayesian classifier is derived from the feature vectors obtained from training images, both the composite operator vector and the classifier are learned by CGP.

5.3.1   Design considerations

To apply genetic programming, there are five major design considerations, which involve determining the set of terminals, the set of primitive operators, the fitness measure, the parameters for controlling the run and the criterion for terminating a run.

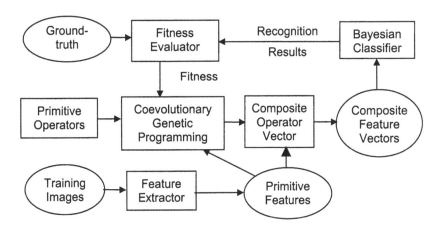

(a) Training module — Learning composite operator
vectors and Bayesian classifier

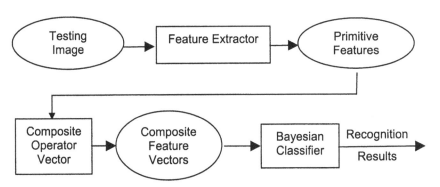

(b) Testing module — Applying learned composite operator
vector and Bayesian classifier to a test image

Figure 5.1. System diagram for object recognition using coevolutionary genetic
programming.

- **The set of terminals**: The set of terminals are the 20 primitive features described in chapter 4.4.2. The first 10 of these features capture the particular characteristics of synthetic aperture radar (SAR) imagery and are found useful for object detection [65]. The other 10 features are common features used widely in image processing and computer vision. In this chapter, we use these same 20 primitive features as in chapter 4.

To extract some primitive features, the CFAR (Constant False Alarm Rate) image of an original image is needed. The CFAR image is generated by applying the method described in chapter 4.4.1. For the detailed description of CFAR detector, the reader is referred to [65].

The set of primitive operators: A primitive operator takes one or two real numbers, performs a simple operation on them and outputs the result. Currently, 12 primitive operators shown in Table 5.1 are used, where a and b are real numbers and input to an operator and c is a constant real number stored in an operator.

Table 5.1. Twelve primitive operators.

Primitive Operator	Description	Primitive Operator	Description
ADD (a, b)	Add a and b.	ADDC (a, c)	Add constant value c to a.
SUB (a, b)	Subtract b from a.	SUBC (a, c)	Subtract constant value c from a.
MUL (a, b)	Multiply a and b.	MUL (a, c)	Multiply a with constant value c.
DIV (a, b)	Divide a by b.	DIVC (a, c)	Divide a by constant value c.
MAX2 (a, b)	Get the larger of a and b.	MIN2 (a, b)	Get the smaller of a and b.
SQRT (a)	Return $\sqrt{a}$ if a $\geq$ 0; otherwise, return $-\sqrt{-a}$.	LOG (a)	Return log(a) if a $\geq$ 0; otherwise, return $-$ log(-a).

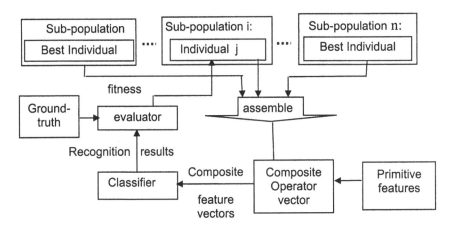

Figure 5.2. Computation of fitness of jth composite operator of ith sub-population.

• **The fitness measure:** The fitness of a composite operator vector is computed in the following way: apply each composite operator of the composite operator vector on the primitive features of training images to obtain composite feature vectors of training images and feed them to a Bayesian classifier. Note that not all the primitive features are necessarily used in feature synthesis. Only the primitive features that appear in the leaf nodes of the composite operator are used to generate composite features. The recognition rate of the classifier is the fitness of the composite operator vector. To evaluate a composite operator evolved in a sub-population (see Figure 5.2), the composite operator is combined with the current best composite operators in other sub-populations to form a complete composite operator vector where composite operator from the *ith* sub-population occupies the *ith* position in the vector and the fitness of the vector is defined as the fitness of the composite operator under evaluation. The fitness values of other composite operators in the vector are not affected. When sub-populations are initially generated, the composite operators in each sub-population are evaluated individually without being combined with composite operators from other sub-populations. In each generation, the composite operators in the first sub-population are evaluated first, then the composite operators in the second sub-population and so on.

• **Parameters and termination:** The key parameters are the number of sub-populations N, the population size M, the number of generations G, the crossover and mutation rates, and the fitness threshold. GP stops whenever it finishes the specified number of generations or the performance of the Bayesian classifier is above the fitness threshold. After termination, CGP selects the best composite operator of each sub-population to form the learned composite operator vector to be used in testing.

5.3.2   Selection, crossover and mutation

The CGP searches through the space of composite operator vectors to generate new composite operator vectors. The search is performed by selection, crossover and mutation operations. The initial sub-populations are randomly generated. Although sub-populations are cooperatively evolved (the fitness of a composite operator in a sub-population is not solely determined by itself, but affected by the composite operators from other sub-populations), selection is performed only on composite operators within a sub-population and crossover is not allowed between two composite operators from different sub-populations.

- **Selection**: The selection operation involves selecting composite operators from the current sub-population. In this chapter, tournament selection is used and the tournament size is five. The higher the fitness value, the more likely the composite operator is selected to survive.

- **Crossover**: Two composite operators, called parents, are selected on the basis of their fitness values. The higher the fitness value, the more likely the composite operator is selected for crossover. One internal node in each of these two parents is randomly selected, and the two subtrees rooted at these two nodes are exchanged between the parents to generate two new composite operators, called offspring. It is easy to see that the size of one offspring (i.e., the number of nodes in the binary tree representing the offspring) may be greater than both parents if crossover is implemented in such a simple way. To prevent code bloat, we specify a hard limit on the composite operator size (called hard size limit). If the size of one offspring exceeds the hard size limit, the crossover is performed again. If the size of an offspring still exceeds the hard size limit after the crossover is performed 10 times, GP selects two subtrees of same size (i.e., the same number of nodes) from two parents and swaps the subtrees between the parents. These two subtrees can always be found, since a leaf node can be viewed as a subtree of size 1.

- **Mutation:** To avoid premature convergence, mutation is introduced to randomly change the structure of some composite operators to maintain the diversity of sub-populations. Candidates for mutation are randomly selected and the mutated composite operators replace the old ones in the sub-populations. There are three mutations invoked with equal probability:

1. Randomly select a node of the composite operator and replace the subtree rooted at this node by a new randomly generated binary tree.

2. Randomly select a node of the composite operator and replace the primitive operator stored in the node with another primitive operator randomly selected from the primitive operators of the same arity as the replaced one.

3. Randomly select two subtrees of the composite operator and swap them. Of course, neither of the two subtrees can be a subtree of the other.

5.3.3   Generational coevolutionary genetic programming

Generational coevolutionary genetic programming is used to evolve composite operators. The GP operations are applied in the order of crossover, mutationand selection. The composite operators in the initial sub-populations are randomly generated. A composite operator is generated in two steps. In the first step, the number of internal nodes of the tree representing the composite operator is randomly determined as long as this number is smaller than half of hard size limit. Suppose the tree has n internal nodes. The tree is generated from top to bottom by a tree generation algorithm. The root node is generated first and the primitive operator stored in the root node is randomly selected. The selected primitive operator determines the number of children the root node has. If it has only one child, the algorithm is recursively invoked to generate a tree of $n-1$ internal nodes; if it has two children, the algorithm is recursively invoked to generate two trees of $\lfloor (n-1)/2 \rfloor$ and $\lceil (n-1)/2 \rceil$ internal nodes, respectively. In the second step, after all the internal nodes are generated, the leaf nodes containing primitive features are attached to those internal nodes that are temporarily the leaf nodes before the real leaf nodes are attached. The number of leaf nodes attached to an internal node is determined by the primitive operator stored in the internal node. In addition, an elitism replacement method is adopted to keep the best composite operator from generation to generation.

Generational Coevolutionary Genetic Programming Algorithms:

1.   randomly generate N sub-populations of size M and evaluate each composite operator in each sub-population individually.
2.   *for gen = 1 to G do*
3.   *for i =1 to N do*
4.   *keep the best composite operator in sub-population P_i.*
5.   *perform crossover on the composite operators in P_i until the crossover rate is satisfied and keep all the offspring from crossover.*
6.   *perform mutation on the composite operators in P_i and the offspring from crossover with the probability of mutation rate.*
7.   *perform selection on P_i to select some composite operators and combine them with the composite operators from crossover to get a new sub-population P_i' of the same size as P_i.*
8.   *evaluate each composite operator C_j in P_i'.*
        to evaluate C_j, select the current best composite operator in each of the other sub-populations, combine C_j with those N-1 best composite operators to form a composite operator vecter where composite operator from the kth sub-population occupy the kth position in the vector (k=1, ..., N). run the composite operator vector on the primitive features of the training images to get composite feature vectors and use them to build a Bayesian classifier. feed the composite feature vectors into the Bayesian classifier and let the recognition rate be the fitness of the composite operator vector and the fitness of C_j.
9.   *perform elitism replacement.*
        let the best composite operator from P_i replace the worst composite operator in P_i' and let $P_i = P_i'$
10.   *form the current best composite operator vector consisting of the best composite operators from corresponding sub-populations and evaluate it. if its fitness is above the fitness threshold, goto 11.*
        endfor // loop 2 iterates on each sub-population. after a new sub-population is generated, the best composite feature vector is changed and we need to find the best composite feature vector and evaluate it to determine if CGP can be terminated
        endfor // loop 1 iterates on each generation.
11.   *select the best composite operator from each sub-population to form the learned composite operator vector and output it.*

Figure 5.3. Generational coevolutionary genetic programming.

5.3.4 Bayesian classifier

For each class C_i (i = 1, 2, 3 or 1, 2, 3, 4, 5 in this chapter), a Bayesian classifier [120] is generated based on GP-learned composite features. A Bayesian classifier consists of a mean feature vector and a covariance matrix of feature vectors of class C_i. Suppose f_{i1}, f_{i2}, ..., f_{in} are the feature vectors extracted from n training images of class C_i, then the mean feature vector and the covariance matrix are computed by:

$$\mu_i = \frac{1}{n}\sum_{j=1}^{n} f_{ij}$$

$$C_i = \frac{1}{n}\sum_{j=1}^{n} (f_{ij} - \mu_i)(f_{ij} - \mu_i)^T \quad i = 1,\ 2,\ 3,\ 4\ or\ 5. \tag{5.1}$$

During testing, for a feature vector f from a testing image, we compute distance d_i ($d_i = (f - \mu_i)^T C_i^{-1}(f - \mu_i)$) and assign the object in the testing image to the class corresponding to the smallest distance. Here, we assume that the prior probability of each class is equal.

5.4 Experiments

Various experiments are performed to test the efficacy of genetic programming in generating composite features for object recognition. All the images used in the experiments are real synthetic aperture radar (SAR) images. These images are divided into training and testing images. The 20 primitive features described in Chapter 4 are extracted from each SAR image. CGP runs on primitive features from training images to generate a composite operator vector and a Bayesian classifier. The composite operator vector and the Bayesian classifier are tested against the testing images. It is worth noting that the ground-truth is used only during training. The experiments are categorized into three classes: (1) distinguishing man-made objects from natural clutters, (2) distinguishing between 3 kinds of man-made objects and (3) distinguishing between 5 kinds of man-made objects. For the purpose of objective comparison, CGP is invoked ten times for each experiment with the same set of parameters and the same set of training images. Only the average performance is used for comparison. Some of the parameters of CGP used throughout the experiments are shown in Table 5.2. The hard size limit is 10 in experiment 1 and 20 in experiments 2 and 3. The real number c stored in primitive operators ADDC, SUBC, MULC and DIVC can be any real number from −20 to 20. When mutation is performed on these primitive operators, the value c stored in these primitive operators may be changed.

Table 5.2. Parameters of CGP used throughout the experiments.

Sub-population size	50	Crossover rate	0.6
Number of generations	50	Mutation rate	0.05
Fitness threshold	1.0	Tournament size	5

5.4.1 Distinguish objects from clutter

• **Data:** The data used here are the same 1048 SAR images containing objects and 1048 SAR images containing natural clutters from the MSTAR public data, as described in chapter 4.5. An example object image and clutter image are shown in Figure 5.4, where white spots indicate scatterers with high magnitude. The 300 object images and 300 clutter images are randomly selected as training images and the rest are used in testing.

• **Experiment 1:** First, the effectiveness of each primitive feature in discriminating the objects from the clutters is examined. Each kind of primitive feature from the training images is used to train a Bayesian classifier and the classifier is tested against the same kind of primitive features from the testing images. The results are shown in Table 5.3. The percent bright CFAR feature (feature 9) is the best single feature with a recognition rate of 0.98.

(a) An object image   (b) A natural clutter image

Figure 5.4. Example object and clutter SAR images.

To show the efficacy of CGP in synthesizing effective composite features, we consider three cases: only the worst two primitive features (blob inertia (6) and mean values of pixels within blob (8)) are used by CGP; five bad primitive features (blob inertia (6), mean values of pixels within blob (8), moments μ_{20} (18), μ_{02} (19) and μ_{22} (20) of scatters) are used by CGP; 10 common features (primitive features 11 to 20) not specifically designed to process SAR images are used by CGP during feature synthesis. The number of sub-populations is 3, which means the dimension of the composite feature vectors is 3. CGP is invoked ten times with the same parameters. The average recognition performance over ten runs is shown in Table 5.4 (first row), where 2f means only features (6) and (8) are used as primitive features (case 1), 5f means features 6, 8, 18, 19 and 20 are used (case 2) and 10f means only 10 common features are used in feature synthesis (case 3). The columns on the left show the training results and those on the right show the testing results. The numbers in the table are the average recognition rates over ten runs. Then the number of sub-population is increased to 5. The same 2, 5 and 10 primitive features are used by CGP to evolve composite features. The average recognition performance over ten runs is shown in Table 5.4 (second row). The performance of synthesized composite features is worse than the feature set selected by GA in chapter 4. It is reasonable, since in chapter 4, a MDL-based GA is applied to select a set of features from all the 20 primitive features to distinguish target from clutter, and effective features are always selected by GA. In this chapter, we deliberately let GP synthesize composite features from 10 common features not specifically designed for SAR images or from 2 or 5 worst primitive features selected from the 20 primitive features.

Table 5.3. Recognition rates of 20 primitive features.

Feature Number	Primitive Feature	Recognition Rate	Feature Number	Primitive Feature	Recognition Rate
1	Standard deviation	0.88	11	Horizontal projection	0.90
2	Fractal dimension	0.91	12	Vertical projection	0.91
3	Weight-rank fill ratio	0.94	13	Major diagonal projection	0.89
4	Blob mass	0.94	14	Minor diagonal projection	0.88
5	Blob diameter	0.94	15	Minimum distance	0.92
6	Blob inertia	0.66	16	Maximum distance	0.95
7	Maximum CFAR	0.97	17	Mean distance	0.94
8	Mean CFAR	0.49	18	Moment μ_{20}	0.80
9	Percent bright CFAR	0.98	19	Moment μ_{02}	0.81
10	Count	0.92	20	Moment μ_{22}	0.75

Table 5.4. Performance of composite and primitive features on object/clutter discrimination.

	Recognition Rate					
	2f		5f		10f	
	Train.	Test	Train.	Test	Train.	Test
3-dimensional composite feature vector	0.989	0.986	0.991	0.989	0.971	0.984
5-dimensional composite feature vector	0.990	0.982	0.994	0.992	0.977	0.986
primitive feature vector	0.625	0.668	0.908	0.947	0.963	0.978

From Table 5.4, it can be seen that composite feature vectors synthesized by CGP are very effective. They are much better than the primitive features upon which they are built. Actually, if both features 6 and 8 from the training images jointly form 2-dimensional primitive feature vectors to train a Bayesian classifier for recognition, the recognition rates on training and testing data are 0.625 and 0.668, respectively; if features 6, 8, 18, 19, and 20 jointly form 5-dimensional primitive feature vectors, the recognition rates on training and testing data are 0.908 and 0.947, respectively; if all the 10 common primitive features are used, the recognition rates on training and testing data are 0.963 and 0.978, respectively. These results are shown in Table 5.4 (third row), where 2f, 5f and 10f indicate both the primitive features used and the dimension of primitive feature vectors. The average recognition rates of composite feature vectors are better than all of the above results and this is the value of using CGP for feature synthesis. Figure 5.5 shows the composite operator vector evolved by CGP maintaining 3 sub-populations in the 6th run when 5 primitive features are used, where PFi means the primitive feature i and so on. In Figure 5.5, the least effective feature (feature 8) is used by the effective composite operator evolved by CGP. This phenomenon is not uncommon, since a feature is not isolated from other features and the interaction of features (covariance) is complicated. Sometimes, a feature is not effective if it is used alone, but when it is used in combination with other features, a high recognition rate may be achieved. At this time, all these features form an effective feature set.

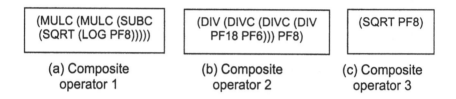

| (MULC (MULC (SUBC (SQRT (LOG PF8))))) | (DIV (DIVC (DIVC (DIV PF18 PF6))) PF8) | (SQRT PF8) |

| (a) Composite operator 1 | (b) Composite operator 2 | (c) Composite operator 3 |

Figure 5.5. Composite operator vector learned by CGP.

5.4.2   Recognize objects

• **Data:** Five objects (BRDM2 armored personnel carrier, D7 bulldozer, T62 tank, ZIL truck and ZSU anti-aircraft gun) are used in the experiments. For each object, 210 real SAR images under 15°-depression angle and various azimuth angles between 0° and 359° are collected from MSTAR public data [104]. Figure 5.6 shows one optical and four SAR images of each object. From Figure 5.6, we can see that it is not easy to distinguish SAR images of different objects. Since SAR images are very sensitive to azimuth angles and training images should represent the characteristics of an object under various azimuth angles, 210 SAR images of each object are sorted in the ascending order of their azimuth angles and the first, fourth, seventh, tenth SAR images and so on are selected for training. Thus, for each object, 70 SAR images are used in training and the rest of the images are used in testing.

- **Experiment 2 - Discriminate three objects:** CGP synthesizes composite features to recognize three objects: BRDM2, D7 and T62. First, the effectiveness of each primitive feature in discriminating these three objects is examined. The results are shown in Table 5.5. The mean CFAR (feature 8) is the best primitive feature with a recognition rate of 0.73. Three series of experiments are performed in which CGP maintains 3, 5 and 8 sub-populations to evolve 3, 5 and 8-dimensional composite feature vectors, respectively. The primitive features used in the experiments are all the 20 primitive features and 10 common primitive features (primitive features 11 to 20). The average recognition rates of 3, 5 and 8-dimensional composite feature vectors over ten runs are shown in Table 5.6, where 10f and 20f mean primitive features 11 to 20 and all the 20 primitive features, respectively.

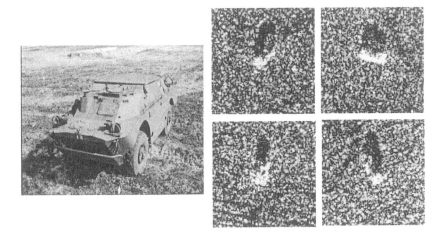

(a) Optical and SAR images of BRDM2.

(b) Optical and SAR images of D7.

(c) Optical and SAR images of T62.

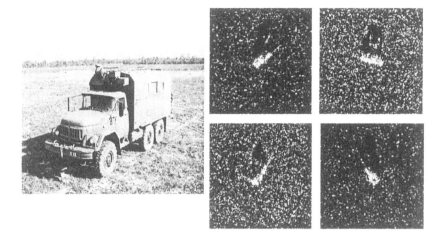

(d) Optical and SAR images of ZIL131.

(e) Optical and SAR images of ZSU.

Figure 5.6. Five objects used in recognition.

From Table 5.5 and Table 5.6, it can be seen that the learned composite feature vectors are more effective than primitive features. If all the 20 primitive features from the training images are used to form 20-dimensional primitive feature vectors to train a Bayesian classifier for recognition, the recognition rates on training and testing data are 0.995 and 0.962, respectively. This result, shown in the 4th row of Table 5.6 under the 20f heading, is a little bit better than the average performance shown in the first and second rows of Table 5.6, but the dimension of the feature vector is 20. However, the dimensions of composite feature vectors in the first and second rows of Table 5.6 are just 3 and 5 respectively. If the dimension of composite feature vector is increased to 8, the CGP results are better. If the last 10 primitive features are used, the recognition rates on training and testing data are 0.863 and 0.812, respectively. From these results, we can see that the effectiveness of the primitive features has an important impact on the composite features synthesized by CGP. In general, with more effective primitive features, CGP can synthesize more effective composite features. Figure 5.7 shows the composite operator vector evolved by CGP with 5 sub-populations in the 10th run using 20 primitive features. The size of the first and second composite operators is 20. The size of the third one and the last one are 9 and 15, respectively. The fourth composite operator is just primitive feature 11. The primitive features used by the learned composite operator vector are primitive features 2, 3, 4, 5, 6, 7, 8, 11, 12, 14, 18, 19, 20. If all these 13 primitive features form 13-dimensional primitive feature vectors for recognition, the recognition rate is 0.960.

Table 5.5. Recognition rates of 20 primitive features (3 objects).

Feature Number	Primitive Feature	Recognition Rate	Feature Number	Primitive Feature	Recognition Rate
1	Standard deviation	0.376	11	Horizontal projection	0.414
2	Fractal dimension	0.662	12	Vertical projection	0.545
3	Weight-rank fill ratio	0.607	13	Major diagonal projection	0.460
4	Blob mass	0.717	14	Minor diagonal projection	0.455
5	Blob diameter	0.643	15	Minimum distance	0.505
6	Blob inertia	0.495	16	Maximum distance	0.417
7	Maximum CFAR	0.588	17	Mean distance	0.376
8	Mean CFAR	0.726	18	Moment μ_{20}	0.421
9	Percent bright CFAR	0.607	19	Moment μ_{02}	0.443
10	Count	0.633	20	Moment μ_{22}	0.512

Table 5.6. Performance of composite and primitive features on 3-object discrimination.

Runs	Recognition Rate			
	10f		20f	
	Training	Testing	Training	Testing
3-dimensional composite feature vector	0.880	0.843	0.969	0.943
5-dimensional composite feature vector	0.921	0.857	0.990	0.961
8-dimensional composite feature vector	0.962	0.870	0.999	0.970
Primitive feature vector	0.863	0.812	0.995	0.962

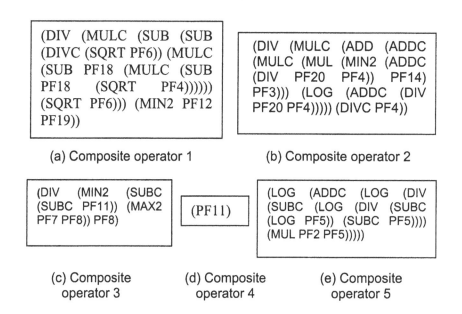

(a) Composite operator 1   (b) Composite operator 2

(c) Composite operator 3   (d) Composite operator 4   (e) Composite operator 5

Figure 5.7. Composite operator vector learned by CGP with 5 sub-populations.

- **Experiment 3 – Discriminate five objects:** With two more objects (ZIL and ZSU) added, the recognition becomes more difficult. This can be seen from Table 5.7, which shows the effectiveness of each primitive feature in discriminating these five objects. Blob mass (feature 4) is the best primitive feature with a recognition rate of 0.486. If all the 20 primitive features from the training images are used jointly to form 20-dimensional primitive feature vectors to train a Bayesian classifier for recognition, the recognition rates on training and testing are 0.914 and 0.812, respectively; if only the 10 common primitive features are used, the recognition rates on training and testing data are 0.737 and 0.623, respectively. These results are shown in the 3rd row of Table 5.8. The composite features built on the primitive features 11 to 20 are not very effective, since these 10 primitive features are common features and are not designed with the characteristics of SAR images taken into consideration.

Table 5.7. Recognition rates of 20 primitive features (5 objects).

Feature Number	Primitive Feature	Recognition Rate	Feature Number	Primitive Feature	Recognition Rate
1	Standard deviation	0.224	11	Horizontal projection	0.273
2	Fractal dimension	0.473	12	Vertical projection	0.343
3	Weight-rank fill ratio	0.361	13	Major diagonal projection	0.281
4	Blob mass	0.486	14	Minor diagonal projection	0.265
5	Blob diameter	0.404	15	Minimum distance	0.277
6	Blob inertia	0.346	16	Maximum distance	0.294
7	Maximum CFAR	0.379	17	Mean distance	0.266
8	Mean CFAR	0.471	18	Moment μ_{20}	0.277
9	Percent bright CFAR	0.449	19	Moment μ_{02}	0.267
10	Count	0.453	20	Moment μ_{22}	0.340

Two series of experiments are performed in which CGP maintains 5 and 8 sub-populations to evolve 5 and 8-dimensional composite feature vectors for recognition. The primitive features used in the experiments are 20 primitive features and 10 common primitive features. The hard size limit is 20. The average recognition rates of 5 and 8-dimensional composite feature vectors over ten runs are shown in the first and second rows of Table 5.8.

Table 5.8. Performance of composite and primitive features on 5-object discrimination.

Runs	Recognition Rate			
	10f		20f	
	Training	Testing	Training	Testing
5-dimensional composite feature vector	0.681	0.579	0.854	0.764
8-dimensional composite feature vector	0.778	0.630	0.926	0.825
Primitive feature vector	0.737	0.623	0.914	0.812

From Table 5.8, we can see that when the dimension of the composite feature vector is 8, the performance of the composite features is good and it is better than using all 20 (0.812) or 10 (0.623) primitive features upon which the composite features are built. When the dimension of the composite feature vector is 5, the recognition is not satisfactory when using just 10 common features as building blocks. Also, when the dimension is 5, the average performance is a little bit worse than using all 20 or 10 primitive features, but the dimension of the composite feature vector is just one-fourth or half of the number of primitive features, saving a lot of computational burden in recognition. When all the 20 primitive features are used and CGP has 8 sub-populations, the composite operators in the best composite operator vector evolved have sizes 19, 1, 16, 19, 15, 7, 16 and 6, respectively and they are shown in Figure 5.8. The primitive features used by the synthesized composite operator vector are primitive features 2, 3, 4, 5, 8, 9, 10, 11, 12, 13, 14, 15, 16, 18, 19 and 20. If all these 16 primitive features directly form 16-dimensional primitive feature vectors to train a Bayesian classifier for recognition, the recognition rate is 0.80 on the testing images, which is lower than the average performance of the composite feature vector shown in Table 5.8.

(MIN2 PF10 (MIN2 (MULC (MUL
PF9 (MIN2 (DIVC PF10) (MUL
PF9 (DIVC PF10))))) (MIN2
(MUL PF9 (DIVC PF10)) PF10)))

(PF3)

(a) Composite operator 1.   (b) Composite operator 2.

(SUB (SUBC (SUB PF14 PF18))
(MAX2 (MAX2 (MAX2 PF14
PF8) PF14) (MAX2 PF14 (MAX2
PF14 PF5))))

(SQRT (DIV PF10 (SQRT (MAX2
(MULC (SUBC (DIV PF5 PF5)))
(MAX2 (SUBC (MULC (SUBC
(MULC (DIV PF15 PF5))))) PF10)))))

(c) Composite operator 3.   (d) Composite operator 4.

(LOG (MUL (LOG (SUB
(ADD PF16 (SQRT (LOG
(MUL (ADD PF16 PF16)
PF12)))) PF12)) PF20))

(SUB (LOG (DIVC
PF2)) (DIV PF9
PF16))

(e) Composite operator 5   (f) Composite operator 6.

(ADDC (ADD PF18 (ADD (MULC (LOG
PF18)) (MIN2 (SUB PF2 PF11) (SUB
PF18 (SUB PF11 PF2))))))

(SQRT(SQRT(SQRT(SQRT
(SQRT PF4)))))

(g) Composite operator 7.   (h) Composite operator 8.

Figure 5.8. Composite operator vector learned by CGP.

5.4.3   Comparison with other classification algorithms

In chapters 5.4.1 and 5.4.2, the effectiveness of CGP-learned composite features is shown and compared with that of original primitive features. The comparison shows that CGP-learned composite features are more effective in object recognition. In this subchapter, the performance of CGP-based approach proposed in this chapter is compared with four other classical classification algorithms: multi-layer feed forward neural networks trained with (a) backpropagation algorithm, (b) stochastic backpropagation algorithm and (c) stochastic backpropagation algorithm with momentum, and (d) the C4.5 classification algorithm. For the detailed description of these algorithms, refer to [28], [40], [78].

Multi-layer feed forward neural networks used in this chapter have three layers: the output layer; the hidden layer; and the input layer. The output layer has only one output node and the hidden layer has 3, 5 or 8 nodes. A node of the input layer contains a primitive feature and the number of nodes in the input layer is equal to the number of primitive features used in recognition. The activation function of nodes in the output and hidden layers is:

$$f(x) = a \frac{e^{bx} - e^{-bx}}{e^{bx} + e^{-bx}} \qquad where \qquad a = 1.716 \quad and \quad b = \frac{2}{3} \qquad (5.2)$$

The inputs to the neural networks are normalized primitive features. The primitive features from training images and testing images are normalized separately. The normalization is performed by the following formula:

$$nf_{ij} = \frac{f_{ij} - \mu_i}{\sigma_i} \qquad\qquad i = 1, 2, \dots or\ 20, \quad j = 1, 2, \dots, n \qquad (5.3)$$

where f_{ij} ($j = 1, 2, \dots, n_i$) are the feature values of original primitive feature i ($i = 1, 2, \dots$ or 20) and nf_{ij} ($j = 1, 2, \dots, n$) are the corresponding normalized feature values, n is the number of training or testing images, μ_i and σ_i are the mean and standard deviation of these n feature values. The reason for feature normalization is that the values of some primitive features are very large, making the value of e^{bx} overflow. The weight values of connections between nodes of different layers are initialized with small randomly generated real numbers in the range of *[-1.0, 1.0]*. The learning rate η of backpropagation algorithms is 0.1 and the momentum α of stochastic backpropagation algorithm with momentum is 0.5. Backpropagation algorithms stop when they finish 300 weight-update loops or when the recognition rate on training data is above 0.9, whichever occurs first. The best recognition rate and its associated weight values are kept from loop to loop, and the trained neural network (the one with the best recognition rate) is applied to the testing data. In each experiment, backpropagation algorithms are invoked ten times with the same parameters and input data to train a neural network. For the purpose of objective comparison, only the average results over ten runs are reported. The original backpropagation algorithm sometimes constructs a neural network with very bad performance (below 0.1) due to the gradient descent convergence to a poor local minimum point. We do not use the results from these runs in the calculation of average performance and invoke the backpropagation algorithm to perform training again.

The input to the C4.5 algorithm is the original set of primitive features, not the normalized ones. For a particular primitive feature, if it has at most 10 unique feature values among the feature values extracted from training images, it is treated as a discrete feature; otherwise, it is treated as a continuous feature [78]. Since C4.5 is a deterministic algorithm, it is invoked only once in each experiments.

Four experiments are performed: distinguishing between 3 objects using all the 20 primitive features or 10 common primitive features; distinguishing between 5 objects using all the 20 primitive features or 10 common primitive features. As previously stated, in each experiment, the backpropagation is invoked ten times to train ten neural networks, the average recognition rates of trained multi-layer neural networks with 3, 5 and 8 hidden layers are shown in Table 5.9 and Table 5.10, where 10f means using the primitive features 11 to 20 and 20f means using all the primitive features. Table 5.9 and Table 5.10 show the performance on distinguishing 3 and 5 objects, respectively, for the three backpropagation algorithms. Table 5.11 shows the performance for the C4.5 algorithm.

From the above tables and Table 5.6 and Table 5.8, it can be seen that the CGP-based approach proposed in this chapter outperforms all the backpropagation and C4.5 algorithms in testing and that the C4.5 algorithm is more effective than all the backpropagation algorithms. Stochastic backpropagation and stochastic backpropagation with momentum outperform the original backpropagation algorithm, since the original backpropagation algorithm is more likely to converge to some local minimum points, yielding a neural network with poor performance. According to our experiments, three hidden nodes are enough, increasing the number of hidden nodes to 5 or 8 does not increase the performance significantly. In fact, sometimes it decreases the recognition performance.

Table 5.9. Average recognition performance of multi-layer neural networks trained by backpropagation algorithms (3 objects).

| Number of hidden nodes | Recognition Rate (Backpropagation) | | | |
| | 10f | | 20f | |
	Training	Testing	Training	Testing
3	0.548	0.526	0.634	0.623
5	0.546	0.532	0.633	0.626
8	0.570	0.552	0.645	0.644

| Number of hidden nodes | Recognition Rate (Backpropagation - Stochastic) | | | |
| | 10f | | 20f | |
	Training	Testing	Training	Testing
3	0.672	0.667	0.792	0.801
5	0.669	0.664	0.801	0.787
8	0.664	0.649	0.765	0.761

| Number of hidden nodes | Recognition Rate (Backpropagation – Stochastic with momentum) | | | |
| | 10f | | 20f | |
	Training	Testing	Training	Testing
3	0.676	0.670	0.831	0.829
5	0.677	0.656	0.823	0.817
8	0.674	0.658	0.751	0.745

10f – means only 10 common primitive features are used in feature synthesis
20f – means all the 20 primitive features are used in feature synthesis

Table 5.10. Average recognition performance of multi-layer neural networks trained by backpropagation algorithms (5 objects).

Number of hidden nodes	Recognition Rate (Backpropagation)			
	10f		20f	
	Training	Testing	Training	Testing
5	0.274	0.267	0.346	0.340
8	0.292	0.290	0.330	0.325
Number of hidden nodes	Recognition Rate (Backpropagation - Stochastic)			
	10f		20f	
	Training	Testing	Training	Testing
5	0.302	0.300	0.370	0.366
8	0.296	0.296	0.366	0.366
Number of hidden nodes	Recognition Rate (Backpropagation – Stochastic with momentum)			
	10f		20f	
	Training	Testing	Training	Testing
5	0.319	0.304	0.376	0.367
8	0.331	0.328	0.369	0.368

10f – means only 10 common primitive features are used in feature synthesis
20f – means all the 20 primitive features are used in feature synthesis

Table 5.11. Recognition performance of C4.5 classification algorithm.

3 objects			
10f		20f	
Training	Testing	Training	Testing
0.962	0.679	0.995	0.917
5 objects			
10f		20f	
Training	Testing	Training	Testing
0.754	0.344	0.917	0.686

5.4.4 Discussion

The above experiments demonstrate that:

- It is important to introduce domain knowledge into the feature synthesis for object recognition by defining the primitive features. In these experiments, we compare the effectiveness of composite features built on both domain-independent primitive features (10 common features) and domain-dependent primitive features encoding demain knowledge (the characteristics of SAR imagery in this chapter). The comparison shows that more effective composite features can be generated in the feature synthesis with primitive features encoding domain knowledge. It is also observed from the experiments that with primitive features encoding domain knowledge, CGP can evolve effective composite features within the fewer number of generations, thus improving the efficiency of CGP search.

- In general, the effectiveness of composite features learned by CGP is dependent on the effectiveness of primitive features. With more effective primitive features available, more effective composite features can be generated by CGP. But this does not mean that ineffective primitive features are never used by CGP in the feature synthesis. As Figure 5.5 shows, an ineffective feature (primitive feature 8) is used to synthesize effective composite features. The reason for the use of one or more ineffective primitive features in the synthesis of effective composite features is due to the interaction between primitive features. Although some features are ineffective when used alone, they can be elements of a primitive feature set that is the building block for effective composite features.

- CGP is a viable tool to synthesize effective composite features from primitive features for object recognition. In general, the synthesized composite features are more effective than the primitive features upon which these composite features are built, although there are a few exceptions in our experiments. In experiment 1, the learned composite features outperform the primitive features or any combination of primitive features upon which they are evolved, although the improvement in recognition rate is not significant when all the 10 common primitive features are used to synthesize composite features, since the performance of these 10 primitive features, when used together, is already very good (0.963 in training and 0.978 in testing). In experiment 2, when 8-dimensional composite feature vectors are evolved or when only 10 common primitive features are used in feature synthesis, the synthesized composite features are more effective. But when all the 20 primitive features are used and the dimension of composite feature vectors is 5 or 3, the performance of primitive features is a little bit higher. However, the dimension of primitive feature vectors is 20, much higher than that of composite feature vectors, which is 5 or 3. In experiment 3, when 8-dimensional composite feature vectors are evolved, the synthesized composite features produce better recognition results. But if the dimension of composite feature vectors is 5, the 10 or 20-dimensional primitive feature vectors yield better performance. Since there is some randomness involved in GP, we can still conclude that CGP can evolve composite features that are more effective than the primitive ones upon which they are evolved. More importantly, to achieve the same or similar recognition rate, the number of composite features needed is smaller than the number of primitive features needed (one-fourth or half), reducing the computational expense during run-time recognition. Thus, the composite features outperform the primitive ones with adequate number of sub-populations.

- The CGP approach synthesizes composite features for recognition that outperform four basic recognition algorithms (three backpropagation algorithms and the C4.5 algorithm).

5.5   Conclusions

This chapter investigates synthesizing composite features for object recognition. Our experimental results using real SAR images show that CGP can evolve composite features that are more effective than the primitive features upon which they are built, although sometimes the improvement in recognition rate may not be significant. To achieve the same recognition performance of primitive features, fewer composite features are needed and this reduces the computational burden during recognition. From the experimental results, it can be seen that primitive features that provide domain knowledge for the evolutionary process have a substantial impact on the performance of the synthesized composite features. Although the effectiveness of synthesized composite features is not solely dependent on the effectiveness of primitive features, on the average, if primitive features do not capture the characteristics of the objects to be recognized, it is difficult, if not impossible, for CGP to synthesize effective composite features. Thus, it is important to design effective primitive features. We cannot entirely rely on CGP to generate good features. However, designing effective primitive features needs human ingenuity. If human experts lack insight into the characteristics of the objects to be recognized, they may not figure out effective primitive features.

Currently, there is only one object in an image during recognition, so all the features come from the same object. If there are multiple overlapped objects [19] in an image, the recognition becomes much more difficult. Some of the features of an object may not be available due to occlusion and we need to distinguish features from different objects before these features are fed into a classifier. Recognizing multiple overlapped objects using this approach is a challenging future research topic.

Chapter 6

LINEAR GENETIC PROGRAMMING FOR OBJECT RECOGNITION

6.1   Introduction

In this chapter, we describe a feature construction method which uses a special linear variety of genetic programming for feature construction. We provide rationale for the design of the method and present its two varieties: using evolutionary computation for evolutionary feature programming (EFP) and cooperative coevolution for coevolutionary feature programming (CFP). We discuss different decomposition strategies for breaking up the feature construction process. The practical utility of EFP and CFP is verified in real-case studies presented in chapter 7.

Evolutionary computation (EC) has several virtues which make it appealing from a computer vision and pattern recognition perspective. As a general template of universal search procedure, it needs relatively little task-specific tailoring to make it work within a specific application. The evolutionary search is usually characterized by low risk of being trapped in local minima, has sound rationale in both computational biology and theory (schemata theorem) [36], [42], and has proven effective in a wide spectrum of benchmarks and real-world applications. In particular, it has found a significant number of applications in image processing and analysis as discussed in the previous chapters. In this chapter we discuss the synthesis of entire feature extraction procedures using linear genetic programming [59], [60], [61].

To make EC work as a search engine for feature construction, two important questions have to be answered: how to represent feature mappings G as solutions $\mathbf{s} \in S$, and how to evaluate individuals. This chapter gives answers to these questions and provides rationale for the proposed EFP method. However, we abstract here from any application-specific knowledge (e.g., knowledge related to computer vision). The particular examples of applying the proposed approach to specific applications will be provided in chapter 7.

6.2   Explicit Feature Construction

In most machine learning and visual learning approaches, EC operates in the space of hypotheses. An outstanding manifestation of this convention are the famous 'Michigan' [43] and 'Pittsburgh' [112] approaches for GA-based rule induction [76], [78]. In EFP, on the contrary, EC is employed to perform a search in the space of feature definition*s*. The evolutionary computation has been also applied to search such spaces, serving the purpose of transformation of training data. Most of the work done, however, concerned feature selection. There are several publications on applying evolutionary computation to feature selection [98], [122], [129]. A new approach was presented in Chapter 4. The superiority of global feature selection methods, EC in particular, over local search methods, was shown experimentally in early 90's [45], [46].

In the framework of learning from examples, a complete description of the learning problem is represented by the (often infinite) universe of examples (instances, objects) $\mathbf{x}$. The learning task posed to the learner (learning algorithm, inducer) consists in finding a hypothesis h (classifier) that optimizes some performance measure f defined with respect to the training data T, which is in fact a sample from the universe. In the following we assume that f is scalar and it is to be maximized, and that the learning is supervised, i.e., a discrete decision class label $d(\mathbf{x})$ is given for each training example $\mathbf{x} \in T$.

From a machine learning (ML) perspective, we focus here on explicit feature construction, i.e., a deliberate process that aims at changing the form of training data. More formally, we are interested in mappings G that transform a given image $\mathbf{x}$ into its representation $G(\mathbf{x})$ in derived feature space:

$$G(\mathbf{x}) = \begin{bmatrix} g_1(\mathbf{x}) & g_2(\mathbf{x}) & \cdots & g_m(\mathbf{x}) \end{bmatrix}, \qquad (6.1)$$

where m denotes the number of features in the transformed representation. The goal of such feature construction process is to improve hypothesis, h, performance (accuracy of classification in the most common case) i.e. to find G such that $h(G(\ ))$ performs better than h alone, with respect to f. The pair (G,h) in the following is referred to as a recognition system or decision system.

Though an example $\mathbf{x} \in T$ could essentially denote any data entity, we identify it with a raster image. In general, the dimensionality m of the derived space is not directly related to the amount of information carried over by $\mathbf{x}$; nevertheless, in most real-world studies the feature transformation method should significantly reduce the dimensionality of the representation to avoid learner's overfitting to the training data at the expense of losing generalization ability. In the proposed approach, the dimensionality m of the resulting space has to be fixed for all images $\mathbf{x} \in T$ to form a so-called attribute-value representation that most learners can work with.

We assume that each g_i represents a real-valued function that is technically realized by a feature extraction procedure and undergoes changes as the system learns. In general, the form of g_i is arbitrary: it could be a polynomial, an artificial neuron, or even a lookup table. We try to maintain the explanatory function of feature construction and aim at its symbolic variety. Therefore, we limit our interest to g_i being a (usually compound) function of $\mathbf{x}$, which may be expressed in terms of some meaningful symbols. We assume that those symbols may be parameterized.

The methods described in this chapter (EFP and CFP) assume that the mapping G is manipulated by an evolutionary process driven by the fitness function f, an estimate of recognition system performance. Now, one has to

decide how to encode G as an EC solution (individual) **s**. Two qualitatively
different methodologies are possible here. One can fix the general form of
each $g_i \in G$ and encode its parameters only. Alternatively, one can encode in
solution **s** the complete information that is required to restore G. The former of
these approaches is obviously less general than the latter one. In EFP and CFP,
to provide a more general approach, we choose the latter method, where the
solution **s** completely determines the actual working of G.

Next, one should decide how to encode the application-related individuals
(solutions) in generic representation used by a particular variant of EC (e.g.,
fixed-length strings over a binary alphabet in the case of GA). In evolutionary
terms, individuals' encoding is commonly referred to as genotype, and its
representation in application-specific terms – phenotype. These entities dwell
in two separate universes, genotypic search space and phenotypic search
space, respectively. In this context, the (maximized) fitness function f:
$S \rightarrow [0,1]$ that evaluates individuals $\mathbf{s} \in S$ is in fact a compound function:

$$f(\mathbf{s}) = f_p(f_g(\mathbf{s})), \quad f = f_g \circ f_p, \tag{6.2}$$

where f_g function implements the mapping from the space of genotypes to the
space of phenotypes (in other words, it decodes the individual). The f_p function
(phenotypic fitness) computes the fitness based on the phenotypic
representation $f_g(\mathbf{s})$ of the solution **s** [105]. Therefore, f_p operates in the
problem domain and is usually much more application-specific than f_g.

Function f_g implements the so-called genotype-phenotype mapping. An
important issue is here the extent to which f_g preserves the topology of the
search space. In EC literature, this issue is usually referred to as the locality of
representation [106]. Locality may be defined as a measure that reflects to
what extent (or, informally, with what probability) the neighbors in the
genotypic space remain neighbors when mapped to the phenotypic space. High
locality representations preserve search space topology to a great extent; low
locality representations do not and resemble more a kind of random mapping.
This notion becomes important in the discussion of properties of the proposed
representation for feature extraction procedures.

6.3   Linear Genetic Programming

Prior to formal presentation of EFP, we devote a few paragraphs to describe the EC paradigm, which inspired the proposed method. Linear Genetic Programming (LGP) was originally proposed by Banzhaff [4]. Essentially, LGP is a variety of GP with simplified, linear representation of individual's code. The representation used in LGP is a hybrid of GA and GP, and combines their advantages. The individual's genome represents a sequential program composed of (possibly parameterized) basic and given *a priori* operators. This feature makes LGP similar to GP. On the other hand, as opposed to GP, where tree-like expressions are maintained (see chapter 2), LGP encodes such procedures in a form of a fixed-length sequence that, at the genome level, is essentially equivalent to GA representation. LGP encoding is, therefore, more positional, i.e. the evolutionary process tends to bind some meaning to particular code fragments. As a consequence, the standard crossover operator used in LGP exchanges mutually corresponding code fragments. In GP, on the contrary, the standard crossover picks at random subtrees in parent solutions and exchanges them, and such an action most often affects unrelated code fragments, leading to deterioration of evolution convergence. Therefore, LGP is more resistant to destructive crossovers than regular GP [4].

Another important concept of LGP is the way the intermediate results are passed from one operation to another. In GP, this is determined by the structure of the expression tree. In LGP, the 'virtual machine' that interprets an LGP program is equipped with extra registers. The registers serve as storage for a program's input data, intermediate results, and a program's output (response).

LGP proved successful in the experimental evaluation on a family of different classification and regression tasks [22]. Another motivation for developing LGP was the possibility of fast individual's compilation into the machine code, which obviously may result in significant speedup of fitness computation [83]. Note also that several other programming-like EC paradigms came into being since GP's advent. These include Grammatical Evolution [87], [107] (a variant of GP with strong control of individuals' syntax), Linear-Tree GP [52] (a hybrid of GP and LGP), and Gene Expression Programming [32] (individuals are represented as fixed-length strings at genotype level, but have tree representation at phenotype level). More general program representations, like graphs, have been also considered [118], [119].

6.4   Evolutionary Feature Programming

The overall architecture of evolutionary feature programming (EFP) is presented in Figure 6.1. It may be briefly characterized as a genetically-driven search in the space of explicit, symbolic feature definitions, aimed at maximizing the expected predictive accuracy of the entire decision (recognition) system. The search is driven by a fitness function f evaluated on the training net, and it uses an LGP-inspired representation to encode the feature definitions. This compound function involves interpretation of encoded feature extraction procedures (genotype-phenotype mapping f_g) followed by the evaluation of the resulting feature extraction procedures in the context of the training data (phenotypic fitness f_p).

Learning takes place at two levels: at the upper level the evolutionary search learns (generates and evaluates) solutions s that encode feature extraction mappings G, i.e., $G \equiv f_g(s)$. At the lower level, the learner built into the fitness function learns (induces and verifies) hypotheses given a particular representation. In other words, the working of the entire approach involves two intertwined loops that provide feedback for corresponding search algorithms: the outer learning loop involves the evaluation cycle and is closed by the fitness function f, whereas the inner learning loop involves hypothesis generation and testing within the fitness function itself.

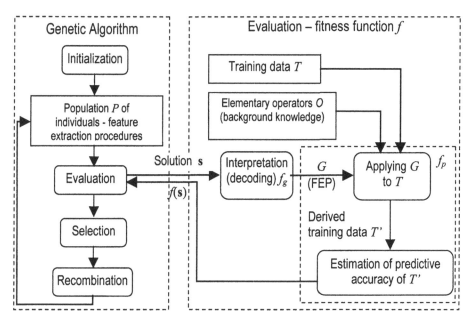

Figure 6.1. The outline of evolutionary feature programming (EFP).

Within the proposed framework, the evolutionary algorithm is used mostly because exact search methods are inappropriate here. The solution space, containing all features that may be expressed as feature extractions procedures, cannot be effectively searched by means of exact methods, mostly for the following two reasons: *Firstly*, the number of possible feature extraction procedures (FEPs) is prohibitively large. Even for the simplest setting of the proposed method, the number of possible realizations is an exponential function of feature extractions procedure's length and the number of operators. This complexity increases if other elements of the approach are taken into account. *Secondly*, we cannot make any assumptions concerning the fitness function f that would simplify the search. As will be shown in following, the EFP representation of solutions has low locality.

Note also that, in the case of feature construction, proving any properties of f is much more difficult than in case the of feature selection, where, e.g., some methods profit from f's monotonicity with respect to the number of features

[25]. Search techniques that would reduce the time complexity by analogously exploiting some properties of the objective function (e.g., branch and bound), are, therefore, not applicable here.

For these two reasons, only exhaustive search guarantees finding the global optimum (with respect to f). Heuristic or metaheuristic search is, therefore, the only plausible method that can be used to approach the feature construction task posed as above, and that can yield reasonably good suboptimal solutions in polynomial time. This is consistent with the rather practical attitude chosen here, where we assume that well-performing suboptimal recognition systems are usually satisfactory. In fact, solutions found during the heuristic search may even be globally optimal; however, as we usually do not know the application-specific upper bound of recognition performance, we cannot discern such solutions from the suboptimal ones.

6.4.1   Representation and its properties

Representation of individuals used in EFP is mostly inspired by LGP but does not strictly implement LGP as proposed by Banzhaff [4]. On the phenotype level, a solution **s** encodes one or more feature extraction procedures; feature definitions, or features for short. Each feature extraction procedure is conceptually equivalent to mapping G defined in (6.1), and is able to yield one or more scalar values $g_i(\mathbf{x})$ given input image **x**. It is encoded by a fixed-length sequence of l elementary steps, or, for short, instructions O_i. Instructions are executed sequentially; the proposed approach does not provide for branching of control flow or iterative computations (loops). Such sophisticated constructs have been introduced in some related approaches [119]; here, to avoid the possible overfitting to the training data, we keep feature extraction procedures simpler.

Instructions are built using operators $o_i \in O$ from the set of elementary operators O. Instruction O_j is a specific instantiation of an elementary operator o_i. Their indices are not related: here, i enumerates operators in O, while j denotes order of instructions within a feature extraction procedure. In other words, an operator is a function that may be called for some set of arguments, whereas an instruction is a particular call to such a function, technically encoded as a fragment of a feature extraction procedure code in individual's genome. In the following operators will be identified with unique ids called opcodes.

The set O constitutes the knowledge base for the feature construction algorithm and is usually domain-dependant. For computer vision and pattern recognition applications, operators from O may be effectively calls to image processing functions, feature extraction functions, and other data processing. For other application domains, O may contain appropriate domain-specific operators. Obviously, the more knowledge is provided in O and the more application-oriented it is, the better. Nevertheless, our goal is to prove that the proposed approach works well even if O contains only general domain-related knowledge, and not necessarily application-related knowledge. In particular, we expect to obtain satisfactory results in different computer vision and pattern recognition applications using general image processing and computer vision knowledge implemented by operators from O.

A specific instruction O_j within a particular feature extraction procedure is composed of two components: an opcode that determines the operator $o_i \in O$ to be used, and arguments, which are usually references to registers and tell where to fetch input data from and store the result. Registers may be thought of as temporary variables (working memory) that are used by instructions as input and output arguments. Registers are typed: the numeric registers (r_j, $j = 1...n_r$) store only scalar values (intermediate results and final feature values). Aiming at computer vision and pattern recognition applications, we define also image registers (r_j', $j = 1...n'_r$), which store input image and processed images (image registers have the same dimensions as the input image **x**).

The number of numeric registers n_r determines the number of scalar features g_i computed by a feature extraction procedure. Commonly, we impose lower bounds on n_r and n'_r, based on the maximum arity of operators from O. Formally, setting even $n_r = n'_r = 1$ is correct, as no constraints are imposed on the way the instructions exchange data with registers. For instance, an operator that requires two input arguments may fetch them both from the same register, and even store the result in the same register. This would, however, seriously limit the computational power of feature extraction procedures, thus in real-world studies we usually set $n_r = n'_r = 2...5$.

Preliminary experiments have also indicated the usefulness of such setting. Though greater values of n_r and n'_r are possible, one should note that the more registers, the less effective is the passing of intermediate results between consecutive instructions, it is less likely that a result produced by instruction O_i will be used by any instruction O_j, $j > i$. To overcome this, a feature extraction procedure has to be longer, that, in turn, increases the processing time. This may be prohibitive in the feature construction phase, because, as it will be shown, each individual's evaluation involves multiple execution of the feature extraction procedure it encodes.

Therefore, a feature extraction procedure may be represented as a directed graph, with nodes corresponding to instructions and arcs representing data flow. Figure 6.2 shows an exemplary graph representing a single feature extraction procedure, with extra nodes (marked by squares) that denote the initial and final register contents (the intermediate register contents are not explicitly depicted here). It can be observed that the proposed representation is flexible and not constrained by strict syntactic rules: feature extraction procedure is allowed to ignore input data (here: contents of register r_1), create dead-ends (instruction O_2), and it is not obliged to produce novel features in all numeric registers (an arrow connecting the initial and final states of r_2 means that its contents remains intact during the execution of feature extraction procedure, so feature g_2 is equivalent to initial contents of r_2).

As register contents may be used more than once by the consecutive instructions, tree representation is, in general, not sufficient to visualize feature extraction procedure processing, though any such graph may be converted into a tree by repeating some code fragments (subexpressions). From another perspective, each feature extraction procedure may be viewed as a compound function made of nested calls of operators $o_i \in O$.

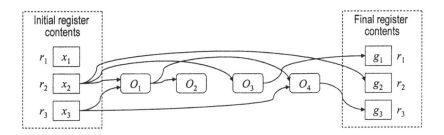

Figure 6.2. Graph representation of an exemplary feature extraction procedure.

The practical applicability of a recognition system based on global features would be very limited. For non-trivial computer vision and pattern recognition applications, local features are required. Therefore, the feature extraction procedure representation allows each instruction to be executed in a local mode. The mask flag, a single bit hidden inside the opcode, decides whether the instruction should be global (work on the entire image register) or local (limited to a mask on the image).

To support this extension, each image register maintains a rectangular mask. The mask may be used by an instruction (if it is local), and limits the processing to its interior. Global instructions ignore masks and operate on the entire image. Mask placement and dimensions, stored as upper left and lower right corner, are initialized prior to the execution of a feature extraction procedure, but may be also changed by instructions.

Given the phenotype representation of a solution s, we are able now to summarize the genotype-phenotype mapping f_g in Figure 6.3. On the genotype level, a feature extraction procedure is encoded as a fixed-length sequence of bits, with consecutive chunks (substrings) of bits encoding successive instructions. On the phenotype level, for each instruction O_i, particular elements of its encoding within EC solution s correspond to separate variables s_i in the formulation of evolutionary search. In EC terminology, these elements are referred to as genes.

Interpretation of genes representing arguments depends on the particular elementary operator. If an operator requires only one input argument, the output argument is stored in the second gene, and the third gene is ignored. Thus, the representation used here is positional in the sense that each instruction component is encoded by a fixed-length bit sequence, and, as a result, each instruction has fixed length. The positional representation implies convenient properties discussed in chapter 6.3.

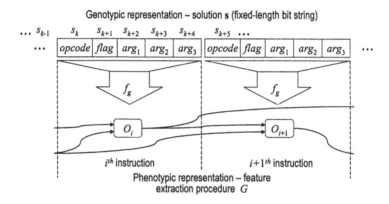

Figure 6.3. Details on genotype-phenotype mapping.

Technically, all instructional elements are binary-encoded integer variables (genes) s_i. For each gene, its upper limit is determined by corresponding parameter setting (the lower limit is always 0). For instance, the number of registers n_r imposes the upper limit on the values of variables s_i encoding arguments (arg_1, arg_2, arg_3), and the number of operators $|O|$ determines the range for the gene representing opcode to $[0,|O|-1]$. However, the number of distinct values of particular gene s_i (alleles in EC terminology) does not necessarily have to be a power of two, which is inconsistent with binary encoding. To resolve this incompatibility, a 'modulo mapping' is used during feature extraction procedure interpretation. f_g maps the corresponding gene by computing the actual gene s_i value *modulo* its upper limit+1. For instance, with $|O| = 70$ elementary operators, the minimal possible number of bits for encoding the opcode is 7 ($2^6 = 64 < 70 < 128 = 2^8$). Therefore, the opcode $1001000_2 = 72_{10}$ will be effectively translated into opcode 2, as 72 modulo 70 amounts to 2.

Except for trivial cases, real-world tasks usually require feature extraction procedures that refer to some constants. Constants are important as, among others, they parameterize instructions and provide fixed components in arithmetic expressions. In EFP, constants are encoded in individual's genome and evolve together with it. In particular, a feature extraction procedure may use constants in two ways. Both methods assume that one bit in binary encoding of each argument ($arg_1 \ldots arg_3$ in Figure 6.3) determines its actual function. In the first method, if this bit is set, the argument is interpreted as a register number; otherwise, the remaining bits of argument encoding are interpreted as a constant integer number. In the latter case, depending on the application, the resulting constant may be directly passed to the phenotype or it may undergo scaling to provide a more appropriate range of values.

This method is simple, but suffers from limited precision and/or range of encoded constants, as each argument is encoded to one byte, i.e., 8 bits. With one bit acting as a register-constant flag, 7 bits are left for constant encoding. This provides only 128 distinct values, which may not be enough to provide both sufficient range and precision. Thus, another, more indirect method of constant encoding is also provided. Similar to the first method, the choice between register reference and constant value is made according to the state of appropriate flag in argument encoding. If the state of the flag indicates constant, the constant value is fetched from an extra part of genome ('tail') that each individual is equipped with, which is exclusively dedicated to constant storage.

In the following, we summarize some properties of the feature extraction procedure representation from the perspective of evolutionary computation, and computer vision and pattern recognition. From an evolutionary computation perspective, the feature extraction procedure representation may be qualified as positional. The proposed representation is also complete and robust, in the sense that all solutions are feasible: any bit string has valid phenotypic representation as a feature extraction procedure. Thus, we do not have to test the solutions for feasibility and use repair algorithms to mend infeasible solutions (see, e.g., [76]), which could be quite time-consuming.

And, last but not the least, feature extraction procedure representation makes some types of problem decomposition easy and elegant (see chapter 6.5).

The genotypic representation of solutions is essentially equivalent to standard GA. As a result, we are able to use the common genetic operators (mutation and crossover) to process the individuals. This allows us to rely on widely accepted EC standards and avoid possible controversies concerning the particular type of genetic operators.

Feature extraction procedure representation supports the schemata theorem [42]. Short bit substrings correspond to conceptually independent elements of solution's phenotype (e.g., single instruction or a sequence of instructions). Therefore, short feature extraction subprograms/subprocedures are less likely to be disrupted by the genetic operators than the long ones. Thus, if a building block contributes positively to the overall performance of the solution, it has more chance to propagate its offspring to the next generations.

The modulo mapping introduced in gene interpretation causes that f_g is not bijective and two different bit strings may represent the same feature extraction procedure. This obviously makes some modifications of the genetic material ineffective, leading, among others, to neutral mutations – changes in the genotype that do not affect individual's fitness. This may apparently be disadvantageous, but, as the experiments show, it has a marginal effect on the convergence of the evolutionary search and may be easily compensated by increasing the mutation rate. Moreover, such encoding is somehow consistent with the working of natural evolution, where most of the genetic material seems to be redundant. Such dead code fragments are usually referred to as introns. It has been shown in the past, that introns may have positive impact on the effectiveness of search, as they enable performing a background search concerning some aspects of the task, without influencing the individual's fitness. More than that, some successful work has been done on explicit introduction of introns into genetic code [75], [81].

Within an instruction, its opcode determines the types of its arguments, and the arguments, being stored in registers, are always accessible. For instance, if the opcode refers to pixel-wise image subtraction, the consecutive genes are interpreted as references to three image registers (two input images, one output image); if the opcode refers to image thresholding, the consecutive genes are interpreted as references to image register (input image), numeric register (threshold), and image register (output image). Therefore, there is no need for extra means that usually have to be undertaken in standard GP. In GP, when genetic operators modify solutions, they have to control the type compatibility: the type of values returned by node of expression tree has to be compatible with its parent's input type. This principle, known as strong typing [57], implies extra computational overhead. As there is no need for such control here, the feature extraction procedure representation may be characterized by weak typing.

From computer vision and pattern recognition perspective, the proposed approach represents the category of feature-based recognition, as opposed to model-based algorithms that recognize an object by measuring its similarity to models from the database of objects. The recognition process is also image-driven (bottom-up, or, more generally, data-driven or example-driven), as opposed to some model-based approaches which implement model-driven (top-down) strategies.

The proposed representation models the processing of visual information in a stepwise manner. This feature is consistent with neurobiology and cognitive science research, which indicates that primates' visual perception is organized and works in a modular way [72], [80]. Many stages of processing and the ability to perform local operations enable grouping, an essential property of any non-trivial vision system [33]. The presence of image registers also helps the EFP to obey the principle of least commitment [72] which states that algorithms, especially those that process imperfect (noisy, incomplete, imprecise) information, should avoid making crisp decisions as long as possible, since it is very difficult (if not impossible) to recover from a wrong crisp decisions made at the early stages of processing. This is particularly true in computer vision and pattern recognition systems, where there are several stages at which decisions are made.

6.4.2   Execution of feature extraction procedure

Given the description of feature extraction procedure encoding, we now explain its execution, i.e., processing of a single training instance. This process, together with evaluation, constitute the second component of the fitness function, the phenotypic fitness f_p.

The processing of an example $\mathbf{x}$ by a feature extraction procedure G encoded by an individual $\mathbf{s}$ proceeds in three steps (Figure 6.4):

1. **Initialization**: The registers are set to values derived from $\mathbf{x}$.

2. **Execution**: The instructions O_i, $i = 1...l$, encoded by $\mathbf{s}$ are carried out one by one; each of them fetches and/or writes some data (intermediate results) from/to registers.

3. **Exploitation**: The scalar values computed in the numeric registers r_j, $j = 1...n_r$, after program execution are interpreted as features $g_j(\mathbf{x})$ that form the feature vector $G(\mathbf{x})$. In particular, if one feature extraction procedure is used, the contents of scalar registers fully determines $G(\mathbf{x})$ (i.e., $m = n_r$).

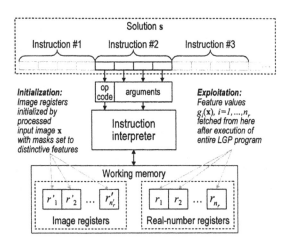

Figure 6.4. Execution of feature extraction procedures for a single training example (image) $\mathbf{x}$.

In the initialization phase, both numeric and image registers have to be prepared for the execution of feature extraction procedure. The simplest way, copying the input image **x** into all the image registers, is correct, yet not optimal from a practical viewpoint. It seems more reasonable to advance the learning process already in its beginning, by providing it with different 'views' of the training data. This effect may be easily obtained by differentiating the initial contents of image registers. Therefore, each of the image registers r'_j is initialized by an image resulting from global processing of **x** by an image filter. All filters used for this purpose are unary image operations (Image → Image) from the set O (see, e.g., list of operators presented in Table 7.1, which serves as a background knowledge base for real-world applications considered in chapter 7). The choice of filters is determined by a separate fragment of feature extraction procedure encoding, which, for clarity, was not shown in Figure 6.3 and Figure 6.4. For each register, its mask is centered on the most distinctive fragment of the image resulting from this preprocessing; in practice, it is the brightest point in the processed image. Initially, the mask is rectangular, and its dimension is determined by a parameter (here: 5 pixels).

The numeric registers r_i are also initialized according to some information derived from the input image **x**. In particular, the center coordinates of the mask of ith image register r'_i determine the contents of numeric registers r_{2i-1} (horizontal coordinate) and r_{2i} (vertical coordinate). This process is obviously limited by the number of available numeric registers n_r; in general, only the coordinates of the first $\lfloor n_r / 2 \rfloor$ image registers may be stored in this way.

Another motivation for making the register initialization rather sophisticated comes from time complexity considerations. The technical implementation of the approach (chapter 7.2) maintains a cache memory for the initial register contents and for all the training examples. Image preprocessing takes place in the initialization phase and is carried out only once, prior to the evolutionary run, for all training examples and all registers, and its results are stored in the cache. When a feature extraction procedure is about to be run on a particular training image **x**, the appropriate part of the cache is copied to registers, which may be done quickly even for relatively large images. This technical trick saves a significant fraction of computation time.

6.4.3   Locality of representation

In this subchapter, we take a closer look at feature extraction procedure representation and its locality. For this purpose we perform a qualitative analysis of the impact genetic modifications (particularly mutations) have on similarities and dissimilarities of solution phenotypes.

As we use common GA recombination operators to manipulate feature extraction procedure representation, the probability of genetic change is distributed evenly across the genome of solution **s**. All stages of information processing are, therefore, equally likely to be subject to genetic change. This is a substantially different than in GP, where initial processing stages (tree leaves and nodes close to them) are more likely to be modified than the final steps (tree nodes close to the root and the root itself). Nevertheless, the influence ('strength') of mutation *does* depend on instruction placement in feature extraction procedure code. Note that some fragments of feature extraction procedure code are potentially 'dead', i.e., the instructions' results stored in registers are overridden by another instruction. The closer O_i to the end of feature extraction procedure code, the less likely its result may be overridden by subsequent instructions, and, therefore, the more important it is. Thus, the mutations taking place close to the end of feature extraction procedure code are more influential, on the average, than the mutations affecting the initial feature extraction procedure fragments.

Within a single instruction, mutation affects a feature extraction procedure in different ways. With respect to the instruction components, a single-bit mutation may be of the following types:

1. change the opcode;

2. change the register the instruction refers to;

3. change the constant arguments used by the instruction;

4. change the mode of instruction (local vs. global).

Mutations of type 1 are potentially the strongest ones in terms of their influence on solution's phenotype and the way the feature extraction procedure processes the training data. They may lead to two qualitatively different effects. The influence of such mutation is minor if it does not change the category (image – scalar) of the operation nor its arity; for instance, when a unary image processing operation is mutated into another unary image processing operation. A major change occurs when the resulting instruction is qualitatively different from its original, e.g., when an image processing operation is replaced by scalar operation or vice versa.

Mutations of type 2 result in a change of the register the operation refers to as an argument. Such mutations are less profound than those of type 1. However, their effects are often stronger for the scalar operations than for the image ones, as the numeric registers usually contain different values. Image registers are initialized with the input image preprocessed by different unary image processing procedures, and are in most cases similar in visual terms, so applying mutation on an argument of an image operation has usually a minor effect.

Mutations on constants (type 3) have the smallest influence on the working of an feature extraction procedure. The particular impact on the working of a feature extraction procedure procedure depends on operation-specific argument interpretation. For most operations, that impact is minor and may consist, for instance, in a change of image binarization threshold or change of mask width and/or height.

Mutations on instruction mode (type 4) may significantly change the working of a feature extraction procedure code. The particular effect of this type of mutation depends on the actual mask placement.

The assumed representation implies that interpretation of some genome fragments is conditional, i.e. it depends on other genome fragments. For many operations, some element's genes are ignored. For instance, the mode of an operation (global/local) is ignored for scalar operations. This, together with the phenomenon of neutral changes ('modulo mapping', chapter 6.4.1), implies that when performing experiments on real-world data, the mutation probability has to be set to rather high values to provide a sufficiently thorough search in the solution space.

In the overall picture, the feature extraction procedure representation cannot be univocally classified as having high or low locality (cf. chapter 6.2; [105]). In general terms, its locality is probably comparable to that of common genetic programming, where application of the standard mutation operator may also lead to qualitative changes (subtree replacement) or quantitative changes (replacement of a constant value in a leaf). Analogously, the locality of feature extraction procedure representation may be characterized as hybrid, as some variables (e.g., those related to constants) exhibit high locality, whereas others, with the opcode, as the most prominent example, demonstrate low locality.

For strong advocates of high-locality representations, we emphasize that lack of high locality is unavoidable for such representations like feature extraction procedure. This is an inherent feature of many knowledge-intensive representations, i.e., representations that heavily relate to background knowledge. With the growing complexity of problems that we attempt to solve by means of EC and, in particular, by means of different varieties of genetic programming, it becomes very difficult to design high-locality representations. Nevertheless, as long as the evolutionary process is not deprived of the possibility of local search, this situation should not be perceived as disadvantageous. For feature extraction procedures, though some actions of genetic operators fundamentally change the working of the procedure, causing warping/switching of fitness landscapes (mutations of type 1, 4 and some of the mutations of type 2), there are still some possibilities of local search (mutations of type 3 and some mutations of type 2).

One could even hypothesize that some extent of low locality is probably advantageous. The way from the genotype to the final evaluation is long and involves feature extraction procedure decoding, its execution on the body of training data, and multiple classifier induction and testing (see chapter 6.4.4). Therefore, the genome has to undergo substantial changes to impact the fitness. This also indicates that the fitness landscape is here probably filled with many flat plateaus, which are extremely inconvenient for pure local search. In this case, 'far-reaching mutations' resulting from low-locality representation may be beneficial.

6.4.4   Evaluation of solutions

The primary objective of the learning process is to provide good predictive accuracy of the recognition system. From the explanatory perspective of knowledge discovery, the second important goal is to promote simple (readable) solutions. For the sake of simplicity, this second objective is not explicitly taken into account in the following, for two reasons. *Firstly*, allowing both objectives requires either their aggregation or solving multi-objective (bi-objective) problem. Aggregation of objectives usually involves parameter setting and often deteriorates the thoroughness of the search. Multi-objective approach, on the other hand, would significantly complicate the entire approach [12], [108], [123], and address topics that are beyond the scope of this book. *Secondly*, there are other means that enable control of the complexity of the evolved solutions: the parameter l that determines the feature extraction procedure length, and the numbers of registers (n_r and n'_r), to mention the most relevant ones.

Therefore, the fitness function f used here relies only on the predictive performance assessment, done in the context of the training set of images T. The feature extraction procedure G encoded in a solution $\mathbf{s}$ is run for all images $\mathbf{x} \in T$ and produces feature vectors $\{G(\mathbf{x}), \mathbf{x} \in T\}$. These vectors, together with decision class labels $d(\mathbf{x})$, constitute the derived dataset with examples given in attribute-value form:

$$T' = \{(G(\mathbf{x}), d(\mathbf{x})), \mathbf{x} \in T\}. \tag{6.3}$$

We want f to promote transformations G that provide better predictive performance. In feature selection and construction, f usually measures the decision class separability, information contents, coherence, statistical properties, or consistency provided by G; the term filter approach has been coined to denote such methods. Alternatively, in a so-called wrapper approach one estimates the accuracy of classification/recognition that may be attained using G, by carrying out an internal multiple train-and-test experiment. The practical superiority of the wrapper approach over the filter approach has been shown in many different contexts [25]. Moreover, wrappers do not make demanding assumptions concerning f's monotonicity and the types of variables (e.g., most consistency measures accept only nominal variables).

For these reasons, EFP relies on a wrapper approach. The derived training set T' is randomly partitioned into n_{cv} *folds* (subsets) T_i of possibly equal size. Given this partitioning, a multiple train-and-test experiment is carried out using an inductive learning algorithm, and the resulting average recognition ratio (accuracy of classification) becomes the fitness of evaluated solution **s** and its phenotypic representation G.

Let us note that the wrapper methodology implies a kind of classifier bias. More formally, given two different learners L_1 and L_1, the corresponding f values are usually different. A representation (mapping) G evaluated in this way usually provides good results with the same classifier; however, for a different classifier good results are less likely.

The above measure is an estimate of predictive accuracy; the actual test-set recognition ratio may be different from $f(\mathbf{s})$. In most cases, overfitting occurs. Fortunately, from the evolutionary perspective, the absolute value of this measure is not as crucial as it appears to be – the mutual relations between fitness values of different individuals are more important. This is particularly true if selection schemes other than fitness-proportional selection are used. For this reason, the random partitioning of T' into folds is static, i.e., it does not change during the evolutionary run. Technically, this partitioning is carried out prior to the evolutionary run and kept fixed.

Another consequence of using a wrapper for evaluation is the discrete character of f: fitness can take on only $|T'|+1$ distinct values. Thus, when the training set is small, the probability of getting equal evaluations for even substantially different solutions is quite high. This weakens the selective pressure, i.e. f's ability to discriminate good solutions from the better ones. This observation is another argument for using large training sets, apart from the obvious argument that a big (and representative) training set increases a learner's chance to produce a well-generalizing classifier. This is, however, in conflict with the computational cost, as the more data, the longer the learning process, and, consequently, the longer the fitness computation. This tradeoff is unfortunate and inescapable; some extra measures that may be taken to avoid it have been elaborated elsewhere [62], but are not used here.

Here the solution evaluation involves inductive learning, i.e. an adaptive process. This makes the proposed approach, and all the approaches based on wrapper-like fitness assessment, belong to the category of so-called Baldwinian learning [3], [76]. The Baldwin effect takes place whenever the genome does not determine directly the working of the phenotype, but offers some space for solution's adaptation. The Baldwin effect is clearly observable in nature, where organisms learn through interaction with an environment during their lifetime. In the approach proposed here, this adaptation affects only the solution's fitness; the traits acquired during learning that takes place within f do not propagate back to the solution being evaluated. Therefore, the learning here is 'Baldwinian' but not 'Lamarckian'. Jean-Baptiste Lamarck (1744-1829) hypothesized that the acquired traits can be inherited. This theory, referred to as 'Lamarckism' or 'Lamarckianism', is currently widely recognized as incorrect (see, e.g., [90], [126] for more details)

6.5   Coevolutionary Feature Programming

Similar to many other applications of EC, the feature construction task is difficult due to the unknown characteristics of the objective function f. More precisely, f *is* known to the feature construction algorithm, but its analytical form is very complex, as it is determined by the training set T and the inductive learner working in a wrapper.

In following we show how to tackle the difficulty of feature construction by exploiting its modularity and decomposing it. Like in Chapter 5 by decomposing the feature construction process, we would like to improve the quality of induced decision/recognition system (G,h). The practical benefits we expect from decomposition include:

- *faster convergence* of the learning process, the possibility of obtaining better recognition systems at the same computational expense, or comparable recognition systems in a shorter computation time,

- *better scalability* of learning with respect to the size of the problem (number of decision classes and/or number of evolved features),

- *better understanding* of obtained solutions (feature extraction procedures).

As formulated earlier in this chapter, explicit feature construction consists in an intertwined search in two spaces: the space of hypotheses and the space of feature definitions. Therefore, one could conceptually consider decomposition concerning both of these spaces. However, as in EFP the hypothesis search is merely an element of fitness computation within a wrapper, so we focus here more on decomposing the search process in the space of feature definitions.

Formally, by a decomposable problem we mean a problem, for which each solution s may be assembled from conceptually disjoint entities called modules s_i, i.e., there exists a mapping C, which, given l modules s_i, $i=1,...,l$, composes them into the overall solution:

$$s = C(s_1,...,s_l).$$
(6.4)

We concentrate on the specific, yet common in practice, case of modules being sets of variables. In this context, by problem decomposition we mean the partitioning of the original set of variables s_i into a set of disjoint modules. In the following, we identify a module with a subset (vector) of original problem variables such that each variable s_i belongs to exactly one module s_j.

When humans apply decomposition, they usually specify a subobjective for each module. By any means, from a practical viewpoint, this is the best approach possible. After decomposition, subobjectives guide the independent searches for particular modules and the overall complexity of the problem is usually reduced. Problems representing this class are sometimes referred to as separable [125].

However, not all decomposable problems are separable, as it is not always possible to define subobjectives, because the existence of C does not automatically imply that there is a way to disassembly the objective function. This is the case when (1) the particular modules are (partially) interdependent and the objective function cannot be decomposed, or (2) there is not enough knowledge available to the human expert to specify subobjectives.

It has been shown recently [124] that decomposition may also be useful for non-separable problems with average interdependency of modules. Such problems have been referred to as nearly decomposable [110], [124] or exhibiting modular dependency [125]. Fortunately, most of the non-separable real-world problems belong to this category of problems with a modest 'amount' of interdependency. A thorough analysis of module interdependency and separability is beyond the scope of this book; the reader is referred to other work that goes into more detail [124].

Cooperative coevolution (CC), one of EC paradigms that this book is devoted to, is especially well-suited for tacking non-separable yet nearly decomposable problems [94], [128]. As already emphasized in Chapter 1 and Chapter 5, the major advantage of CC is that it provides the possibility of breaking up a complex problem into subproblems without specifying explicitly the objectives for them. This makes CC especially appealing to a broad class of practical problems, where it is possible to design a decomposition of the problem into subproblems, however, the objective functions for the particular subproblems are not known. The way the individuals from populations cooperate emerges as the evolution proceeds.

In this chapter, we propose a way to decompose the task of evolutionary feature programming of linear feature extraction procedures by means of CC. This leads us to coevolutionary variety of the proposed methodology, coevolutionary feature programming (CFP).

In CFP, the CC search engine is responsible for searching the space of mappings G [63]. Similar to EFP, this search is guided by a fitness function f, which consists in cross-validation on the training data (a wrapper approach). The best feature mapping G found in the search, together with the trained classifier h, constitute the resulting recognition system (G,h). However, G is not encoded in a single solution/individual s. Rather than that, particular individuals s_i from populations P_i describe components of the mapping G. The populations and their semi-independent evolutionary processes correspond to modules in the terminology introduced here. In the next subchapter, we discuss and present four different ways of defining those components (modules) and their composition method C.

6.6   Decomposition of Explicit Feature Construction

Problem decomposition consists in designing a mapping C that allows for assembling the complete solution from some modules (Equation 6.4). For most problems, the total number of possible problem decompositions is very large. However, only some of them are reasonable in the sense that they enable the genotype-phenotype mapping to preserve the modularity (or the 'degree' of modularity). To design successful decompositions, i.e. such that they increase the chance of finding feature transformations that are (a) feasible, and (b) outperform the feature transformations obtained without referring to decomposition, we use the background knowledge about the nature of the feature construction task and the way the solutions are evaluated. In the following, we attempt to investigate the 'reasonable' decomposition strategies, though we do not claim that all the possible strategies are considered here.

We describe four qualitatively different decompositions, in the same order as the stage at which they take place within solution evaluation process. In CC-related terms, they correspond to different levels on which the cooperation takes place: instruction, feature, class and decision levels.

• **Instruction Level Decomposition:** The lowest possible level at which decomposition may be applied is the instruction level. In this decomposition strategy, each population is delegated to specific fragment of feature extraction procedure. A module s_i is equivalent to a continuous fragment of feature extraction procedure, which constitutes the entire solution s (organism). The compositional mapping C is a straightforward concatenation of modules that preserves the order of instructions as given by module indices. As the subsequences of feature extraction procedure instructions correspond directly to substrings of bits in the genotype, this way of decomposition may be characterized as genotypic.

For this type of decomposition, no matter what the number of modules, the number of evolved features m is determined by the number of numeric registers n_r: $m = n_r$. Note also that, as this type of decomposition is genotypic, it may significantly affect the purely evolutionary aspects of the search/learning; for instance, the more populations, the shorter individuals' genome, and the less effective the crossover.

In case of nontrivial real-world applications, there is usually need for using *multiple* features g_i. Even for binary learning tasks, one scalar feature is usually not enough to discriminate decision classes if they are entangled in decision space in a complex way. The importance of possible inter-feature influences is obvious and present in almost all real-world application (see, for instance [25], [26]).

Note that the non-coevolutionary EFP already enables simultaneous computation of multiple features, as one feature extraction procedure may potentially compute up to n_r features g_i, where n_r denotes the number of numeric registers. However, in most cases, one cannot expect obtaining a single FEP that implements qualitatively different features that would lead to useful synergy. Moreover, as already discussed in chapter 6.4.1, a large number of registers calls for longer FEPs, which, in turn, increases prohibitively the search/learning time.

Features should discriminate the decision classes as well as possible on one hand, and be mutually non-redundant on the other. A desirable phenomenon here is synergy, i.e., working together of two or more elements to produce an effect greater than their individual effects.

More precisely, the mutually redundant features cause their combined effect to be smaller than or equal to the individual contributions. For a simple case two features g_1 and g_2, this means:

$$f([g_1 \ g_2]) \leq \max(f(g_1), f(g_2))$$ (6.5)

In a simple case, such redundancy may usually be detected using, for instance, statistical tools like correlation (for continuous features) or χ^2 statistics (for nominal features). However, the statistical approach fails if the dependencies are difficult (e.g., complex non-linear), affected by noise, or when the sample (training set T) size is not large enough to provide statistical evidence. The synergy of features, on the contrary, provides a better value of the objective function than any of the features attains individually:

$$f([g_1 \ g_2]) > \max(f(g_1), f(g_2)).$$ (6.6)

Apparently, to stimulate synergy, one could construct several different features independently, but the chance that such features would complement each other in discriminating decision classes is rather scant. More likely, the resulting features, being drawn from similar 'traits' in the training data T, would be highly correlated. To benefit from feature synergy, the processes that elaborate particular features have to exchange some information. This, together with the pressure on discrimination mentioned earlier, shows that the task of explicit feature construction at feature level exhibits intermediate interdependency of modules. This makes it an excellent candidate for application of cooperative coevolution.

• **Feature Level Decomposition:** The decomposition at feature level consists of delegating each population P_i to work on a separate feature extraction procedure. To evaluate a solution **s** within CC, the following steps are undertaken. For each module $\mathbf{s}_i$, we first decode it and obtain the feature extraction procedure G_i, and then run it on the training data to produce the derived training data T'_i. These steps proceed for each module separately as in regular EFP. The fusion of information takes place *after* all the modules $\mathbf{s}_i$ produce their T'_i's: the composition mapping C performs a concatenation of the feature vectors $G_i(\mathbf{x})$ produced by particular modules $\mathbf{s}_i$ for all training images $\mathbf{x} \in T$ (feature fusion). Here the number of evolved features m is a multiple of the number of populations n_p: for n_r numeric registers, $m = n_p n_r$.

• **Class Level Decomposition:** The multi-class learning problems exhibit another kind of inherent modularity that consists of the presence of many decision classes $(n_d > 2)$. To correctly classify an unknown example, the learner has to discriminate it from examples representing *all* the remaining decision classes. Instead of solving this as one learning task, one can decompose it into binary base learning tasks. The base learners produce so-called base classifiers. Usually, one obtains such decomposition by applying a one-vs.-all approach (each base classifier discriminates one decision class from the remaining ones) or a pairwise approach (each base classifier discriminates between a pair of decision classes). Though other decomposition schemes are conceptually possible, these two have been most extensively studied in past.

Such class-level decomposition leads to separable modules: by maximizing discrimination of a pair of decision classes (or discrimination of ith decision class and the remaining classes), the overall recognition system performance is improved too. Thus, a feature construction process is run separately for each base learning task and yields a base decision system (G_i,h_i). The composition C takes place off-line here, after all the learning processes related to particular subproblems produce (G_i,h_i), and consists in assembling them into one decision system (G,h) in a way that depends on the particular architecture chosen.

The particular form of C may vary; within the real-world case studies described in chapter 7, we use the one-vs.-all decomposition and a simple aggregation rule that produces univocal class assignment if and only if one base classifier yields positive response (i.e., votes for the decision class it is assigned to). Other response patterns (no base classifier responding or more than one base classifier responding) are interpreted as 'no-decision', and counted as errors in the final results. This setting implies that the number of base decision systems is equal to the number of decision classes n_d.

As this decomposition leads to separable subproblems, the number of evolved features m is not directly related to any parameter of EFP. However, if we assume that the base learners are homogenous, i.e., each of them produces the same number of features k, m amounts to kn_d for the one-vs.-all decomposition.

• **Decision level Decomposition:** The last decomposition method considered here relates to the concept of multiple (compound) classifiers. This way of decomposition resembles the class-level decomposition to some extent. In decomposition at decision level, each module encodes a complete base decision system that solves the entire learning task (including all decision classes). The responses of particular base systems (classification decisions) are aggregated by a decision rule (e.g., simple voting) to yield the overall decision.

This setting implies reducibility, provided each base system does its best, any module may be dropped (cancelled) without significant deterioration of the result (fitness). The objective of decomposition is not mere enabling the learning process to find a satisfactory decision system, rather the goal here is boosting the recognition performance. The decompositions produced by this approach are also symmetric: if all modules attempt to solve the entire task, their roles are interchangeable, provided that the aggregating decision rule is symmetric too.

The separability of decision level decompositions is difficult to assess. Apparently, this method is similar to feature-level decomposition. As each base decision system attempts to solve the entire learning task, the objective function for each module is known, the marginal search may be thus performed, and the decomposition should be claimed separable. On the other hand, if no other means are applied, base decision systems are identical or very similar, as they optimize virtually *the same* objective, so they yield no synergy when combined.

A more thorough analysis shows that the similarity of this decomposition method to feature-level decomposition is only apparent. In feature level, the synthesized features cooperate and span together a common feature space $g_1 \times g_2 \times \ldots \times g_m$. The placement of each training example $\mathbf{x}$ in that space does matter, because, with high probability, it has direct influence on the resulting fitness. In decision level decomposition, on the contrary, each module produces features that are used for *separate* learning process and the cooperation takes place in the space of decisions. As the base decision systems cooperate by majority-vote decision rule, it is much more likely that an erroneous decision made by a particular base decision system will not affect the overall system performance (fitness). In other words, the poor module's performance may be concealed by the other modules. Thus, we hypothesize that the cooperation is difficult at this level, and we label this type of decomposition as separable.

To clarify possible misinterpretations, Figure 6.5 compares the four decomposition methods described in this section: instruction-level, feature-level, class-level, and decision level. It presents data flows that start with individuals (modules) in sub-populations P_i and end up with complete recognition systems (G,h). In this presentation, class-level and decision level decomposition look the same, as they differ only in data used for training.

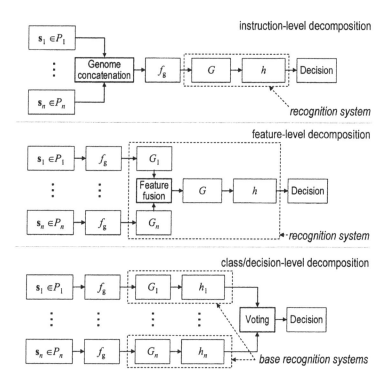

Figure 6.5. Comparison of particular decomposition levels for evolutionary feature programming.

6.7   Conclusions

In this chapter, we described evolutionary feature programming, an evolutionary approach to explicit synthesis of recognition systems that uses linear representation of feature extraction procedures. We discussed properties of the assumed feature extraction procedure representation and its genetic encoding. We also proposed a general framework for coevolutionary approach to decomposition of feature construction task, and outlined four different decomposition schemes, providing rationale for each of them. In the following chapter 7, we verify practical utility of different varieties of this methodology in an extensive computational experiment concerning view-independent recognition of real-world 3D objects imaged using passive and active sensing techniques.

Chapter 7

APPLICATIONS OF LINEAR GENETIC PROGRAMMING FOR OBJECT RECOGNITION

7.1   Introduction

This chapter is a logical continuation of chapter 6 and presents results of applying the methodology described there to real-world computer vision and pattern recognition problems. In particular, the configurations verified here include basic, single-population evolutionary feature programming (EFP), and selected variants of coevolutionary feature programming (CFP) working on different decomposition levels.

To provide experimental evidence for the generality of the proposed approach, we verify it on two different tasks. First of them is the recognition of common household objects, a popular benchmark used in computer vision community. It concerns the visible part of the electromagnetic spectrum and relates to so-called passive sensing, as usually no active dedicated source of light is required to acquire the images. On the contrary, the second considered application concerns the non-visual modality of radar imaging and represents active sensing, as the source of radiation (radar wave transmitter) is required. Therefore, the problems considered are entirely different; the only features they have in common are (a) recognition of 3D objects from different viewpoints, and (b) using mid-size one-channel raster images.

7.2   Technical Implementation

To provide an experimental testbed we developed a software environment named CVGP (Computer Vision by Genetic Programming). CVGP, written in Java and C, is a universal platform for experimenting with explicit feature construction in both machine learning and computer vision. To conform to the existing standards and benefit from the ready-to-use background knowledge, CVGP integrates several existing libraries:

- Soft-computing libraries written in Java:
  - machine learning library WEKA [127],
  - evolutionary computation library ECJ [70].
- Image processing and computer vision libraries (C and machine code):
  - Intel Image Processing Library (IPL) [47],
  - Open Computer Vision Library (OpenCV) [88],

Figure 7.1 presents the overall software architecture of the system. Java Native Interface (JNI) has been used to integrate modules and libraries written in Java with those written in C. Thanks to this choice of components, the most time-consuming evaluation of Feature Extraction Procedures (FEP) is efficiently carried out in well optimized libraries written in C and machine code, whereas the less computationally demanding ML and EC computation takes place in Java. The IPL and OpenCV libraries function as a repository of background knowledge. Though originally designed to serve explicit feature construction in CV, CVGP may also be applied to ML problems; in such a case, WEKA and ECJ are sufficient to run an experiment. On the other hand, CVGP may be easily combined with other libraries to use background knowledge and input representation relating to other domains (sound, video, etc.).

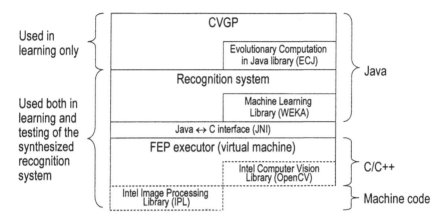

Figure 7.1. Software implementation of CVGP. Dashed-line components implement background knowledge.

7.3   Common Experimental Framework

7.3.1   Background knowledge

For the proposed methods (EFP and CFP), the only source of background vision knowledge is the set of elementary operators O provided by the human expert (see Figure 7.1). This set could be tailored independently to each visual learning task presented here. However, to demonstrate generality of EFP/CFP, we use the same set O for both CV tasks and make it contain only general-purpose image processing and feature extraction operations. Therefore, both applications share the same vision-related background knowledge and do not refer to any application-specific domain knowledge. For instance, though the concept of scattering point is usually applied in analysis of radar images (see, e.g., [10]), there is no ready-to-use operation in O that could detect such features in the image.

The set O contains approximately 70 elementary operations listed in Table 7.1. Technically, operations refer to functions implemented in Intel Image

Processing library [47] and OpenCV library [88]. They embrace image processing, feature extraction, mask-related operations, and arithmetic and logic operations.

Table 7.1. Elementary operations used in the visual learning experiments (k and l denote the number of the input and output arguments, respectively).

Category	Operations
Image → Image	
Convolution filters (for mask sizes 3x3 and 5x5)	Prewitt, Sobel, Laplacian, Gaussian, Highpass, Lowpass, Sharpening
Other filters	Median filter, Min filter, Thresholding, Normalized cross-correlation
Image transforms	2-D Fast Fourier Transform
Morphological operations	Erosion, Dilatation, Opening, Closing
Image arithmetic (pixelwise)	Absolute difference, Addition, Subtraction, Multiplication
Image logic operations (pixelwise)	And, Or, Xor
Image^k → $\Re^l$	
Image norms	Dot product, L1 (city-block), L2 (Euclidean)
Feature extraction operations	Spatial 2D moments (up to 3rd order), Central 2D moments (up to 3rd order), Normalized central 2D moments (up to 3rd order), Mass center, Location of the brightest pixel, Location of the darkest pixel. Number of non-zero pixels, Sum/Average/Standard deviation of pixel intensities
$\Re^k → \Re^l$	
Scalar arithmetic	+, -, *, % (protected division)
Scalar functions	Max, Min, Abs, Sgn, If (conditional expression) Sin, Cos, Tan, Exp, Log
Other	
Mask-related operations	Set rectangular mask, Set mask upper left corner, Set mask lower right corner, Shift mask in specific direction, Get mask height, Get mask width, Get mask mid X, Get mask mid Y

The experiments presented in the following may be roughly divided into two categories: basic study experiments focus on the dynamics of evolutionary search, its sensitivity to different parameter setting, and the convergence of evolutionary process; performance experiments focus on maximizing the overall recognition performance and on the predictive (related to the test set) properties of evolved recognition systems. Quite obviously, the latter experiments are usually much more time-consuming.

7.3.2   Parameter settings and performance measures

EFP and CFP use the wrapper approach to estimate the fitness of a particular set of features. Unfortunately, the wrapper approach, widely recognized as very accurate, is quite time-consuming. As n_{cv}-fold cross-validation involves n_{cv}-times classifier induction and n_{cv}-times classifier querying, we need to use an inducer that is fast in both of these aspects.

In the following experiments, the popular tree induction algorithm C4.5 [96] is used for that purpose. Precisely, we use the last public release of C4.5 implemented in WEKA under the name J4.8 [127]. C4.5 has low computational complexity of learning and linear (with respect to tree depth) complexity of querying. Another advantage of this inducer is that its bias/variance trade-off may be easily controlled by the pruning confidence level. In following experiments, we use C4.5's default settings: pruning confidence level: 0.25, node evaluation measure: gain ratio, subsetting: off. The cross-validation runs with $n_{cv} = 3$ folds. The feature construction is the time-critical phase of EFP. After the evolutionary run is over, we use the best feature transformation G found for training the classifier for the final recognition system. As this is a single event, for some of the final recognition systems presented in the following, we use a sophisticated, yet more time-consuming in training, support vector machine (SVM) classifier. In particular, we rely here on SVM trained by means of the sequential minimal optimization algorithm [91] implemented in WEKA library [127]. The SVM classifier uses polynomial kernels of degree 3 and is trained with the complexity parameter set to 10.

Peformance is measured by the recognition ratio which measures the classification performance on the training or testing data for all the classes under consideration. The value of recognition ratio on the training data is the fitness value. True positive ratio, TP = P (positive decision | positive example) and False Positive ratio, FP = P (positive decision | negative example).

7.4   Recognition of Common Household Objects

7.4.1   Problem and data

For the test of passive sensing, we use the COIL20 database [79], a popular computer vision benchmark. COIL20 contains a total of 1440 grayscale (one-channel) images of 20 household objects taken at different aspects (72 images of each object taken at 5° aspect intervals). Figure 7.2 depicts the representatives of all decision classes.

Figure 7.2. Exemplary images from COIL20 database (one representative per class).

We use the processed version of COIL20. Each image in this collection was obtained from the unprocessed image by cropping its contents to a minimum bounding rectangle (MBR) embracing the object, and scaling it to 128×128 pixels (see [77] for details). To speedup the computation, we downsample the original images to 64×64 pixels. The downsampled images are directly used by the learning system; they do not undergo any other processing.

Appearances to the contrary, recognition of processed images may be more difficult than the unprocessed ones, as (i) the actual size differences between particular objects are lost in scaling, and (ii) the use of MBR cropping may cause an object to have apparently different sizes for different aspects (see Figure 7.3). Due to (i), inter-class differences of size-related features are possibly reduced. Due to (ii), the intra-class variance of some features is larger than for the unprocessed data.

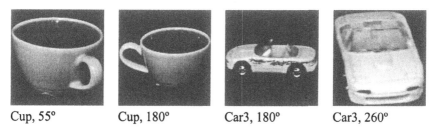

Cup, 55°   Cup, 180°   Car3, 180°   Car3, 260°

Figure 7.3. Apparent size changes resulting from MBR cropping for different aspects of two selected objects from the COIL20 database.

The COIL20 database comes with a predefined partitioning of data into a training set T and testing set W. In particular, for each object class, the training set T contains every fifth image from the entire collection (15 images per class, aspect every 24°), and the testing set W gathers all the 57 remaining images of that object. Such partitioning provides that the training data well represents the entire learning task.

7.4.2   Parameter settings

In this COIL20 experiment, we use feature level CFP. The detailed parameter settings are presented in Table 7.2. This experiment runs in a minimum configuration, with $n_P = 2$ populations and $n_r = n'_r = 2$ registers. Small n_P allows us to verify the approach in a simple setting and provides relatively high search mobility. Standard genetic operators are used for recombination and selection. The probability of mutation refers to single bits. Therefore, given fixed mutation probability, the longer the feature extraction procedure code, the more mutations it undergoes on the average. The crossover probability 1.0, what implies that all individuals undergo recombination and none of them is directly transferred to the subsequent generation (i.e., there is no *elitist* sampling [76]). To motivate this choice, we argue that the primary task of evolutionary algorithm within EFP/CFP is to perform effective search, and that maintaining continuity between consecutive generations is of secondary importance.

No constraints have been imposed on genome loci where the one-point crossover operator starts to exchange the 'tails' of genetic material. As a result, recombination may break apart the feature extraction procedure instructions (for instance, opcode may be detached from its arguments and replaced by different arguments). This setting may seem strange at first sight, as apparently one should treat entire operations as genes and not allow recombination to break them apart. Nevertheless, the preliminary experiments have shown that such an approach is much more effective as far as search convergence is concerned, because it provides more flexibility.

Setting the tournament pool size to 5 is a compromise between values 2 and 7 used commonly in genetic algorithms and genetic programming, respectively. In each experiment, if no ideal individual is found, evolutionary search stops after 4000 seconds (from a practical viewpoint, about an hour seemed to be a reasonable amount of time to be devoted to the design of a recognition system). The results presented have been obtained using computers equipped with a Pentium 1.4 GHz processor.

To provide for statistical significance, each evolutionary run is repeated 10 times, starting from different initial populations. Technically, this is provided by changing the seed of the random number generator. Therefore, if not otherwise stated, the following tables and graphs show the mean performance of best individuals obtained from ten independent runs.

Table 7.2. Parameter settings for COIL20 experiments.

Parameter	Setting
Single population size $|P_i|$	500
# of populations n_P	2
# of registers $(n_r=n'_r)$	2
Mutation operator	bit flip, probability 0.1
Crossover operator	one point, probability 1.0
Selection operator	tournament selection, pool size: 5
Time limit for evolutionary search	4000 seconds

7.4.3   Results

• **Binary classification tasks.** In this setting, we evolve recognition systems to recognize one class (positive class, d^+) against the remaining 19 classes of COIL20 objects, which are temporarily grouped to form the negative class d^-. Figure 7.4 and Figure 7.5 present the results of training the feature-level CFP on the COIL20 data (means over 10 runs). For brevity, classes are referenced by numbers with respect to the order they appear in Figure 7.2 (rows, then columns). Figure 7.4 presents final fitness, test set recognition ratio, and test set true positive ratio of evolved binary recognition systems for particular binary problems. Figure 7.5 depicts test set false positive ratio (left vertical axis) and mean decision tree size (right vertical axis). For selected data series, these figures also present 0.95 confidence intervals.

For 13 out of 20 binary problems, CFP yields recognition systems having perfect fitness 1.0 (with respect to the training data). In the remaining cases, the training-set performance of evolved recognition systems is very close to ideal. Note however, that the *a priori* probability for the negative class d^- amounts here to 0.95 ($n_d = 20$), and this is the reference point for recognition ratio assessment (the performance of the so-called *default classifier*). The evolutionary runs last for 12.5 generations on the average.

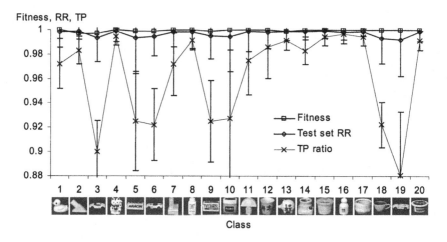

Figure 7.4. Fitness of the best individual, test set recognition ratio, and test set TP ratio for binary COIL20 experiments (means over 10 runs and 0.95 confidence intervals).

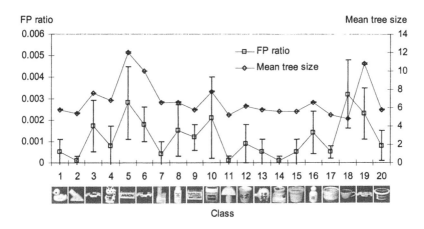

Figure 7.5. Test set FP ratio and tree size for binary COIL20 experiments (means over 10 runs and 0.95 confidence intervals).

For each binary task, after the evolutionary search is over, we build a simple recognition system (G, h) using the best representation G evolved in the run and the C4.5 decision tree classifier h trained on this representation. Therefore, the final recognition system uses the same inducer as the wrapper-based fitness function and may benefit from concordance of inductive biases.

As expected, training set-based estimate (fitness function) is in most cases overoptimistic: test-set recognition ratio is usually inferior to solution's fitness value. Nevertheless, this deterioration does not exceed 0.01, and for class 2 ('Block1') even some improvement may be observed (from 0.997 to 0.999). Thus, for the COIL20 problem, CFP seems to generalize well and no significant overfitting is observed.

Also in terms of true positive (TP = $\Pr(h(\mathbf{x}) = d^+ \mid d(\mathbf{x}) = d^+)$) and false positive (FP = $\Pr(h(\mathbf{x}) = d^+ \mid d(\mathbf{x}) = d^-)$) ratios, the charts vote in favor of CFP. Only a few cases exhibit significantly worse performance when compared to other classes. The classes most affected by this are those for which there are visually similar objects in the database: classes 3 and 19 (cars), and 5 and 9 (elongated boxes). Nevertheless, the overall performance is still sound. Even for the worst case (decision class 19), the mean TP value is 0.8804, that means that only about 12% of positive class instances are not detected by the recognition system. Taking into account that the negative decision class comprises in fact images of 19 different objects, and that the approach is feature-based, the obtained rates should be regarded as good.

The FP results are even more appealing. In the worst case (class 18, 'Cup'), the mean FP rate is 0.0032. Thus, only 0.32% images of other 19 objects are identified as cups on the average. For many other classes, this figure is much smaller. Among the total of 200 recognition systems considered in this experiment ($n_d = 20$ decision classes × 10 runs per class), 109 recognition systems attained *zero FP rate*. These results are comparable and, in some cases, superior to past experimental studies concerning COIL20 database which, in most cases, use a model-based approach (e.g., [1], [73]). The confidence intervals are narrow and ensure stability of the results obtained. This is especially important from a practical viewpoint, where the method is expected to yield a reasonable result in one run, without any need for redesigning the settings and repeating computation.

These encouraging results have been obtained using simple decision tree classifiers. Figure 7.5 presents (on the right vertical axis) the average number of tree nodes used by decision trees induced from the transformed training data. In particular, difficult problems (e.g., for decision classes 6, 9, and 19) result in larger trees. Figure 7.6 shows one of the induced trees. Numbers in parenthesis denote leaf weight (number of training examples that reached tree node; the total number of training examples is $|T| = 15n_d = 300$). Due to uneven distribution of decision classes in the data (19:1), the tree is heavily imbalanced and classifies the greater part of the examples in the root node. Most of the remaining trees induced for this binary problem and for other binary COIL20 problems have a similar structure. Relatively small trees (6.8 nodes for all 200 experiments on the average) clearly indicate, that the most difficult part of recognition takes place within feature extraction procedures. Otherwise, the results would be probably much worse, as C4.5 often fails when faced with highly imbalanced decision classes. The readable structures of trees enable human inspection and analysis.

$g_0(\mathbf{x}) \;<=\; 3849\colon\; h(\mathbf{x}) = d^-\; (270)$
$g_0(\mathbf{x}) \;>\; 3849$
$|\; g_1(\mathbf{x}) \;<=\; 361962\colon\; h(\mathbf{x}) = d^-\; (13)$
$|\; g_1(\mathbf{x}) \;>\; 361962$
$|\; |\; g_2(\mathbf{x}) \;<=\; 2853.808333\colon\; h(\mathbf{x}) = d^+\; (15)$
$|\; |\; g_2(\mathbf{x}) \;>\; 2853.808333\colon\; h(\mathbf{x}) = d^-\; (2)$

Figure 7.6. Decision tree h used by the final recognition system evolved in one of the COIL20 binary experiments.

- **Complete recognition task.** For the complete recognition task, we use CFP to discriminate all 20 decision classes present in the COIL20 dataset, that is obviously much more difficult than the binary recognition tasks. For this purpose, we treat the evolved binary recognition systems synthesized in the previous experiment as base classifiers, and combine their votes. Therefore, in fact we apply off-line one-versus-all problem decomposition on class level; such proceeding is fully justified as class-level decomposition leads to separable modules (cf. chapter 6.6). The assembled compound classifier comprises 20 base classifiers, one for each decision class. We build 10 such compound recognition systems (each binary CFP run was repeated 10 times). The resulting mean accuracy of classification for these compound recognition systems on the test set amounts to 0.9877 ± 0.0036. Thus, only about 1% of the images are mistakenly labeled by the compound recognition system. Analysis of error occurrences in test-set confusion matrices confirms the conclusions of the binary experiments: the most often confused classes are the ones that exhibit visual similarity: 3 'Car' and 5 'Box1', 3 'Car' and 6 'Car2', 3 'Car' and 18 'Cup', 3 'Car' and 19 'Car3' , 5 'Box1' and 6 'Car2' .

7.5 Object Recognition in Radar Modality

As another experimental testbed, we chose the task of object (vehicle) recognition in synthetic aperture radar (SAR) images [88]. Imaging in radar modality, due to particular wavelengths and their properties (specular reflections), is fundamentally different from the general diffuse reflection for the visible spectrum. Radar senses in wavelengths outside the visible and infrared spectrum, providing information on surface roughness, and other shape properties. Radar waves may penetrate some materials, e.g., vegetation, sand, and snow. Radar imaging is *active* in the sense that it requires illumination (source of radiation).

Synthetic aperture radar (SAR) imaging is a specific technology [86] that makes a relatively small antenna work like it is much larger, due to the receiver (aircraft) motion and the Doppler principle. SAR sensors can operate 24 hours a day; there are many other interesting properties of SAR images and the reader is referred to [86]. Nevertheless, from the viewpoint of human perception, the subjective quality of the acquired images is generally disappointedly low. In particular:

- SAR images are *non-literal*. There is not 1:1 appearance similarity with visible imagery and one needs to understand the physics of SAR image formation to interpret the imagery.

- Usually only so-called *scattering centers* are visible.

- The features do not persist under rotation (aspect change).

- SAR images are noisy and have low resolution.

These properties make SAR image interpretation difficult. This is particularly true for this study, which concerns recognition of relatively small (when compared to one foot image resolution) man-made objects like vehicles.

We use the MSTAR public database [104] as the benchmark for evolutionary feature programming. The MSTAR database contains SAR images of several objects, mostly vehicles, taken at different elevation angles and azimuth (aspect) angles. In this study, we consider only images acquired at 15° elevation angle (MSTAR contains also images for different elevation angles). The spatial resolution is 1 foot and the objects are centered in the image. Figure 7.7 presents selected images of the vehicles considered: BRDM armored personnel carrier (APC), ZSU anti-aircraft gun, T62 tank, ZIL truck, T72 tank, 2S1 gun, BMP2 (APC), and BTR70 (APC). Figure 7.8 shows selected SAR views of particular object classes. Note also the presence of radar shadow behind each object. Table 7.3 shows the image data used for the experiments on three selected objects (Figure 7.9).

SAR images are originally two-channel (complex), with each image pixel described by signal amplitude/magnitude and signal phase [88]. We use the magnitude component only. The images are cropped to 48×48 pixel window centered in the original image. No other form of preprocessing (e.g., speckle removal) is applied.

7.5.1   Problem decomposition at instruction level

In this experiment, we compare the performance of evolutionary feature programming (EFP) and coevolutionary feature programming (CFP), where the cooperation in CFP takes place at the instruction level. To make this comparison reliable, we consider equal total genome length: for EFP experiment with code length l, in the corresponding CFP experiment each of n_P populations works on code fragment of length l/n_P. Similarly, we fix the total number of individuals: the total number of individuals in all n_P populations in CFP is equal to the number of individuals maintained in the single population of the corresponding EFP run (see Table 7.4).

The task is to recognize three different objects: BRDM2, D7, and T62 (see Figure 7.9). From the MSTAR database, 507 images of these objects have been selected by means of appropriate sampling procedure. The resulting set of images has been split into disjoint training and testing parts to provide reliable estimate of the recognition ratio of the learned recognition system (see Table 7.3). This selection was aimed at providing uniform coverage of the azimuth; for each class, there is a training image for approximately every 5.62° of azimuth (aspect), and a testing image every 2.9°-5.37°, on the average.

Table 7.4 compares the recognition performance obtained by the proposed coevolutionary approach (CFP) and its regular counterpart (EFP). To estimate the performance the learning algorithm is able to attain in a limited time, if no ideal solution is found, we stop evolution when its run time reaches a predefined limit. Two different limits have been imposed on the evolutionary learning time, 1000 and 2000 seconds. To obtain statistical evidence, all evolutionary runs are repeated 10 times, so the table presents the average performance of the best individuals found. The results presented in Table 7.4 show the superiority of the instruction-level CFP to instruction-level EFP. This applies to both the performance of the synthesized systems on the training as well as on the test set. In all cases, the observed increases in accuracy are statistically significant with respect to the one-sided t-Student test at the confidence level 0.05. Though it is not shown in the table, CFP usually ran for a smaller number of generations on the average, due to the extra time required to maintain (perform selection and mating) multiple populations. Table 7.5 and Table 7.6 show, respectively, the confusion matrices for the best individuals found in the first two test set of experiments in Table 7.4 (time limit: 2000 seconds, total # of individuals: 300).

Figure 7.7. Selected vehicles represented in MSTAR database.

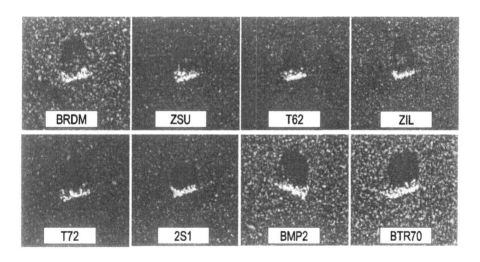

Figure 7.8. Exemplary images from the MSTAR database.

Figure 7.9. Three vehicles and their correspondings SAR images.

Table 7.3. Description of data for the experiment concerning cooperation on genome level.

Class	Number of images				
	Total	Training set	Aspect interval	Testing set	Aspect interval
BRDM2	188	64	5.62°	124	2.90°
D7	188	64	5.62°	124	2.90°
T62	131	64	5.62°	67	5.37°
Total	507	192		315	

Table 7.4. Performance of recognition systems evolved by means of cooperation at genome level.

Method	Parameter setting			Recognition ratio			
				1000 seconds		2000 seconds	
	n_P	l	P_i	Training set	Test set	Training set	Test set
EFP	1	72	300	0.806	0.747	0.843	0.801
CFP	3	24	100	0.915	0.867	0.933	0.890
EFP	1	72	900	0.839	0.795	0.881	0.830
CFP	3	24	300	0.927	0.874	0.940	0.883

Table 7.5. Test set confusion matrix for selected EFP recognition system.

Actual class	Predicted class			
	BRDM2	D7	T62	None
BRDM2	97	3	22	2
D7	0	115	9	0
T62	1	0	66	0

Table 7.6. Test set confusion matrix for selected CFP recognition system.

Actual class	Predicted class			
	BRDM2	D7	T62	None
BRDM2	118	1	4	1
D7	5	114	3	2
T62	5	1	61	0

7.5.2   Binary classification tasks

To illustrate the performance of the proposed approach let us first consider the simple two-class experimental setting. The overall architecture of the recognition system is straightforward in this case: it consists of two modules: the best feature extraction procedure G and classifier h trained using those features.

For this performance experiment, we designed a more thorough dataset sampling procedure. To provide for good representation of the problem in the training data, we implemented an aspect-aware division procedure of the original MSTAR collection into training and test data. Similarly to COIL20 database partitioning, we attempt to build the training set so that a representative spectrum of different view angles (aspects) is present in T. For each decision class, its representation in the training data T consists of *two* subsets of images sampled from the original MSTAR database; two subsets are necessary to provide proper operation of the cross-validation experiment involved by the fitness function. For both subsets, the images are selected from MSTAR collection as uniformly as possible with respect to 6° azimuth step. Note that as opposed to the COIL20 database, MSTAR images do not observe precisely equidistant view angles. Therefore, the training set T contains $2 \times 360/6 = 120$ images from each decision class, so its total size is $120n_d$, where n_d denotes the number of decision classes.

The corresponding test set W contains all the remaining images from the original MSTAR collection (for the decision classes considered with 15° elevation angle). In this way, the T and W are disjoint, yet the learning task is well represented by the training set as far as aspect is concerned. Thus, we can be confident in the credibility of the results; performing time-consuming multiple train-and-test experiment would probably not change the overall picture much. For simplicity, we keep the numbers of numeric registers and image registers as low as possible, similar to COIL20 experiment. This implies setting $n_r = n'_r = 2$, as some of the elementary operations from O are binary and need two registers to fetch input arguments. The number of coevolving populations n_P is 4 this time, as the SAR task is more difficult than the COIL20 problem. This implies $m = n_P n'_r = 8$ scalar features g_i computed by the four coevolving feature extraction procedures. The settings of remaining parameters are the same as in COIL20 experiments.

The task is the recognition of the positive decision class d^+ represented here by the BRDM vehicle. The objects representing the remaining categories build up the negative class d^-. We run several experiments of different difficulty, starting with d^- containing images from a single decision class ZSU; let us denote this task by B1. Next, we define subsequent tasks, denoted, hereafter, B2 to B7, by extending d^- by other vehicles in the following order: T62, ZIL, T72, 2S1, BMP2, and BTR70. In all these tasks, d^+ remains fixed and contains exclusively images of the BRDM vehicle.

On each of these seven binary classification problems from B1 to B7, ten independent CFP processes have been run to provide statistical significance. Each run started with different, randomly created, initial population of solutions. Figure 7.10 presents fitness graphs of the best individuals for evolutionary learning process run on the B2 problem, i.e. BRDM (d^+) versus ZSU and T62 (d^-). Particular data series depict 10 independent evolutionary runs starting from different initial states. All learning processes attain fitness over 0.9 within the first three generations. The fitness f of the best solutions found varies from 0.964 to 0.992, depending on the run. Runs end up in different generations (57th to 75th), as the stopping condition concerns time limit (4000 seconds), and particular individuals contain feature extraction procedures that require different amounts of time when executed. Note that this learning process seems to be quite resistant to the problem of local minima: after long periods of leveling-off, several runs show improvement.

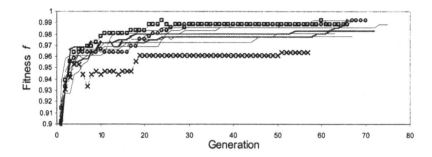

Figure 7.10. Fitness graph for binary experiment (fitness of the best individual for each generation).

   The fitness graphs presented in Figure 7.10 reflect the behavior of the recognition systems on the training data. The performance of the synthesized recognition systems on the test data is shown in Table 7.7 and Figure 7.11. Two variants of recognition systems are considered here: those using C4.5 classifier and those using support vector machine (SVM). In each learning task, the recognition systems use the same best solution evolved in the training phase. Figure 7.11 and Table 7.7 present true positive (TP) and false positive (FP) ratios that the recognition systems attain on test set (averages and 0.95 confidence intervals for 10 independent runs). It may be observed that in all experiments, recognition systems using C4.5 and SVM perform similarly. At first sight this may seem surprising, taking into account the simplicity of C4.5, especially its limited capability of fusing and combining attributes. On the other hand, the synthesized features are especially well-suited for C4.5, as this induction algorithm is used for fitness computation in the process of feature synthesis. In terms of machine learning, the features generated are biased towards C4.5.

Table 7.7. True positive (TP) and false positive (FP) ratios for SAR binary recognition tasks (testing set). Table presents averages over 10 independent synthesis processes and their 0.95 confidence intervals.

Task	C4.5				SVM			
	TP		FP		TP		FP	
B1	.987 ± .007		.042 ± .016		.966 ± .032		.022 ± .019	
B2	.960 ± .013		.040 ± .011		.935 ± .027		.010 ± .005	
B3	.892 ± .025		.035 ± .005		.929 ± .030		.017 ± .005	
B4	.901 ± .023		.036 ± .007		.929 ± .032		.013 ± .002	
B5	.860 ± .030		.033 ± .007		.880 ± .039		.014 ± .005	
B6	.733 ± .055		.026 ± .004		.762 ± .063		.018 ± .009	
B7	.654 ± .041		.039 ± .006		.610 ± .069		.012 ± .004	

The number of decision classes in the negative class controls the complexity of this learning task. More decision classes lower the *a priori* probability of the positive class (Figure 7.11). The TP ratios of synthesized recognition systems also decrease with growing task complexity. Nevertheless, the results obtained are still impressive if we keep in mind that the classifier operates in the space spanned over only 8 scalar features computed by the best solution from raw, difficult to recognize, raster images. Let us also point out, that objects BMP2 and BTR70, used in problems B6 and B7, the last two instances of the problem, are visually very similar to the positive class BRDM (see Figure 7.7 and Figure 7.8). Note also that *a priori* probabilities of the positive class in these instances are relatively low, amounting to 0.15 and 0.14, respectively.

In terms of false positives, all the synthesized systems perform well. Here, SVM outperforms C4.5 in a statistically significant way (significance level 0.01), exceeding 2% FP ratio only for the simplest problem B1 (BRDM (d^+) versus ZSU (d)). Compared to C4.5, SVM reduces the FP rate from by 32% (B6) to by 75% (B2).

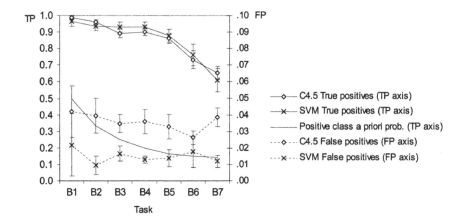

Figure 7.11. True positive (TP) and false positive (FP) ratios for binary recognition tasks (testing set, single recognition systems). Chart presents averages over 10 independent synthesis processes and their .95 confidence intervals.

7.5.3   On-line adaptation of population number

The results presented in Table 7.7 and Figure 7.11 have been obtained with $n_P = 4$ populations, each of them evolving $n_r = 2$ features. Determining the number of populations n required to attain acceptable performance on a particular task prior to test set evaluation may be difficult in general. Therefore, we developed a variant of the approach, *adaptive cooperative feature programming* (CFP-A), which adapts the number of cooperating populations to the problem difficulty. The coevolutionary algorithm starts with a single population. In this special case, the solution the algorithm works on, is composed of a single part (individual). In this configuration, evolution proceeds until saturation, i.e. until the fitness of the best solution does not improve for a certain number of generations (here: 5). In such a case, a new, randomly initialized population is added to the cooperation ($n_P \leftarrow n_P + 1$), and the evolutionary process continues with two populations. Consecutive saturations of the evolutionary search cause addition of other populations. However, with n_P populations at hand, the extension to $n_P + 1$ populations is allowed only if the best solution has been improved since the insertion of n_P th population.

Table 7.8 and Figure 7.12 present results of the evolutionary runs carried out using the above algorithm. Also Table 7.9 depicts the mean and maximum number of populations in various experiments. These figures decrease as the complexity of the problem grows. This is due to the fact, that the runs on more difficult problems last usually for a smaller number of generations (fitness function is more time-consuming). As a result, within the fixed time limit of 4000 seconds per evolutionary run, the CFP-A algorithm has fewer opportunities to add new populations on the difficult problems.

Table 7.8. True positive (TP) and false positive (FP) ratios for SAR binary recognition tasks (testing set, CFP-A; means over 10 independent synthesis processes and 0.95 confidence intervals).

Task	C4.5				SVM			
	TP		FP		TP		FP	
B1	.973 ± .012		.050 ±	.019	.981 ± .010		.012 ±	.008
B2	.969 ± .011		.033 ±	.010	.972 ± .012		.013 ±	.008
B3	.904 ± .025		.036 ±	.008	.940 ± .026		.014 ±	.006
B4	.888 ± .031		.026 ±	.006	.908 ± .035		.021 ±	.011
B5	.816 ± .036		.028 ±	.006	.856 ± .038		.015 ±	.003
B6	.736 ± .038		.037 ±	.008	.723 ± .058		.018 ±	.006
B7	.652 ± .062		.027 ±	.007	.698 ± .082		.014 ±	.003

Table 7.9. Mean and maximum number of populations for SAR binary recognition tasks (CFP-A).

Task	# of learned populations	
	Mean	Maximum
B1	5.6	7
B2	5.1	7
B3	5.8	6
B4	5.3	6
B5	5.0	6
B6	4.9	6
B7	4.4	5

The results suggest that the test set performance of the recognition systems synthesized using CFP-A do not differ much from those obtained using CFP. The observed slight differences in both TP and FP ratios are not statistically significant. We can, therefore, draw a positive conclusion that CFP-A allows attaining results that are not worse than those obtained by CC, with the advantage of relieving the system designer from fixing the number of cooperating populations.

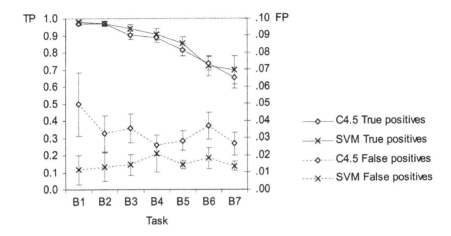

Figure 7.12. True positive (TP) and false positive (FP) ratios for binary recognition tasks (testing set, single recognition systems, adaptive CC). Chart presents averages over 10 independent synthesis processes and their 0.95 confidence intervals.

7.5.4   Scalability

From a practical viewpoint, our interest is not limited to binary classification only. To investigate the ability of the proposed approach to handle multiple class recognition tasks [49], in this section we consider several problems with increasing number of decision classes, similar to the binary classification experiments. The simplest problem involves $n_d = 2$ decision classes: BRDM (D1) and ZSU (D2). Consecutive problems are created by adding decision classes in the following order: T62 (D3), ZIL (D4), T72 (D5), 2S1 (D6), BMP2 (D7), and BTR70 (D8). In this task, the architecture of the compound recognition system is the same as the one used in Chapter 7.5.2, however, this time each base recognition system makes a decision concerning $n_d > 2$ decision classes. The number of base systems (voters) is 10; each of them is a result of an independent evolutionary run that started from different initial population. Simple voting (argmax-like) is used.

Figure 7.13 presents the accuracy of classification (recognition) rate as a function of the number of decision classes n_d. It can be observed, that the scalability of the proposed approach with respect to the number of decision classes depends heavily on the base classifier. Here, SVM clearly outperforms C4.5. The major drop-offs of accuracy occur when T72 tank and 2S1 self-propelled gun (classes D5 and D6, respectively), are added to the training data; this is probably due to the fact that these objects are similar to each other (e.g., both have gun turrets) and significantly resemble the T62 tank (class D3). On the contrary, introducing consecutive classes D7 and D8 (BMP2 and BTR60) did not affect the performance much; more than this, an improvement is even observable for class D7.

Figure 7.14 shows the curves obtained, for the recognition systems using SVM as a base classifier [91], by introducing and modifying the confidence threshold that controls voting among base classifiers. The higher this threshold, the more classifiers are required to vote for particular class to make the final decision. Too small a number of votes causes an example to remain unclassified. The curves in Figure 7.14 may be regarded as generalization of ROC (receiver operator characteristics) curves to $n_d > 2$ decision classes. Let n_c, n_e, and n_u denote respectively the numbers of test objects correctly classified, erroneously classified, and unclassified by the recognition system. In this chart, the error rate is defined as $n_e/(n_c+n_e+n_u)$, and the accuracy of classification as $n_c/(n_c+n_e+n_u)$. Also here the results are encouraging, as the curves do not drop rapidly as the error rate decreases. By modifying the confidence threshold, one can easily control the characteristics of the recognition system, for instance, to lower the error rate by accepting a reasonable rejection rate $n_u/(n_c+n_e+n_u)$.

7.5.5   Recognizing object variants

From a computer vision perspective, a desirable property of an object recognition system is an ability to recognize different variants of the same object, i.e. to generalize the knowledge acquired from the training data. In vehicle recognition in SAR modality, different configuration variants of the same vehicle often vary significantly; major differences result from the presence of extra equipment mounted on the vehicle. The MSTAR database contains images of different configuration variants for selected vehicles; these variants will be distinguished in following by the pound (#) sign and vehicles' serial number following class name. For instance, 'BMP2#C21' denotes variant C21 of BMP2 APC.

To provide comparison with human-designed recognition systems, we use the experimental setting as in [8]. In particular, we synthesize two separate recognition systems using the following training data:

1) a 2-class recognition system trained with BMP2#C21, T72#132;

2) a 4-class recognition system trained with BMP2#C21, T72#132, BTR70#C71, and ZSU#d08.

Figure 7.16 shows the representative images of objects. After training, these systems are tested on a testing set that contains two *other* variants of BMP2 (#9563 and #9566), and two *other* variants of T72 (#812 and #s7). Therefore, the testing set is not only disjoint with the training sets, but it also contains significantly different variations of the objects to be recognized.

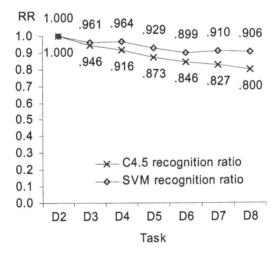

Figure 7.13. Test set recognition ratios of compound recognition systems for different number of decision classes.

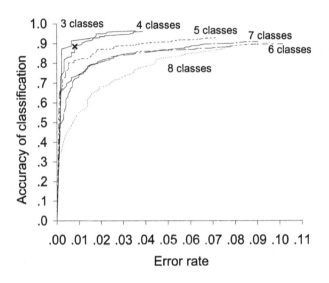

Figure 7.14. Curves for different number of decision classes (base classifier: SVM).

Table 7.10. Confusion matrices for recognition of object variants for 2-class recognition system.

Object (class)	Predicted class		
	BMP2#C21	T72#132	No decision
BMP2#9563,9566	**295**	18	78
T72#812,s7	4	**330**	52

Table 7.11. Confusion matrices for recognition of object variants for 4-class recognition system.

Object	Predicted class				
	BMP2#C21	T72#132	BTR#C71	ZSU#d08	No decision
BMP2#9563,9566	**293**	27	27	1	43
T72#812,s7	12	**323**	1	9	41

Table 7.10 and Table 7.11 present test set evaluation of the synthesized recognition systems shown in the form of confusion matrices. The results suggest that, even when the recognized objects differ significantly from the models provided in the training data, the approach is still able to maintain high performance. The true positive rate equals 0.804 and 0.793, for 2- and 4-class systems, respectively. If we consider only test cases for which the systems make any decision (83.3% and 89.2% of test examples for 2-class and 4-class decision system, respectively), then the classification accuracy amounts to 0.966 and 0.940, respectively. These figures are comparable to the forced recognition results of the human-designed recognition algorithms reported in [9], [10], which are 0.958 and 0.942, respectively. However, for a fair comparision we must force a recognition decision on the "no decision" class in Table 7.10 and Table 7.11. Without other information, a random choice applied to the no decision results (with 50% and 25% success rates for the 2 and 4 class decisions) yields forced recognition accuracies of 0.888 and 0.820, which are less than the comparable human-designed recognition algorithm results. Note that in this experiment we do not use *confusers*, i.e. test images from different classes than those present in the training set. In [8] the BRDM class has been used for that purpose. Synthesizing features for recognizing object variants is challenging and further work is needed.

7.5.6   Problem decomposition at decision level

Some preliminary experiments have been run for the vehicle recognition task decomposed at decision level. For this purpose, we design an evolutionary experiment as described in chapter 7.5.4: each individual in population P_i implements one or more *complete* feature extraction procedures. For evaluation, the feature extraction procedures encoded by the individual are run on the training data T and produce the derived dataset T', which is subsequently passed to the wrapper-based within fitness function f. Till this stage, the evaluation process is independent from the remaining populations.

In each cross-validation fold, the wrapper induces a compound classifier from the training data. The number of voters is equal to the number of populations n_P, and each base classifier h_i works exclusively with features developed by the corresponding population P_i (precisely speaking, the remaining base classifiers work with features computed by the representatives of the remaining populations). In testing, the base classifiers cooperate by voting on the class assignment of each example; their votes are aggregated into overall decision by simple (unweighted) majority rule. This process is repeated for each cross validation fold. As in all other cooperation levels, the predictive accuracy resulting from this cross-validation is assigned to the evaluated individual as a fitness.

This process resembles the class-level decomposition used in some COIL20 experiments (cf. chapter 7.4). Here, however, each of the base classifiers solves the complete, multi-class training task; in class-level decomposition, base classifiers handle (usually simpler) binary classification tasks. As a result, the computational cost of individual evaluations is much higher here.

In decision level decomposition the cooperation is postponed as long as possible. The cooperating individuals (and representatives) do the prevailing part of their work prior to cooperation. As already predicted in chapter 6.6, some properties of this cooperation model may prevent it from providing significant improvements in comparison to EFP. In particular, voting makes it probable that a base classifier's incorrect decision is concealed by its peers: the 'bad and ugly' will not show up in the crowd of 'goods'. This becomes especially probable when the number of voters is high.

The computational experiment we performed with decision level CFP confirmed this hypothesis. The fitness of the best solutions found during evolutionary search and the test set performance of the resulting recognition systems usually did not show significant improvement in comparison to EFP. Even worse, in time-complexity terms, the results obtained with decision level cooperation were usually inferior to other CFP decomposition methods and EFP, as the computational overhead resulting from the presence of a compound classifier inside the fitness function is overwhelming. Therefore, the results concerning this cooperation model are not presented in detail here.

Note that these observations may be interestingly related to Marr's principle of least commitment [72], which states that reasoning should postpone making crisp (qualitative, discrete) decisions as long as possible, because erroneous crisp decisions are difficult to withdraw. This principle, though formulated within vision science, is applicable to all decision-making systems that perform reasoning in stages, especially those that work with imperfect real-world data. In decision level decomposition, cooperating populations make their crisp choices *prior* to decision aggregation. As the aggregation consists in simple voting and does not involve any adaptation, these decisions cannot be withdrawn and, if incorrect, deteriorate the overall performance.

An important conclusion of this decision level CFP experiment is that, with the cooperation taking place on such a high abstraction level, the CC does not seem to be able to provide for successful decomposition of the training task, or, more precisely, for enough diversification among voting recognition subsystems. A natural question that may be asked at this point is: why not treat the modules in this decomposition method as separable and enforce diversification of voters by other means?

Such diversification may be naturally provided by the random nature of genetic search. For this purpose, we detach, in a sense, the populations that would run in the framework described above, and run many *independent* genetic searches that start from different initial states (initial populations). The best solution evolved in each run gives rise to a separate recognition system, which serves as a voter in the overall recognition system architecture. This assembling of the final recognition system takes place off-line, i.e., after all genetic searches come to an end. The base recognition systems are, therefore, homogenuous as far as their structure is concerned.

Table 7.12. True positive and false positive ratios for binary recognition tasks (testing set, off-line decision level decomposition).

Task	C4.5		SVM	
	TP	FP	TP	FP
B1	1.000	.000	1.000	.000
B2	1.000	.000	.981	.000
B3	.955	.006	.981	.002
B4	.955	.006	.974	.000
B5	.955	.004	.961	.001
B6	.792	.002	.896	.004
B7	.721	.005	.708	.001

In this experiment, we attempt to maximize the predictive performance and verify scalability of the resulting recognition system. Thus, 10 recognition subsystems are engaged. In particular, as base recognition systems we use here the solutions obtained in the experiments described in chapter 7.5.2.

Table 7.12 and Figure 7.15 present test-set TP and FP ratios of the compound recognition systems built using the described procedure. Quite naturally, the cooperation of ten classifiers using different features makes the compound recognition system superior to all the single recognition systems examined in earlier in this section. This applies to both C4.5 and SVM, as well as to both performance measures: true positives and false positives. In particular, the FP ratios are here approximately one order of magnitude smaller than in the case of single recognition systems.

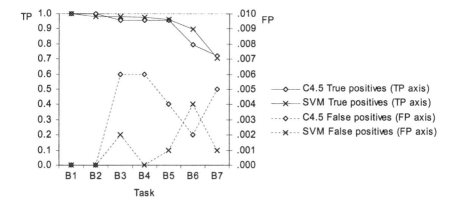

Figure 7.15. True positive and false positive ratios for binary recognition tasks (testing set, compound recognition systems).

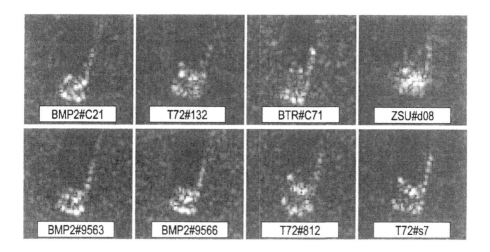

Figure 7.16. Representative images of objects used in experiments concerning object variants (all pictures taken at 191° aspect/azimuth, cropped to central 64×64 pixels, and magnified to show details).

7.6   Analysis of Evolved Solutions

One of the advantages of symbolic feature construction is the readable form of the acquired knowledge. To illustrate this virtue, we present an example of a complete evolved recognition system. The recognition system considered here is the best solution found in one of the learning processes concerning binary classification tasks described in the beginning of Chapter 7.5.2, more precisely the B1 task (BRDM versus ZSU). This particular solution has perfect fitness ($f = 1.0$) on the training set, and attains test set TP and FP ratios of, 0.974 and 0.058, respectively, when combined with C4.5 classifier, and .974 and 0.0, respectively, when used together with a SVM classifier.

The experiment referenced here concerned CFP with 4 populations cooperating at the feature-level. Therefore, in Figure 7.18 to Figure 7.21, we present four feature extraction procedures, each of them working with two image registers and two numeric registers. The figures depict feature extraction procedures encoded by particular individuals that the solution is composed of. Each row in these figures corresponds to execution of a single elementary operation. The figures depict the processing carried out for a selected image representing the negative class (ZSU in this experiment), taken at 6° azimuth (see Figure 7.17).

In all the figures from Figure 7.18 to Figure 7.21 the first row presents the initial register contents, which is determined by initial fragment of solution encoding (see chapter 6.4.2). Before carrying out the feature extraction procedure, the image registers are initialized by passing the original input image through one of the predefined filters. The masks of the registers are initially set to the brightest spot, and the numeric registers are initialized by mask coordinates. This genome-dependent initialization method proved useful in preliminary experiments, speeding up the convergence by enabling feature extraction procedure to start with an already preprocessed image. It also provides more diversity among individuals and causes the effective code to be shorter by one chunk (4 bytes). This is why, though originally the parameter determining feature extraction procedure length has been set to 9 operations (implying genome length of 36 bytes), the effective number of operations is 8.

Figure 7.17. Image of the ZSU class taken at 6° azimuth angle (cropped to input size, i.e. 48×48 pixels).

In Figure 7.18 to Figure 7.21, the original binary code (solution genome) is not presented, as it would not be readable. Rather than that, in each row, the first column presents the textual description of the operation being carried out, whereas the second column contains the argument lists. An argument list contains references to registers; for better readability, numeric registers are denoted here by lower-case symbols (r_1 and r_2), and image registers by upper-case symbols (R_1 and R_2). Registers in square brackets are output or input-output arguments, i.e. their contents changes when the operation is executed; lack of brackets denotes an input (read only) argument. Each subsequent table column corresponds to a particular register and illustrates how its contents changes during feature extraction procedure execution. For clarity, only register changes are shown in the figures; blank table cells denote no change of register contents. Arrows illustrate data flow or, in other words, dependencies between particular nodes of the processing graph.

Small gray boxes mark the current position of the image mask. Local operations process the image within that mask only; global ones ignore them. Mask position and size may be controlled by the feature extraction procedure, either explicitly (see, for instance, operation #7 in Figure 7.18 and operation #5 in Figure 7.21), or as a side effect of some image processing operations (e.g., operation #4 in Figure 7.19). As a consequence, a particular feature extraction procedure may apply and use a different mask position/size depending on the input image. Any violations of required ranges of scalar values (e.g., mask corner coordinate exceeding the actual image dimension) are handled by modulo operation.

Note that some operations involve *constants* that are not fetched from the registers but are encoded directly in the feature extraction procedure code. For clarity, such constant parameters are not shown in these examples. For instance, they determine the orders of geometrical moments to be computed (see operation #3 in Figure 7.18, and operation #6 in Figure 7.20).

It may be observed that, due to the heuristic nature of evolutionary search, only a part of feature extraction procedure code is effective, i.e. produces feature values that are fetched from numeric registers after execution of the entire procedure. As mentioned in chapter 6.4.1, feature extraction procedure fragments may constitute dead code that does not influence the final feature values. This phenomenon takes place when an operation writes to a image register that is not being read until the end of the entire procedure execution (e.g., operations #7 and #8 in Figure 7.18), or the register contents (image or numeric) becomes overwritten by a subsequent operation without being read (e.g., operation #1 in Figure 7.18). Seemingly superfluous, this redundancy is a normal and positive phenomenon characteristic to all variants of genetic programming.

For the input image $\mathbf{x}$ considered here, the four individuals described above return feature values $g_i(\mathbf{x})$ of, respectively, 2.1 and 2577, 14.2 and 7.0, 343 and 4386817, and 0 and 0. These eight feature values build up the final feature vector $G(\mathbf{x})$ that is subsequently passed to the classifier h. Both C4.5 and SVM yield correct decisions for this image, pointing to the ZSU decision class.

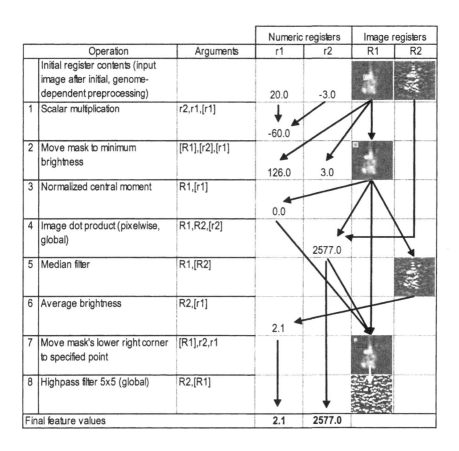

Figure 7.18. Processing carried out by one of the evolved solutions (individual 1 of 4; see text for details).

	Operation	Arguments	Numeric registers		Image registers	
			r1	r2	R1	R2
	Initial register contents (input image after initial, genome-dependent preprocessing)		19.0	14.0		
1	Scalar multiplication	r1,r2,[r2]		266.0		
2	L2 norm between image and itself	R2,[r2]		1128.3		
3	Logarithm (ln)	r2,[r2]		7.0		
4	Morphologic erosion	R2,[R1]				
5	Scalar maximum	r2,r2,[r2]		7.0		
6	Median filter	R1,[R2]				
7	Erase entire image (global)	[R2]				
8	Standard deviation of pixel values	R1,[r1]	14.2			
Final feature values			14.2	7.0		

Figure 7.19. Processing carried out by one of the evolved solutions (individual 2 of 4; see text for details).

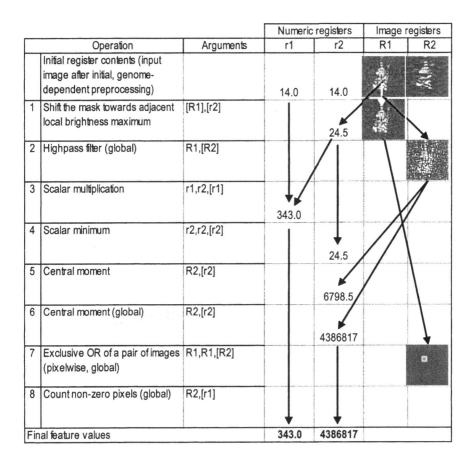

	Operation	Arguments	Numeric registers		Image registers	
			r1	r2	R1	R2
	Initial register contents (input image after initial, genome-dependent preprocessing)		14.0	14.0		
1	Shift the mask towards adjacent local brightness maximum	[R1],[r2]		24.5		
2	Highpass filter (global)	R1,[R2]				
3	Scalar multiplication	r1,r2,[r1]	343.0			
4	Scalar minimum	r2,r2,[r2]		24.5		
5	Central moment	R2,[r2]		6798.5		
6	Central moment (global)	R2,[r2]		4386817		
7	Exclusive OR of a pair of images (pixelwise, global)	R1,R1,[R2]				
8	Count non-zero pixels (global)	R2,[r1]				
Final feature values			343.0	4386817		

Figure 7.20. Processing carried out by one of the evolved solutions (individual 3 of 4; see text for details).

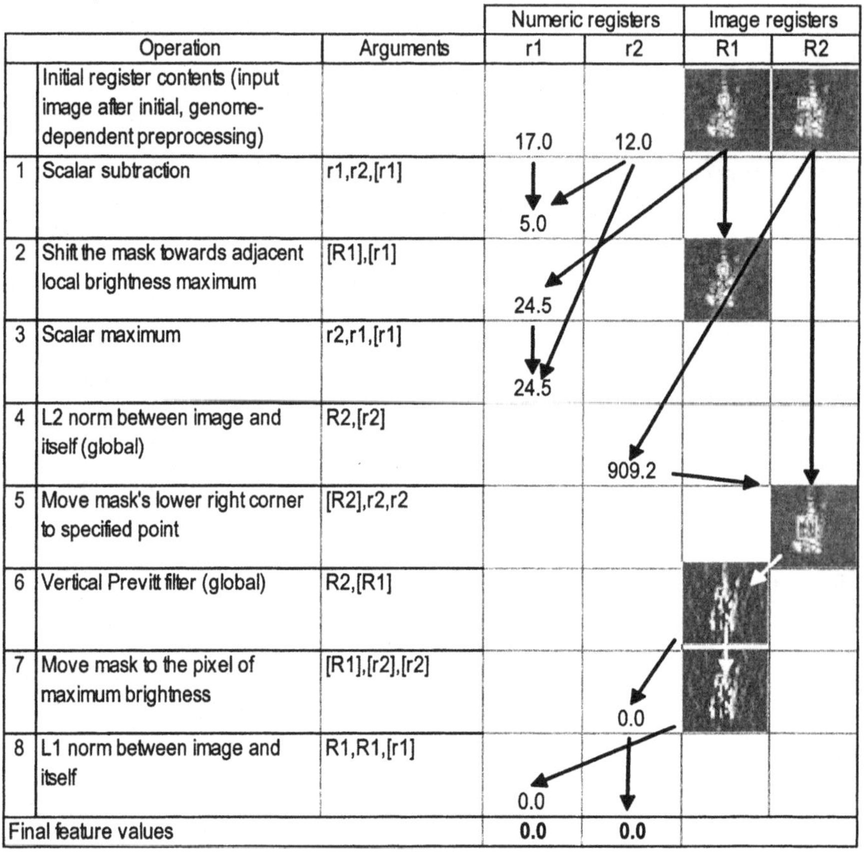

	Operation	Arguments	Numeric registers		Image registers	
			r1	r2	R1	R2
	Initial register contents (input image after initial, genome-dependent preprocessing)		17.0	12.0		
1	Scalar subtraction	r1,r2,[r1]	5.0			
2	Shift the mask towards adjacent local brightness maximum	[R1],[r1]	24.5			
3	Scalar maximum	r2,r1,[r1]	24.5			
4	L2 norm between image and itself (global)	R2,[r2]		909.2		
5	Move mask's lower right corner to specified point	[R2],r2,r2				
6	Vertical Previtt filter (global)	R2,[R1]				
7	Move mask to the pixel of maximum brightness	[R1],[r2],[r2]		0.0		
8	L1 norm between image and itself	R1,R1,[r1]	0.0			
Final feature values			0.0	0.0		

Figure 7.21. Processing carried out by one of the evolved solutions (individual 4 of 4; see text for details).

7.7   Conclusions

The results presented show that the proposed methodology of visual learning is a promising tool for automatic and semi-automatic synthesis of robust computer vision and pattern recognition systems operating in real-world environments.

In particular, the results show that EFP and its coevolutionary variety, CFP, meet demands of different imaging frameworks: passive and active sensing, visual and invisible spectrum. They yield good results for difficult real-world problems, where one has to rely on imperfect (especially noisy) training data. Recognition statistics are comparable superior to approaches discussed in the literature.

Without an explicit database of object models and 3D vision knowledge, EFP/CFP perform effective view-independent visual learning and recognition using a feature-based recognition algorithm. They are able to capture relevant patterns in multidimensional sparse spaces of images, discarding the details of secondary importance. Small sizes of investigated decision trees for the COIL20 problem indicate, that the evolutionary process is able to elaborate compact yet efficient view-independent internal representations. These representations generalize well to novel examples.

No application-specific tuning is required to maintain high quality of results – both visual learning studies use the same background knowledge comprising a set O of general-purpose vision operators. The evolved feature extraction procedures may be conveniently represented as data-flow diagrams that give good insight into the inner wiring of the recognition system. Such graphs represent explicitly the knowledge acquired by the learner (recognition system) and may be analyzed and tuned by the human expert. Further re-use in other applications is also possible.

Cooperative coevolution enables decomposition of the EFP task at different levels of abstraction. For levels that exhibit average interdependency (mainly instruction-level decomposition and feature-level decomposition), CFP delivers recognition statistics that outperform the non-coevolutionary approach in a statistically significant way. For other cooperation levels (class and decision), EFP and CFP deliver robust base recognition systems that cooperate off-line (post-learning). The random nature of genetic search provides natural diversification of evolved image features. That, in turn, enables performance boosting and good scalability with respect to problem difficulty and with respect to the number of decision classes. CFP may also be equipped with automatic adaptation of the number of coevolving populations, without significant performance decrease of resulting recognition systems.

As there is no need for matching the recognized image with models from a database, EFP and CFP offer high recognition speed. The average time required by the entire recognition process for a single 48×48 image, starting from the raw image and ending up at the decision, ranged on the average from 2.2 ms to 20.5 ms for single classifiers and compound recognition systems, respectively. This impressive recognition speed makes our approach suitable for real-time applications.

Despite the impressive results presented in this chapter, the methodology needs to be extended so that it can be easily generalized to a greater number of categories (decision classes) – model-based extension seems to be desirable. Further research is necessary to investigate the issues of interdependency and modularity in CFP is more-depth and to identify more precisely the prerequisites for more deterministic success.

Chapter 8

SUMMARY AND FUTURE WORK

8.1   Summary

This book investigates the efficacy of evolutionary computation such as a variety of genetic programming and genetic algorithms in learning programs/procedures and selecting features for object detection and object recognition. The reason for incorporating learning into object detection and recognition is to avoid the time consuming process of feature generation and selection. With learning incorporated, an object detection and recognition system can automatically explore many unconventional features that may yield exceptionally good detection and recognition performance, thus overcoming human expert limitations of concentrating only on a small number of conventional features. A learning integrated system is more flexible and is able to automatically generate features on the fly that are particularly effective to the type of objects and images to which it is applied. The ultimate goal is to lower the cost of designing object detection and recognition systems and to build more robust and flexible systems with human-competitive performance.

The contributions of this book include:

- Investigates the effectiveness of genetic programming in synthesizing composite operators and composite features for object detection. It shows that GP is effective in synthesizing effective composite operators based on domain-independent primitive operators and domain-independent primitive feature images that can be easily generated from the original image for object detection. The synthesized composite operators can be applied to other testing images that are similar to the training images. The composite features discovered by GP are much more effective than the human-designed primitive features from which they are built. The GP learned composite features are generally unconventional features and different than the features designed by human experts. Thus, the learning method will be of a great help in the design of practical object detection and recognition systems.

- Proposes an MDL-based fitness function and smart GP operators to improve the efficiency of genetic programming. An MDL-based fitness function is proposed to address the well-known code bloat problem of GP. The MDL-based fitness function takes the size of a composite operator into the fitness evaluation process to prevent composite operators from growing too large without setting a hard limit on the size of a composite operator, imposing relatively less restrictions on the GP search and greatly improving the GP efficiency. To further improve the efficiency of genetic programming, smart crossover and smart mutation are proposed to identify and prevent the effective components of composite operators from being disrupted by destructive crossover and mutation. Also, a public library is set up to keep effective components for later reuse. Compared to traditional genetic programming, the smart GP, driven by the MDL-based fitness function and equipped with smart crossover and smart mutation, synthesizes composite operators with better performance and smaller size, reducing the computational expense during recognition and the possibility of overfitting the training images.

- Proposes an MDL-based fitness function to drive GA in the selection of features for object detection and recognition. The performance of the MDL-based fitness function is compared with those of three other fitness functions. The MDL-based fitness function balances the number of features selected and the recognition error rate very well and it is the best fitness function compared to other three functions. With fewer features selected, the computational expense and the possibility of overfitting the training data is reduced.

- Investigates coevolutionary genetic programming to synthesize composite feature vectors for object recognition. The experimental results show that CGP can evolve composite features based on domain-independent primitive features and the learned composite features are more effective than the primitive features upon which they are built. The book explores the role of domain knowledge and public library in evolutionary computation by providing general and domain specific primitive features. To achieve the same recognition performance of primitive features, fewer composite features are needed and this greatly reduces the computational burden during recognition. Applications and extensions of these ideas to fingerprint classification [117], facial expression recognition [8], and imge databases [27] have been highly encouraging.

- Investigates evolutionary and coevolutionary linear genetic programming (LGP) techniques to synthesize feature extraction procedures to generate features for object recognition. LGP is a variety of GP with simplified, linear representation of individuals and it is a hybrid of GA and GP and combines their advantages. LGP is similar to GP in the sense that each individual actually contains a sequence of interrelated operators. On the other hand, a feature extraction procedure has a fixed number of instructions and an instruction is encoded into a fixed-length binary string at the genome level, which is essentially equivalent to GA representation. A feature extraction procedure consists of a sequence of instructions, which are primitive image processing operators that are executed sequentially one after another. Each instruction in a procedure is composed of an opcode determining the operator to be used and arguments referring to registers from which to fetch the input data and to which to store the result of the instruction. LGP encoding is, therefore, more positional and more resistant to destructive crossovers. When coevolutionary computation is applied, the problem of feature construction can be decomposed at different levels. We explore decomposition at the instruction, feature, class and decision levels. The experiments on visible and SAR images show the superiority of decomposition at the instruction level. With different segments of a feature extraction procedure evolved by sub-populations of coevolutionary computation, a better feature extraction procedure can be synthesized by concatenating the segments from sub-populations. The benefits we expect from the decomposition of feature construction by coevolutionary computation include faster convergence, better scalability and better understanding of the obtained solutions.

8.2   Future Work

Although this book covers a deep and extensive research on using a variety of genetic programming and genetic algorithms for feature generation and selection, there are still issues that merit further consideration.

In this book, smart crossover and smart mutation determine the interactions among the nodes of a composite operator based on their performance. The fitness value at each node is used to determine the crossover and mutation points. Currently, in order to get the fitness at each node, its output image has to be evaluated against the ground-truth during the training, which is a time consuming and inefficient process. To further improve the efficiency of GP, it is important to find a way to estimate the fitness of internal nodes based on the fitness of the root node.

From the experiments with SAR images containing road in chapters 2 and 3, it can be seen that the relations and interactions between different nodes of a composite operator is very complicated. Thus, it is difficult to determine how the performance of a node is dependent on the performance of descendent nodes.

Currently, there is only one object in an image or a ROI during recognition, so all the features come from the same object. If there are multiple overlapped objects in an image or a ROI, the recognition becomes much more difficult. Some of the features of an object may not be available due to occlusion and we need to distinguish features from different objects before these features are used into a classifier. How to extend the approach to recognize multiple overlapped objects is a challenging future research topic.

From chapter 5, it can be seen that primitive features still have a substantial impact on the goodness of the synthesized composite features. It will be difficult for CGP to yield effective composite features based on ineffective primitive features. If primitive features do not capture the characteristics of the objects to be recognized and cannot discriminate between them, no matter how hard CGP works, it still cannot yield effective composite features. However, designing effective primitive features needs human ingenuity. If human experts lack insight into the characteristics of the objects to be detected and recognized, they may not figure out effective primitive features. Sometimes, due to various factors, including noise, it is very difficult, to extract effective primitive features from images. How to let CGP evolve relatively effective composite features based on those somewhat ineffective primitive ones using a variety of sophisticated operators is an important and challenging future research area. Also synthesizing highly effective features for the recognition of articulated and oculated objects [20], [51] will be very interesting

For coevolutionary feature programming presented in Chapter 7, the most interesting future research direction is the further exploration of the possible approaches to problem decomposition. This may include exploring higher-order decomposition schemes (hierarchies of subprocedures), or even explicit preservation of useful code chunks (subprocedures), similarly to automatically defined functions in standard genetic programming [59], [60]. In particular, it would be interesting to verify if the knowledge (e.g., subprocedures) acquired in the training process related to one application may be somehow reused in (ported to) another vision application.

As far as technical aspects of evolutionary feature programming and coevolutionary feature programming are concerned, it would be nice to further reduce the number of parameters that control the feature synthesis procedure; this may include on-line adaptation of procedure length and number of registers. It would be interesting to reduce the time complexity of the fitness function, i.e., by caching and re-using intermediate processing results (images).

Lastly, concerning applications, it would be interesting to extend the approach to problems that change with time and/or analysis of video streams. Extension to vision tasks other than recognition, like object tracking, will also be interesting.

References

[1] A. Ahmadyfard and J. Kittler. A comparative study of two object recognition methods. In P.L. Rosin and A.D. Marshall (editors), *Proceedings of the British Machine Vision Conference 2002*, Cardiff, UK, 2002.

[2] P. Angeline. Subtree crossover: Building block engine or macromutation? In J. Koza et al. (editor), Genetic Programming 1997: *Proceedings of the Second Annual Conference* (GP97), pages 240–248, San Francisco, 1997. Morgan Kaufmann.

[3] J.M. Baldwin. A new factor in evolution, *American Naturalist*, 30, 441-451, 1896.

[4] W. Banzhaf, P. Nordin, R. Keller, and F. Francone. Genetic Programming: An Introduction: On the Automatic Evolution of Computer Programs and its Application. Morgan Kaufmann, 1998.

[5] T. Belpaeme. Evolution of visual feature detectors, *Proc. Evolutionary Computation in Image Analysis and Signal Processing*, Göteburg, Sweden, pp. 1-10, 1999.

[6] H.N. Bensusan and I. Kuscu. Constructive induction using genetic programming. In T. Fogarty and G. Venturini (editors), *Proc. Int. Conf. Machine Learning, Evolutionary Computing and Machine Learning Workshop*, 1996.

[7] B. Bhanu, D. Dudgeon, E. Zelnio, A. Rosenfeld, D. Casasent and I. Reed (editors), *IEEE Trans. on Image Processing, Special Issue on Automatic Target Recognition,* Vol. 6, No. 1, New York, USA, Jan. 1997.

[8] B. Bhanu, J.Yu, X. Tan and Y. Lin, Feature synthesis using genetic programming for facial expression recognitions, *Proc. Genetic and Evolutionary Computation Conference*, pp. 896-907, Seattle, WA, June 26-30, 2004.

[9] B. Bhanu and G. Jones. Increasing the discrimination of SAR recognition models, *Optical Engineering*, 12:3298–3306, 2002.

[10] B. Bhanu and G. Jones. Recognizing target variants and articulations in SAR images, *Optical Engineering*, 39(3):712–723, 1999.

[11] B. Bhanu and S. Fonder. Functional template-based SAR image segmentation, *Pattern Recognition*, Vol. 37, No. 1, pp. 61-77, 2004.

[12] B. Bhanu and S. Lee. Genetic Learning for Adaptive Image Segmentation. Kluwer Academic Publishers, 1994.

[13] B. Bhanu and T. Poggio (editors), Special section on machine learning in computer vision, *IEEE Trans. on Pattern Analysis and Machine Intelligence,* Vol. 16, No. 9, pp. 865-919, September, 1994.

[14] B. Bhanu and Y. Lin. Object detection in multi-modal images using genetic programming, *Applied Soft Computing,* Vol. 4, pp. 175-201, 2004.

[15] B. Bhanu and Y. Lin. Genetic algorithm based feature selection for target detection in SAR images, *Image and Vision Computing*, Vol. 21, No. 7, pp. 591-608, 2003.

[16] B. Bhanu and Y. Lin. Learning feature agents for extracting terrain regions in remotely sensed images, *Proc. Pattern Recognition for Remote Sensing Workshop*, Niagara Falls, NY, USA, pp 1-6, August 12, 2002.

[17] B. Bhanu and Y. Lin. Learning composite operators for object detection, *Proc. Genetic and Evolutionary Computation Conference*, New York, USA, pp. 1003-1010, July 2002.

[18] B. Bhanu and I. Pavlidis (editors), Computer Vision Beyond the Visible Spectrum. Springer, 2004.

[19] B. Bhanu and Y. Lin. Stochastic models for recognition of occluded objects, *Pattern Recognition,* Vol. 36, No. 12, pp. 2855-2873, Dec. 2003.

[20] B. Bhanu, Y. Lin, G. Jones, J. Peng. Adaptive target recognition, *Int. Journal of Machine Vision and Application*, Vol. 11, No. 6, pp. 289-299, 2000.

[21] B. Bhanu and Y. Lin. Synthesizing feature agents using evolutionary computation, *Pattern Recognition Letters,* Special Issue on Remote Sensing, Vol. 25, pp. 1519-1531, Oct. 2004.

[22] M. Brameier and W. Banzhaf. Evolving teams of predictors with linear genetic programming. *Genetic Programming and Evolvable Machines*, 2:381-407, 2001.

[23] S. Cagnoni, A. Dobrzeniecki, R. Poli and J. Yanch. Genetic algorithm-based interactive segmentation of 3D medical images, *Image and Vision Computing,* Vol. 17, No. 12, pp. 881-895, October 1999.

[24] P. D'haeseleer. Context preserving crossover in genetic programming, *Proc. IEEE World Congress on Computational Intelligence*, Vol. 1, pp. 256-261, 1994.

[25] M. Dash and H. Liu. Feature selection for classification. *Intelligent Data Analysis*, 1(3):131–156, 1997.

[26] V. Dhar, D. Chou, and F. Provost. Discovering interesting patterns for investment decision making with GLOWER – a genetic learner overlaid with entropy reduction, *Data Mining and Knowledge Discovery*, 4:251–280, 2000.

[27] A. Dong, B. Bhanu and Y. Lin, Evolutionary feature synthesis for image databases, *Proc. IEEE Workshop on Application of Computer Vision*, Breckenridge, Colorado, Jan. 5-7, 2005.

[28] R. Duda, P. Hart and D. Stork. Pattern Recognition (2nd edition). A Wiley-Interscience Publication, 2001.

[29] M. Ebner and A. Zell. Evolving a task specific image operator, *Proc. Evolutionary Image Analysis, Signal Processing and Telecommunications*, First

European Workshops, EvoIASP'99 and EuroEcTel'99, Berlin, Germany, pp. 74-89. Springer-Verlag, 1999.

[30] C. Emmanouilidis, A. Hunter, J. MacIntyre, and C. Cox. Multiple-criteria genetic algorithms for feature selection in neuro-fuzzy modeling, *Proc. Int. Joint Conf. on Neural Networks,* Vol. 6, pp. 4387-4392, Piscataway, NJ, USA, 1999.

[31] P. Estevez and R. Caballero. A niching genetic algorithm for selecting features for neural classifiers, *Proc. 8th Int. Conf. on Artificial Neural Networks*, Vol. 1, pp. 311-316. Springer-Verlag, London, 1998.

[32] C. Ferreira. Gene expression programming: A new adaptive algorithm for solving problems. *Complex Systems*, 13(2):87–129, 2001.

[33] D. Forsyth, J. Mundy V. Gesu, and R. Cipolla (editors), Shape, contour and grouping in computer vision, lecture notes in computer science, Vol. 1681. Springer, Berlin, 1999.

[34] Q. Gao, M. Li and P. Vitanyi. Applying MDL to learn best model granularity, *Artificial Intelligence*, Vol. 121, pp. 1-29, 2000.

[35] A. Ghosh and S. Tsutsui (editors), Advances in Evolutionary Computing – Theory and Application. Springer-Verlag, 2003.

[36] D. Goldberg. Genetic Algorithms in Search, Optimization and Machine Learning. Addison–Wesley, Reading, 1989.

[37] R.C. Gonzalez and R.E. Woods. Digital Image Processing. Addison–Wesley, Reading, 1992.

[38] S. Halversen. Calculating the orientation of a rectangular target in SAR imagery, *Proc. IEEE National Aerospace and Electronics Conf.*, pp. 260-264, May 1992.

[39] C. Harris and B. Buxton. Evolving edge detectors with genetic programming, *Proc. Genetic Programming, 1st Annual Conference*, Cambridge, MA, USA, pp. 309-314, MIT Press, 1996.

[40] J. Hertz, A. Krogh, and R.G. Palmer. Introduction to the Theory of Neural Computation. Addison–Wesley, Redwood City CA, 1991.

[41] J.H. Holland. Escaping brittleness: the possibilities of general–purpose learning algorithms applied to parallel rule–based systems. In R.S. Michalski, J.G. Carnoell, and T.M. Mitchell (editors), Machine Learning: An Artificial Intelligence Approach 2, pages 48-78. Morgan Kaufmann, 1986.

[42] J.H. Holland. Adaptation in Natural and Artificial Systems (2nd edition), The MIT Press, 1992.

[43] J.H. Holland and J.S. Reitman. Cognitive systems based on adaptive algorithms. In D.A. Waterman and F. Hayes-Roth (editors), Pattern–Directed Inference Systems. Academic Press, New York, 1978.

[44] D. Howard, S. C. Roberts, and R. Brankin. Target detection in SAR imagery by genetic programming, *Advances in Engineering Software*, Vol. 30, No. 5, pp. 303-311, Elsevier, May 1999.

[45] J. Huang J. Bala, H. Vafaie, K. DeJong, and H. Wechsler. Hybrid learning using genetic algorithms and decision trees for pattern classification, in *International*

Joint Conference on Aritifical Intelligence, pp. 719-724, Montreal, August 19–25, 1995.

[46] I.F. Imam and H. Vafaie. An empirical comparison between global and greedy-like search for feature selection, in *Proceedings of the Florida AI Research Symposium–FLAIRS*, 1994.

[47] Intel® image processing library: Reference manual, 2000.

[48] T. Ito, H. Iba and S. Sato. Depth-dependent crossover for genetic programming. *Proc. IEEE Int. Conf. on Evolutionary Computation*, pp. 775-780, 1998.

[49] J. Jelonek and J. Stefanowski. Experiments on solving multiclass learning problems by n2–classifier, in *Proceedings 10th European Conference on Machine Learning*, Volume 1398, Springer Lecture Notes in AI, pages 172–177. Chemnitz, 1998.

[50] M. Johnson, P. Maes and T. Darrell. Evolving visual routines, *Artificial Life*, 1:4, 1994.

[51] G. Jones and B. Bhanu. Recognition of articulated and occluded objects, *IEEE Trans. on Patern Analysis and Machine Intelligence*, Vol. 21, No. 7, pp. 603-613, 1999.

[52] W. Kantschik and W. Banzhaf. Linear–tree GP and its comparison with other GP. In Julian F. Miller, Marco Tomassini, Pier Luca Lanzi, Conor Ryan, Andrea G. B. Tettamanzi, and William B. Langdon (editors), Genetic Programming, Proceedings of EuroGP'2001, Volume 2038 of LNCS, pages 302–312. Springer–Verlag, Lake Como, Italy, 18–20 2001.

[53] A. Katz and P. Thrift. Generating image filters for target recognition by genetic learning, *IEEE Trans. on Pattern Analysis and Machine Intelligence,* Vol. 16, No. 9, September, 1994.

[54] M. Koppen and B. Nickolay. Genetic programming based texture filtering framework. In N.R. Pal (editor), Pattern Recognition in Soft Computing Paradigm, Chapter 12, pp. 275-305, World Scientific, 2001.

[55] J.R. Koza. Human–competitive applications of genetic programming. In A. Ghosh and S. Tsutsui (editors), Advances in Evolutionary Computing, pages 663–682. Springer, 2003.

[56] J.R. Koza et al. Genetic Programming IV: Routine Human - Competitive Machine Intelligence. Kluwer Academic Publishers, 2003.

[57] J.R. Koza. Genetic Programming II: Automatic Discovery of Reusable Programs. MIT Press, 1994.

[58] J.R. Koza. Genetic Programming: On the Programming of Computer by Means of Natural Selection. MIT Press, Cambridge, MA, 1992.

[59] K. Krawiec. Genetic programming–based construction of features for machine learning and knowledge discovery tasks, *Genetic Programming and Evolvable Machines*, 4:329–343, 2002.

[60] K. Krawiec. Genetic programming with local improvement for visual learning from examples. In W. Skarbek (editor), *Computer Analysis of Images and*

Patterns, Lecture Notes in Computer Science (LNCS), Volume 2124, pages 209–216. Springer Verlag, Berlin, 2001.

[61] K. Krawiec. On the use of pairwise comparison of hypotheses in evolutionary learning applied to learning from visual examples. In P. Perner, editor, *Machine Learning and Data Mining in Pattern Recognition*, Lecture Notes in Artificial Intelligence, Volume 2123, pages 307–321. Springer Verlag, Berlin, 2001.

[62] K. Krawiec. Pairwise comparison of hypotheses in evolutionary learning. In C.E. Brodley and A. Danyluk (editors), *Proc. Eighteenth International Conference on Machine Learning*, pages 266–273. Morgan Kaufmann San Francisco, 2001.

[63] K. Krawiec and B. Bhanu. Coevolution and linear genetic programming for visual learning, *Genetic and Evolutionary Computation Conference*, Part I, pp. 332-343, Chicago, IL, July 12-16, 2003.

[64] K. Krawiec and B. Bhanu. Visual learning by evolutionary feature synthesis. *Proc. International Conference on Machine* Learning, pp. 376-383, Washington D. C., August 21-24, 2003.

[65] D. Kreithen, S. Halversen, and G. Owirka. Discriminating targets from clutter, *Lincoln Laboratory Journal*, Vol. 6, No. 1, pp. 25 – 52, Spring 1993.

[66] W.B. Langdon and R. Poli, Foundations of Genetic Programming, Springer 2002.

[67] Y. Lin and B. Bhanu. Learning composite features for object recognition, *Genetic and Evolutionary Computation Conference*, Part II, pp. 2227-2239, Chicago, IL, July 12-16, 2003. An extended version, "Evolutionary feature synthesis for object recognition," *IEEE Trans. on Systems, Man and Cybernetics,* Part C, Special Issue on Knowledge Extraction and Incorporation in Evolutionary Computation (In Press).

[68] Y. Lin and B. Bhanu. Discovering operators and features for object detection, *Proc. 16th International Conference on Pattern Recognition*, Vol. 3, pp. 339-342, August 2002.

[69] Y. Lin and B. Bhanu. MDL-based genetic programming for object detection, *Proc. IEEE Workshop on Learning in Computer Vision and Pattern Recognition*, Madison, WI, June 22, 2003. A modified version, Object detection via feature synthesis using MDL-based genetic programming, *IEEE Trans. on Systems, Man and Cybernetics Part B*, (accepted), In press.

[70] S. Luke. ECJ evolutionary computation system, 2002.

[71] S. Luke and L. Spector. A revised comparison of crossover and mutation in genetic programming. In J. Koza et al. (editor), *Proc. of the Third Annual Genetic Programming Conference* (GP98), pages 208–213. Morgan Kaufmann, San Fransisco, 1998.

[72] D. Marr. Vision. W.H. Freeman, San Francisco, CA, 1982.

[73] J. Matas, J. Burianek, and J. Kittler. Object recognition using the invariant pixel–set signature. In M. Mirmehdi and B.T. Thomas (editors), *Proc. of the British Machine Vision Conference*, Bristol, UK, 2000.

[74] K. Matsui, Y. Suganami, and Y. Kosugi. Feature selection by genetic algorithm for MRI segmentation, *Systems and Computers in Japan*, Vol. 30, No. 7, pp. 69-78, Scripta technical, June 30 1999.

[75] H.A. Mayer. ptGAs–genetic algorithms evolving noncoding segments by means of promoter/terminator sequences, *Evolutionary Computation*, 6(4):361–386, Winter 1998.

[76] Z. Michalewicz. Genetic Algorithms + Data Structures = Evolution Programs. Springer Verlag, Berlin Heidelberg, 1994.

[77] M. Mitchell. An introduction to genetic algorithms. MIT Press: Cambridge, 1998.

[78] T. Mitchell, Machine Learning. McGraw-Hill, 1997.

[79] S.A. Nene, S.K. Nayar, and H. Murase. Columbia object image library (COIL–20). Technical Book CUCS–005–96, Columbia University, February 1996.

[80] A. Noë and E. Thompson (editors), Vision & Mind: Selected Readings in the Philosophy of Perception. The MIT Press, Cambridge MA, 2002.

[81] P. Nordin. Explicitly defined introns in genetic programming. In J. P. Rosca, F. Francone, and W. Banzhaf (editors), *Proc. Workshop on Genetic Programming: From Theory to Real–World Applications – Twelfth Int. Conf. Machine Learning*, pages 6–22, Tahoe City CA, July 9, 1995.

[82] P. Nordin and W. Banzhaf. Complexity compression and evolution, *Proc. Sixth Int. Conf. on Genetic Algorithms*, pp 310 – 317, 1995.

[83] P. Nordin, W. Banzhaf, and F. Francone. Efficient evolution of machine code for CISC architectures using blocks and homologous crossover. In L. Spector, W. Langdon, U. O'Reilly, and P. Angeline (editors), Advances in Genetic Programming III, pages 275 – 299. MIT Press, Cambridge, MA, 1999.

[84] L. Novak, G. Owirka, and C. Netishen. Performance of a high-resolution polarimetric SAR automatic target recognition system, *Lincoln Laboratory Journal*, Vol. 6, No. 1, pp. 11–24, Spring 1993.

[85] L. Novak, M. Burl, and W. Irving. Optimal polarimetric processing for enhanced target detection. *IEEE Trans. Aerosp. Electron. Syst.* 29, pp. 234 - 244, 1993.

[86] C. Oliver and S. Quegan, Understanding Synthetic Aperture Radar Images, Artech House, Inc. 1998.

[87] M. O'Neill and C. Ryan. Grammatical Evolution. Evolutionary Automatic Programming in an Arbitrary Language. Kluwer Academic Publishers, Boston, 2003.

[88] Open Source Computer Vision Library: Reference Manual, 2001.

[89] E. Ozcan and C. Mohan. Partial shape matching using genetic algorithms, *Pattern Recognition Letters*, Vol. 18, pp. 987-992, 1997.

[90] P.V. Parthasarathy, D.E. Goldberg, and S.A. Burns. Tackling multimodal problems in hybrid genetic algorithms. Technical Book 2001012, March 2001.

[91] J. Platt. Fast training of support vector machines using sequential minimal optimization. In B. Scholkopf, C. Burges and A. Smola (editors), Advances in

Kernel Methods -- Support Vector Learning. MIT Press, Cambridge, Mass., 1998

[92] R. Poli. Genetic programming for feature detection and image segmentation. In T. C. Forgarty (editor), Evolutionary Computation, pp. 110-125. Springer-Verlag, Berlin, Germany, 1996.

[93] R. Poli. Exact schema theory for genetic programming and variable–length genetic algorithms with one–point crossover, *Genetic Programming and Evolvable Machines*, 2(2):123–163, June 2001.

[94] M.A. Potter and K.A. De Jong. Cooperative Coevolution: An architecture for evolving coadapted subcomponents, *Evolutionary Computation*, Vol. 8(1), pp. 1-29, 2000.

[95] W. Punch and E. Goodman. Further research on feature selection and classification using genetic algorithms, *Proc. 5th Int. Conf. on Genetic Algorithms*, pp. 557-564, 1993.

[96] J. Quinlan. C4.5: Programs for Machine Learning. Morgan Kaufmann: San Mateo, 1992

[97] J. Quinlan and R. Rivest. Inferring decision tree using the minimum description length principle, *Information and Computation,* Vol. 80, pp. 227-248, 1989.

[98] M.L. Raymer, W.F. Punch, E.D. Goodman, L.A. Kuhn, and A.K. Jain. Dimensionality reduction using genetic algorithm, *IEEE Trans. on Evolutionary Computation*, 4(2):164–171, 2000.

[99] F. Rhee and Y. Lee. Unsupervised feature selection using a fuzzy-genetic algorithm, *Proc. IEEE Int. Fuzzy Systems Conf., V*ol. 3, pp. 1266-1269, Piscataway, NJ, 1999.

[100] J. Rissanen. A universal prior for integers and estimation by minimum description length, *Ann. of Statist*, Vol. 11, No. 2, pp. 416-431, 1983.

[101] M. Rizki, L. Tamburino and M. Zmuda. Multi-resolution feature extraction from Gabor filtered images, *Proc. of the IEEE National Aerospace and Electronics Conference*, Dayton, OH, USA, pp. 24-28, May 1993.

[102] M. Rizki, M. Zmuda and L. Tamburino, Evoluting pattern recognition systems, *IEEE Trans. on Evolutionary Computation*, 6, pp. 594-609, 2002.

[103] S.C. Roberts and D. Howard. Evolution of vehicle detectors for infrared line scan imagery, *Proc. Evolutionary Image Analysis, Signal Processing and Telecommunications, First European Workshops*, EvoIASP'99 and EuroEcTel'99, Berlin, Germany, pp. 110-125, Springer-Verlag, 1999.

[104] T. Ross, S. Worell, V. Velten, J. Mossing, and M. Bryant. Standard SAR ATR evaluation experiments using the MSTAR public release data set, in *SPIE Proceedings: Algorithms for Synthetic Aperture Radar Imagery V*, Vol. 3370, pages 566–573, April 1998.

[105] F. Rothlauf. On the locality of representations. Technical book, University of Mannheim, Department of Information Systems 1, 2003.

[106] F. Rothlauf. Representations for Genetic and Evolutionary Algorithms. Physica–Verlag Heidelberg New York, 2002.

[107] C. Ryan C., J.J. Collins, and M. O'Neill. Grammatical evolution: Evolving programs for an arbitrary language, in *First European Workshop on Genetic Programming*, Lecture Notes in Computer Science. Vol. 1391, 1998.

[108] J.D. Schaffer. Multiple objective optimization with vector evaluated genetic algorithms, In *Proc. First International Conference on Genetic Algorithms and their Applications*, Hillsdale, 1985. Lawrence Erlbaum Associates.

[109] W. Siedlecki and J. Sklansky. A note on genetic algorithms for large-scale feature selection, *Pattern Recognition Letters*, Vol. 10, pp. 335-347, November 1989.

[110] H.A. Simon. The Sciences of the Artificial. MIT Press, Cambridge, MA, 1969.

[111] P. Smith. Conjugation – A bacterially inspired form of genetic recombination. In J. R. Koza (editor), Late Breaking Chapters at the Genetic Programming Conf., pp. 167 – 176, 1996.

[112] S.F. Smith. A learning system based on genetic algorithms. Ph.D. thesis, University of Pittsburgh, 1980.

[113] R. Srikanth, R. George, N. Warsi, D. Prabhu, F. Petry and B. Buckles. A variable-length genetic algorithm for clustering and classification, *Pattern Recognition Letters*, Vol. 16, pp. 789-800, 1995.

[114] S.A. Stanhope and J. M. Daida. Genetic programming for automatic target classification and recognition in synthetic aperture radar imagery, *Proc. Seventh Conference on Evolutionary Programming VII*, Springer-Verlag, Berlin, Germmany, pp. 735-744, 1998.

[115] W. Tackett. Genetic programming for feature discovery and image discrimination, *Proc. Fifth International Conference on Genetic Algorithm*, Morgan Kaufmann, San Mateo, CA, USA, pp. 303-311, 1993.

[116] W. Tackett. Recombination election and the genetic construction of computer programs. Ph.D. thesis, Univ. of Southern California, Dept. of Electr. Engg. Systems, 1994.

[117] X. Tan, B. Bhanu and Y. Lin. Learning features for fingerprint classification. *International Conference on Audio- and Video-based Person Authentication*, pp. 318-326, Guildford, UK, June 9-11, 2003. An extended version, Fingerprint classification based on learned features, *IEEE Transactions on Systems, Man and Cybernetics Part C*, Special issue on Biometrics (In Press).

[118] A. Teller. Algorithm evolution with internal reinforcement for signal understanding, Ph.D. thesis, School of Computer Science, Carnegie Mellon University, Pittsburgh, PA, 1998.

[119] A. Teller and M.M. Veloso. PADO: A new learning architecture for object recognition. In K. Ikeuchi and M. Veloso (editors), Symbolic Visual Learning, pages 77–112. Oxford University Press, 1997.

[120] S. Theodoridis and K. Koutroumbas. Pattern Recognition. Academic Press, 1999.

[121] S. Ullman. Visual routines, *Cognition*, Vol. 18, pp. 97-159, 1984.

[122] H. Vafaie and I.F. Imam. Feature selection methods: Genetic algorithms vs. greedy–like search, in *Proc. of International Conference on Fuzzy and Intelligent Control Systems*, 1994.

[123] D.A. van Veldhuizen. Multiobjective evolutionary algorithms: Classifications, analyses, and new innovations. Ph.D. thesis, Department of Electrical and Computer Engineering. Graduate School of Engineering, Wright–Patterson AFB, Ohio, 1999.

[124] R.A. Watson. Modular interdependency in complex dynamical systems. In Bilotta et al. (editor), *Workshop Proceedings of the 8th International Conference on the Simulation and Synthesis of Living Systems*, UNSW Australia, December 2003.

[125] R.A. Watson. Compositional Evolution. Ph.D. thesis, Brandeis University, 2002.

[126] D. Whitley, V.S. Gordon, and K. Mathias. Lamarckian evolution, the Baldwin effect and function optimization. In Y. Davidor, H.-P. Schwefel, and R. Maenner (editors), *Proc. Third International Conference on Parallel Problem Solving from Nature (PPSN)*, Lecture Notes in Computer Science, Vol. 866. Springer Verlag, New York, 1994.

[127] I.H. Witten and E. Frank. Data Mining: Practical Machine Learning Tools and Techniques with Java Implementations. Morgan Kaufmann: San Francisco, 1999.

[128] L. Włodarski. Coevolution in decomposition of machine learning problems. Master's thesis, Institute of Computing Science, Poznań University of Technology, 2003.

[129] J. Yang and V. Honavar. Feature subset selection using a genetic algorithm. In H. Motoda and H. Liu (editors), Feature Extraction, Construction, and Subset Selection: A Data Mining Perspective. Kluwer Academic: New York, 1998.

Index